DATE DUE

HIGHSMITH #45115

THE DEADLOCKED ELECTION OF 1800

American Presidential Elections

MICHAEL NELSON

JOHN M. MCCARDELL, JR.

THE DEADLOCKED ELECTION
OF 1800

JEFFERSON, BURR,
AND THE UNION
IN THE BALANCE
JAMES ROGER SHARP

UNIVERSITY PRESS OF KANSAS

Published
by the
University
Press of Kansas
(Lawrence,
Kansas 66045),
which was
organized by the
Kansas Board of
Regents and is
operated and
funded by
Emporia State
University,
Fort Hays State
University,
Kansas State
University,
Pittsburg State
University,
the University
of Kansas, and
Wichita State
University

© 2010 by the University Press of Kansas

Library of Congress Cataloging-in-Publication Data

Sharp, James Roger, 1936–
   The deadlocked election of 1800 : Jefferson, Burr, and the
union in the balance / James Roger Sharp.
       p.   cm. — (American presidential elections)
   Includes bibliographical references and index.
   ISBN 978-0-7006-1742-5 (cloth : alk. paper)
   1. Presidents—United States—Election—1800. 2. United
States—Politics and government—1797–1801. 3. Jefferson,
Thomas, 1743–1826. 4. Burr, Aaron, 1756–1836. 5. Adams, John,
1735–1826. 6. Hamilton, Alexander, 1757–1804. I. Title.
   E330.S53 2010
   324.909'034—dc22   2010027343

British Library Cataloguing-in-Publication Data is available.

Printed in Canada

10 9 8 7 6 5 4 3 2 1

The paper used in this publication is recycled and
contains 30 percent postconsumer waste. It is acid free
and meets the minimum requirements of the American
National Standard for Permanence of Paper for Printed
Library Materials Z39.48-1992.

To Sandy, Matt, Martha, Topher, Lee Lee, Meredith,
and, above all, Nancy

CONTENTS

Eighteenth-century Americans who knew their history knew that republican experiments were ultimately doomed. In creating the United States of America, the founders tried to put in place as many mechanisms as they could to impede the process of inevitable decline they knew somewhere, in the distant future, loomed. Yet for all its genius, its system of checks and balances, and its exquisite division and distribution of sovereignty, there was something the Constitution, and its framers, failed to anticipate: the creation of organized political parties.

The founders believed that "party" and "faction" were synonymous. As the first decade of nationhood unfolded, and disputes over policy led to the creation of parties, the early warning signs were unmistakable. Beginning with the ambitiously nationalistic economic plans of Alexander Hamilton as secretary of the treasury, continuing with the vexatiously complex issue of maintaining neutrality in a war between two European powers, and culminating with a genuine crisis over civil liberties, Americans found themselves lining up on one side or the other of a set of issues that seemed, in the heat of partisan debate, irreconcilable.

Nomenclature mattered. The incumbent administration called itself "Federalist," making the connection between its policies and the successful campaign to ratify the Constitution. Its opponents, fearing identification as "Antifederalist," losers in the ratification debate or, worse still, members of a subversive faction, chose the name "Republican."

Troubling, seemingly intractable problems arose as partisan lines were drawn. How reconcile majority rule and minority rights? How define the line that separates dissent and disloyalty? How assert and then uphold a policy of diplomatic neutrality? How and by what agency determine the constitutionality of a particular legislative act?

By the time of the presidential election of 1800, as James Roger Sharp details in this elegant, thorough, masterful study, the American voting public found itself bitterly divided. In so many ways the questions seemed inverse. Either France or England. Either strict construction or loose construction. Either loyalty or disloyalty. Either states or nation. Either Republican or Federalist. Either Jefferson or Adams.

In telling this fascinating, riveting, and consequential story, Sharp covers the political history of the 1790s in detail, thereby providing a necessary context for the 1800 campaign. In his capable hands, characters come to life, issues emerge with searing clarity, the stakes are high, and the outcome far from certain. When the votes are counted, there is no clear winner, nor has the constitutional mechanism for selecting the president and vice president worked as planned. At almost literally the last minute, disinterested statesmanship and magnanimity combine to avoid a crisis and allow for the peaceful and orderly transfer of power from one party to the other. As the narrative concludes, readers will realize that, as a new president representing a new party takes the oath of office on March 4, 1801, Americans have secured their revolution.

One distinguished political scientist has concluded that the "right of an organized opposition to appeal for votes against the government in election and in parliament" is one of the "three great milestones in the development of democratic institutions."[1] But that milestone had not yet been reached in the United States at the time of the election of 1800. And it was this failure to reach that crucial milestone that caused the election to be so dangerously acrimonious and bitter.

In order for the right of opposition to have taken root in the country, all sides would have had to recognize that they shared a widely held consensus of loyalty to republicanism, the Constitution, and the Union and an acknowledgment that conflict would take place within the boundaries of those shared beliefs.

But this shared consensus that was to become clearly apparent to Americans of later generations was not evident to political leaders in 1800. Indeed, the perilous polarization and frenzied antagonisms that developed in the decade after the installation of the new government under the Constitution were unexpected—yet almost inevitable given the failure of the Founders to accurately foresee how conflict could be managed. As a result, this right of opposition was not accepted by the two embryonic political parties that began to emerge in the 1790s under the names Republican and Federalist. This acceptance only developed slowly, incrementally, after the widespread sense of the new republic's fragility had ebbed.

The fact that Americans in the 1790s failed to make the critical distinction between a political party that would temporarily hold power and the government itself was of fundamental importance. This is because what has come to be "the concept that the party is a conveyer of the people's will through the institutions of government, but is not [itself] the repository of state power," is seen as an essential component of democratic government.[2]

Thus, as Americans fought with each other over seemingly intractable issues at the time of the election of 1800, they also became alarmed that their republic might not endure. Although hoping for the best, they shared a pervasive unease and skepticism about the future—envisioning a number of possible scenarios playing out—many of them bad. Even former President George Washington, only months before the election got under way and right before his death, lamented that the grave political situation he had been observing "with an anxious, and painful eye" appeared "to be moving by hasty strides to some awful crisis."[3]

This, then, was the setting for the election of 1800, one of the two most critical elections in American history. While the other, the election of Abraham Lincoln in 1860, led to the Civil War, the election of 1800 also held the potential for violence, secession, and armed conflict.

The catalysts for the dangerous divisiveness in 1800 stemmed from several factors.

First, the Constitution was then hardly more than a decade old, and many Americans feared that it and the Union ultimately would founder, just as the short-lived Articles of Confederation government had.

Second, the federal government under the Constitution had been given unprecedented powers compared to those in the previous Articles government. This had produced an almost reflexive alarm among many citizens against any federal proposal or action that might increase the authority of the central government at the expense of the states. As one historian has pointed out, most Americans today would take for granted "a strong national government," and "thus we tend to miss the radicalness of the Constitution." Further, "from the vantage point of the late twentieth century, allegiance to the nation, to the union, seems a matter of course; we can scarcely conceive of the United States without a powerful central government. . . . But if we change our vantage point and stand in 1776, then a strong national government is not something we can take for granted."[4]

Third, the great war between revolutionary France and Great Britain threatened to engulf the United States and divide Americans into two opposing groups, supporters of France and supporters of England, with each side questioning the other's loyalty to the United States.

And finally, the election ended up a tie in the Electoral College between the two Republican candidates, Virginian Thomas Jefferson for president and his vice presidential running mate, Aaron Burr from New York. And in the midst of rumors of potential violence, civil war, and secession, the House of Representatives—rather than the electors—ended up having the responsibility for resolving the deadlock and electing a president. These unexpected complications added fuel to an already combustible situation. The Union hung in the balance.

This book is primarily a synthetic work resting on the labors of dozens of historians whose research has made the early republic one of the most fascinating and intellectually rich periods in American history. And that is entirely appropriate. Quite simply, the period from 1788 to 1815 *was* one of the most challenging and difficult times in the nation's history.[5] There was a real question whether the nation would survive.

As a result of this excellent historical work, there are many whom I need to acknowledge. My bibliographic essay provides a long list of those to whom I am deeply grateful. And all of the historians of the early republic are in the debt of Philip J. Lampi of the First Democracy Project at the American Antiquarian Society. The marvelous collection of political data he amassed is unrivaled for this period.

Beyond that, as a graduate student at Berkeley years ago, I profited immensely from my graduate colleagues as we sat in the California sun at the student union looking across the Bay to San Francisco and the Golden Gate Bridge while we discussed politics or the latest books in our fields—more often than not challenging the opinions of each other. And I, too, was greatly influenced by my mentor, Charles G. Sellers, Jr., who is a brilliant teacher and scholar.

While this book was in preparation I also had great help from a number of graduate and undergraduate students at Syracuse University, but most especially Michelle Orihel, who did research for me at the American Antiquarian Society, and Judd Olshan, my research assistant, who tirelessly helped me edit my footnotes, track sources in the bibliographic essay, find illustrations, and worked creatively to produce a map of Washington in 1800. Timely research funds were provided by Associate Dean Michael Wasylenko of the Maxwell School.

The University Press of Kansas has also been splendidly supportive. I have benefited a great deal from the suggestions of John McCardell and Mike Nelson, the editors of this series. Jenny Bennett did a great job in copyediting the manuscript, while Jennifer A. Dropkin, the production editor, has been wonderfully helpful in all aspects of the preparation of this manuscript. Cartographer Bill Nelson was especially helpful in finalizing the map of Washington, D.C. And Fred M. Woodward, director of the press, has, from the very beginning, been very supportive, patient, and nurturing throughout this project.

Finally, my wife Nancy's influence is on every page of this book. She has read and line edited the manuscript numerous times, always willingly and enthusiastically. A superb editor and writer in her own right, she does not just tell me what is wrong or not clear but also suggests creative reformulations. Unswerving in her independence and courage, she does not hesitate to tell me what I might not want to hear at midnight—about the need to reorganize a section. Her love, support, and encouragement have been indispensable.

I am, of course, solely responsible for any errors of commission or omission.

1

INAUGURATION DAY, MARCH 4, 1801

I

Inauguration Day, March 4, 1801, dawned bright and chilly in the raw, new capital of Washington, D.C., with temperatures later in the day reaching the middle fifties. At noon, after a breakfast at his Conrad and McMunn's boarding house near the south side of the unfinished Capitol, the newly elected president, Thomas Jefferson, traveled on foot the two hundred paces to the Capitol. He was attended by the Virginia militia, some members of Congress, and other officials. Once inside he was received by Chief Justice John Marshall, who would administer the oath of office, and the newly sworn in vice president Aaron Burr.[1]

The occasion had none of the pomp and ceremony that had accompanied George Washington's majestic, imposing, almost coronation-like inauguration in 1789. Then, the soon-to-be inaugurated first president had been feted by throngs of cheering well-wishers as he had made his week-long celebratory journey from Mount Vernon to New York.[2] In contrast, the festivities surrounding Jefferson's inaugural were simple, low-key, and informal—although for the first time the Marine Corps Band played, establishing a custom that has been carried on at each and every presidential inauguration since.

In keeping with the lack of formality, the president-elect dressed plainly. He did not powder his hair, nor did he carry a sword, as his two predecessors had. The only fanfare was the artillery salute that greeted him and his party as they arrived at the north wing of the Capitol—the only wing whose construction was complete at the time. They entered a senate chamber crowded to capacity by members of Congress and citizens for the inauguration.[3]

Later, after Jefferson had presented his inaugural address and had been sworn in, the new president returned to Conrad and McMunn's to welcome guests. At dinner that night the newly installed president unpretentiously insisted upon sitting at his usual place at the foot of the table, the furthest seat away from the warmth of the fire.

As Jefferson was poised to exercise power, there must have been a huge collective sigh of relief on the part of most Americans—but especially Jefferson's supporters—that the bitter and dangerous political crisis arising from the deadlocked election had been settled without violence. In the late fall of 1800 and the early winter of 1801, a peaceful transition of power had seemed uncertain as the political storm, which had been building for several years, struck with full fury.

In fact, the presidential election of 1800 and the election of Abraham Lincoln in 1860 stand as the two most critical presidential elections in American history. Before a winner was chosen in February 1801, the country seemed for a time to be poised at the brink of an abyss, with the real possibility that the republic might disintegrate or, even worse, slide into civil war, as it would after Lincoln's election.

The antagonists, John Adams and Thomas Jefferson, had run against each other in 1796, with Adams winning the presidency and Jefferson the vice presidency. But by 1800, the two old colleagues who had collaborated on the writing of the Declaration of Independence and had served together for a time in the Continental Congress had become increasingly estranged. And the country itself had become dangerously polarized, pervaded by a feverish atmosphere of suspicion and apprehension.

II

As was the custom at the time, the two presidential candidates in 1800 played relatively passive roles in the election, especially in the summer and fall, when they mostly stayed at home, writing letters and receiving reports from supporters. Yet both men must have pondered the great significance of the contest and the turmoil and uncertainty that had increasingly plagued the federal government since the ratification of the Constitution. They were certainly well aware of the intensifying acrimony and hysteria that were casting a shadow over the balloting that had begun in the spring and would continue until early December—acrimony and hysteria due in large part to deeply divisive domestic and foreign policy questions and to a development that had not been foreseen by the Founders. By 1800 two competing, what can only be seen as protoparties had emerged in the nation, and their visions of the future of the country differed radically.[4]

The Republicans, who backed Jefferson, received the core of their support from the South, were suspicious of the power of the federal government, and tended to embrace an image of a rural agrarian republic. In contrast, the Federalists, who supported Adams, drew most of their strength from New England and believed that the survival of the republic depended on a strong national government that encouraged commercial and industrial development.

But in December, Americans of all political persuasions were stunned when the unofficial results of the balloting were made known. They indicated that, although the Republicans had won, there was a tie in the Electoral College between Jefferson and his running mate, Aaron Burr of New York. The stalemate had arisen because under the Constitution (until the passage of the Twelfth Amendment in 1804) each elector was to cast two votes. The person receiving the highest number of votes, provided it was a majority of the total vote, was to become president and the person receiving the second highest number, vice president.

But Republican electors had erred. They had each given one vote to Jefferson, the designated presidential nominee, and one to Burr, the designated vice-presidential nominee. This meant that, as specified by the Constitution, the Federalist-controlled House of Representatives would be called upon to resolve the deadlock and decide which of the candidates would become the president and which the vice president.[5]

Jefferson may have experienced temporary exhilaration after the electoral results revealed his defeat of Adams. If so, his initial reaction quickly turned to one of apprehension and then alarm as the implications of his tie with Burr became more obvious.

Distressing rumors were circulating that the Federalists might support Burr, and Jefferson himself sensed that the New Yorker was becoming progressively coy. While assuring Jefferson of his loyalty, on the one hand, Burr seemed to be allowing himself to be courted by Federalist leaders, on the other. Reportedly, the strategy of the Federalists was either to elect Burr in the House of Representatives and make him their creature or else to forestall the election of any president at all and usurp power outright.

Thus, Burr's unexpected refusal to acquiesce and publicly deny any claims to the presidency in favor of Jefferson led to ever-deepening distrust and hostility between Jefferson's Republicans and the governing Federalists. From December 1800 until late February 1801, the Union teetered at the verge of collapse as a result of political tensions fueled by sectional jealousies as well as almost paranoid fears of foreign influence and domestic sedition. Federalists and Republicans were willing to believe that their opponents were capable of virtually any action, no matter how treacherous or violent, in order to gain or retain power. Talk was also rife about state militias arming and a possible breakup of the Union and civil war. It was even alleged that Jefferson would be assassinated.

Could the country, whose first form of government under the Articles of Confederation had failed, survive under its new Constitution that was only twelve years old? That was the question in many American minds.

From the perspective of the twenty-first century, it might appear as if the Republican and Federalist parties were engaged in exaggerated and over-heated rhetoric about their own virtues and the evils of their opponents—rhetoric that would become typical of many subsequent political campaigns in our nation's history.

Yet, that would be a fundamental misreading of the history of that period. That the stalemate was resolved peacefully does not mean that it did not have the real potential for violence and the possible disintegration of the Union. Certainly the participants believed that this was a possibility. Much later in life John Adams admitted that during that time of crisis in 1801 he had thought that the Federalists and Republicans were looking into a disastrous chasm and that "a civil war was expected."[6]

Americans living at the turn of the nineteenth century obviously did not know what the future would hold. Most, if not all, desperately hoped that republicanism, the Union, and the new Constitution would survive. But, while they hoped for the best, the potential for armed conflict was real.

III

The bitter and acrimonious struggle surrounding the election of 1800 had been shaped and framed by challenges that faced Americans as they struggled to sustain a republican form of government and to create a cohesive and unified nation in a world of powerful monarchies. It was a daunting undertaking and one made even more so by the vast, almost overwhelming, American physical environment that led to feelings of isolation and separateness among a people whose cultures, although similar, were also dissimilar in many critical ways. In fact, the differing past experiences and political institutions of the various states and communities made up a political culture that, although generally derived from English practices, was also diverse because of local histories and traditions.

As a consequence of this patchwork quilt of beliefs, practices, and institutions deeply rooted in pre-Revolutionary America, early efforts to establish a stable and effective national government had been discouraging. The Articles of Confederation (1781–1788), with its decentralized structure and lack of authority, had foundered in its inability to stabilize the nation's finances and to pay its debts. To many Americans, especially the country's elites, the Articles government seemed dangerously weak and incapable of controlling the democratic excesses of the various state legislatures.[7]

The ratification of the Constitution in 1788, then, raised the hopes of many Americans that the new, more powerful frame of government would bring stability and unity to the country. However, many, if not most, Americans were still localists and remained wary of ceding control to any outside or higher authority. And this presented the new government with almost insurmountable problems—problems that were magnified and exaggerated by grave domestic and foreign policy challenges.

One Massachusetts Antifederalist expressed the fears that were shared by many Americans when he warned during the debate over the ratification of the Constitution that a republican form of government was impossible in such a large empire as the United States, which extended from the Atlantic Ocean on the east to the Mississippi River on the west, from the Great Lakes on the north to the northern boundary of Spanish Florida on the south. "Such a government will degenerate to a despotism," he wrote, "unless it be made up of a confederacy of smaller states, each having the full powers of internal regulation." Sectional differences, it was percipiently argued, could be fatally divisive, for in "large states the same principles of legislation will not apply to all parts." Indeed, there were sharp differences between the sections, he observed, saying with a bit of sectional chauvinism that "inhabitants of warmer climates are more dissolute in their manners, and less industrious, than in colder countries."[8]

IV

Looking back over the sectional and partisan divisions that wracked the country in the almost quarter of a century spanning from the Declaration of Independence down to the election of 1800, it is obvious that an extraordinary group of leaders played major roles in the creation of the American republic. But it was the dominant force of the personality and character of George Washington that was the most crucial. Washington, as commander in chief of the Continental Army, symbolized to most Americans the success of the American Revolution. After that, his looming presence as the nation's first president had had the effect of tempering the hard edges of the geographic, cultural, sectional, and political conflicts in the 1790s and keeping them from destroying the young republic. The strife surrounding the election of 1800, however, would have to be dealt with without the unifying presence of Washington, who died in 1799.

Through Washington's acceptance of the presidency, the government of the new republic was significantly strengthened, for he was truly a national figure with a popularity that transcended sectionalism. Towering six inches or so over most of his male contemporaries, the Virginia land speculator and scientific farmer had an impressive physical bearing and, in the words of one historian, a "noble carriage and regal gravitas."[9]

Assuming the presidency when he was 57, the American commander in chief during the Revolution had fought alongside British troops as a young lieutenant colonel during the French and Indian War in the Ohio Country from 1754 to 1759. He had also been politically active, serving in the Virginia House of Burgesses and later as president of the country's Constitutional Convention.

However, unlike two of his distinguished cabinet members, Thomas Jefferson and Alexander Hamilton, Washington was not the gentleman scholar. Instead, he enjoyed the physical aspects of the planter's life, riding horseback around his property, overseeing the planting and harvesting as well as working on various projects to improve his plantation. He has been described by some who knew him as forthright, blunt, thin-skinned, hot tempered, strong willed, and dogmatic. Others of his contemporaries, however, thought of him as shy, although this may have been due to a hearing loss that inhibited him from being fully engaged in conversation, particularly in a crowded setting. Abigail, John Adams's wife, described Washington as having a "dignity which forbids familiarity mixed with an easy affability which creates love and reverence."[10]

In a long critical letter years after Washington had died, Jefferson described his fellow Virginian as someone whose "mind was great and powerful, without being of the very first order." And someone who was slow and deliberate in making up his mind, but, once having made it up, found it difficult to change. His sense of justice was "the most inflexible" Jefferson had "ever known." Washington, Jefferson continued, also was a man capable of "tremendous . . . wrath," someone whose "heart was not warm in

President George Washington. Despite his transcendent popularity, a divisive factionalism emerged during his two terms of office. Nonetheless, his matchless reputation and strength of character mitigated and blunted the sharper edges of conflict until his death in 1799. George Washington (Lansdowne Portrait) by Gilbert Stuart, 1796. National Portrait Gallery, Smithsonian Institution; acquired as a gift to the nation through the generosity of the Donald W. Reynolds Foundation. NPG.2001.13.

its affections" and whose conversation exhibited neither a "copiousness of ideas, nor fluency of words." Reading little outside of agricultural journals and English history, Jefferson observed, Washington was "halting and embarrassing in his public pronouncements." However, in private among friends, he was more at ease, Jefferson added. Nonetheless, Jefferson saw Washington as "a wise, a good, and a great man" and one whose integrity was "most pure."[11]

Historian Joseph Ellis writes that "Benjamin Franklin was wiser than Washington; Alexander Hamilton was more brilliant; John Adams was better read; Thomas Jefferson was more intellectually sophisticated; James Madison was more politically astute." Nonetheless, "each and all of these prominent figures acknowledged that Washington was their unquestioned superior."[12] And one contemporary captured the almost universal esteem that Americans had for Washington by declaring that he was "first in war, first in peace, and first in the hearts of his countrymen."[13]

The monument constructed in the national capital to honor the first president in many ways reflects the prevailing image of Washington. Dominating the Washington, D.C., skyline, the large marble obelisk is best seen from afar. The closer you get, the less perspective you have. Unlike the Lincoln and Jefferson memorials that convey a sense of personal intimacy, the Washington Monument, while commanding, stately, and extraordinarily imposing, remains distant, remote, and aloof.

Washington's cabinet, though small, was the most brilliant and talented in American history. The president's choice for secretary of treasury was Alexander Hamilton (1757–1804), who, as a staff officer, had become almost like a son to the general during the American Revolution.

Born in the British West Indies, Hamilton was the illegitimate son of a Scottish merchant. It was an ignoble birth that haunted him all of his life and did not go unnoticed by his contemporaries. For example, John Adams, who developed a passionate hatred for Hamilton over the years, once referred to him as "the bastard brat of a Scottish peddler."

Coming to New York as a young man in 1772, Hamilton was educated in New York City at King's College (Columbia). Later, during the American Revolution, he served as Washington's secretary and aide-de-camp and, as such, became the general's trusted adviser. Short of stature at five feet, seven inches, and rather frail and slim, Hamilton was often quick tempered and intense in his relationships with both friends and foes. He was, however, irresistible to women. One short but disastrous affair with a woman by the name of Maria Reynolds ultimately resulted in his public humiliation, although not his political banishment.

Alexander Hamilton. The secretary of treasury under President George Washington, he authored the bold financial plan that led to the first major political division in the Washington administration. In 1800, the New Yorker was at the forefront of Federalist opposition to the reelection of President John Adams. Alexander Hamilton by John Trumbull, after 1804, oil on canvas, 30½ × 25½ inches. Collection of the New-York Historical Society. Accession no. 1867.305.

Mercurial and indiscreet as well as extraordinarily gifted, Hamilton had a wide-ranging intelligence that allowed him to discuss the finer points of domestic and international law as well as the intricacies of finance and more practical matters.

One of the most controversial public men of the early republic, Hamilton was once characterized by Woodrow Wilson as "a very great man, but not a great American."[14] Wilson's frank assessment of Hamilton reflected the prevailing opinion of historians down to the recent past. Hamilton, it was agreed, was somehow outside the American tradition of democracy, with its healthy skepticism of power.

Critical of the Constitution for being too weak rather than too strong, Hamilton feared democracy. He was an admirer of the British monarchical system, believing it to be the "best in the world" although not possible in the United States. Nonetheless, the United States, he argued, needed a strong and vigorous national government, and that could only be accomplished if the executive and the upper house served for good behavior and the executive had absolute veto power over legislation. In addition, he advocated that all state governors be appointed by the federal government.[15]

Washington's secretary of state, Jefferson (1743–1826), had reddish hair and freckled skin and was taller than most of his contemporaries, standing a bit more than six feet. Like Hamilton, he was extraordinarily gifted. The Virginian's vast correspondence over time reveals a man of great intellect, who, through a lifetime of reading and study, acquired a wide-ranging expertise on an enormous variety of subjects. Conversant with classical history, natural history, philosophy, international law, and scientific agriculture, among other topics, he had a truly remarkable depth and breadth of knowledge.

Drafter of the Declaration of Independence, governor of Virginia during the Revolutionary War, and minister to France in the 1780s, he would have preferred to return to France and serve again as the minister there rather than assume the post in the cabinet. But after some hesitation, he felt duty bound to accept Washington's invitation and joined the cabinet.

Jefferson was hampered as a politician by his hatred of personal conflict and confrontation as well as his rather diffident and reserved manner. And this avoidance of dissension sometimes led to charges of dissembling by his critics.

Thus, throughout his career Jefferson grappled with how to balance his extreme sensitivity to public criticism with his strong sense of obligation to play an active and visible role in the public life of the new nation. As wartime governor of Virginia from 1779 to 1781, he had suffered the humiliation of a British invasion of the state that resulted in the burning of the capital at

President Thomas Jefferson. As secretary of state in George Washington's first administration, he found himself constantly at odds with Secretary of Treasury Alexander Hamilton over both domestic and foreign policy issues. Later, after a brief retirement, he reentered political life and became the center of opposition to the Federalists, running for president in 1796 and 1800. Thomas Jefferson at the National Bridge *by Caleb Boyle, ca. 1801, oil on canvas, 92 × 60.75 inches. Kirby Collection of Historical Paintings, Lafayette College, Easton, Pennsylvania.*

Richmond and his own near-capture. His ignominious escape on horseback from his home, Monticello, later brought charges of personal cowardliness and malfeasance in office. Although the charges were ultimately dismissed by the Virginia legislature, they continued to haunt Jefferson for the rest of his public career. In 1782, he mournfully wrote a friend that the experience had "inflicted a wound on my spirit that will only be cured by the all-healing grave."[16]

Senator William Maclay of Pennsylvania, who was not awed by the reputations of any of the Revolutionary elite who staffed the new government, saw Jefferson as having other flaws and offered a rather harsh appraisal of him. The secretary of state, he wrote, was a "slender man" with clothes "too small for him" and with an "air of stiffness in his manner." A man with a "sunny" face, Maclay observed, he sat "in a lounging manner, on one hip commonly, with one of his shoulders elevated much above the other," and had a "loose, shackling air" and "a rambling, vacant look" with "nothing of that firm, collected deportment which I expected would dignify the presence of a secretary or minister." And there was, Maclay pointed out, a "laxity of manner" in his personal bearing. Not only was he reserved and ill at ease in large public settings, according to Macclay, but in more intimate surroundings Jefferson "spoke almost without ceasing" in a "loose and rambling" way.[17]

The least distinguished member of the cabinet was Henry Knox (1750–1806), secretary of war. The chief of artillery during the Revolution, Knox was best known for his dogged loyalty to Washington.

As vice president, John Adams was not a member of the cabinet. In fact, he had no formal or informal duties in the Washington administration. Vice presidents then and up to the recent past had no official responsibilities outside of their constitutional role of presiding over the Senate.

v

As the government first assembled under the new Constitution, James Madison of Virginia expressed what surely must have been the majority sentiment. "We are in a wilderness," he said, "without a single footstep to guide us."[18] Despite the remarkable talents and skills of the leaders, there were no familiar signposts or precedents that could be turned to for support and direction. The domestic and foreign policy matters that had to be faced during the early days of the Washington administration were intractable and irreconcilable ones. In essence, they were closely related to the issues that would frame the election of 1800 eleven years later.

The most pressing and controversial question was how to finance the new federal government. It was a question that heightened sectional jealousies and raised grave concerns about the distribution of power between the federal government and the states. And revenue problems had, in fact, crippled the nation from the beginning. Washington himself had bitter memories of the Continental Congress failing to provide adequate financial support for his Continental Army. And the Articles of Confederation government had faltered as a result of not being able to raise adequate revenue.

To meet this challenge, Hamilton offered a bold plan that called for the national government to assume the debts of the states incurred during the Revolution, fund the national domestic and foreign debt inherited from the Confederation government, and create a national bank. To raise revenue, the plan proposed levying an excise tax.

Each component of the plan was controversial. In short, Hamilton's plan was an intensely political document with winners and losers—and thus staunch supporters and fierce opponents. For in defining the debt, in determining how to fund it, and in deciding whom to pay and how much, Hamilton favored certain economic groups and geographic areas over others.

Furthermore, there were profound implications regarding the power relationships between the federal government and the states. As one historian has pointed out, "Groups used to getting their way at home were unused to being thwarted in the new arena," which "aroused suspicions that 'the general welfare' was being sacrificed to faction."[19]

Moreover, bitter sectional fears, especially in the South, also were ignited by the scheme. Patrick Henry had earlier warned that the new government under the Constitution would lead to a "subserviency of Southern to Northern interests."[20] Now Hamilton's proposals seemed to be confirming those suspicions. Richard Henry (Light Horse Harry) Lee wrote James Madison in the early years of Washington's administration that he would rather "submit to all the hazards of war and risk the loss of everything dear to me in life . . . [than] to live under the rule of an . . . insolent northern majority."[21]

This sectional and state suspicion and fear of federal power were deeply entrenched. And it does not take a stretch of the imagination to understand the shock and horror that Virginians must have felt when it seemed to them as if their state, the wealthiest and most populous in the Union, was becoming subservient to the new federal government, or worse, the northeastern states.[22]

With a largely sectional vote in Congress—the representatives from northern states voting in favor and southern representatives in opposition—Hamilton's financial system did become law. For Jefferson and his more agrarian-minded colleagues, however, the Hamiltonian program was an anathema. To them it represented a bold scheme to transform and subvert the Constitution and to corrupt representatives of the new government by inducing them to support policies out of avarice and self-interest rather than the promotion of the public good. Even worse, they feared, it would lead to the creation of an overly strong and menacing central government that would, through the stimulation of commerce and industry, align itself with men of wealth and influence. Furthermore, they saw it as a disturbing reminder of the political and economic system in the British empire that Americans had repudiated—but that they now believed was serving as Hamilton's model.

VI

Even before the battle over Hamilton's financial program had divided Congress and the country, a historic chain of events had begun that would eventually alter the face of Europe and further destabilize American politics in the 1790s. Only a few months after Washington took the oath of office as the country's first president, the world was stunned to hear the reports from France about the fall of the Bastille on July 14, 1789, and the beginning of the French Revolution. Ultimately, in fact, it was the French Revolution that, by intensifying and hardening political differences, would become the major polarizing force in American politics, especially in the election of 1800.

At first, news of the revolution was greeted with euphoria by most Americans. There was an outpouring of sympathy and support for France as Americans embraced the idea that the French were following in America's footsteps by seeking their freedom from autocratic rule. This almost inevitable search for freedom, Americans were convinced, would now begin to be emulated throughout the world. Led by both America and France, they hoped, other countries mired in monarchism and aristocracy would inexorably shed their outmoded authoritarian governments and adopt republicanism as the wave of the future. Jefferson, who served as the U.S. minister to France from 1785 to 1789, even went so far as proclaiming that the "liberty of the whole earth" depended on the French Revolution's success.[23]

Therefore, as events unfolded in the early days of the revolution, Americans celebrated French successes and rued French failures, seeing France as a kind of yardstick for measuring and evaluating the future course of republicanism not only elsewhere but at home as well.

So, when the French Revolution turned more radical and violent with the execution of Louis XVI in January 1793, considerable fears were raised in the United States about the possible exportation of the contagion of extremism, brutality, and chaos beyond French borders.

The concern about France deepened further when a worldwide war broke out between the forces of England and revolutionary France. Desperate to stay out of the hostilities, which would end up lasting—with only intermittent truces—until 1815, the Washington administration issued a controversial Proclamation of Neutrality. Although Washington's action was supposedly an effort to prevent the United States from being pulled into the war between two of the world's great powers, many Americans condemned it, seeing it as a betrayal of both the ally who had come to America's aid against England during the American Revolution and also to the cause of republicanism. The "cause of France is the cause of man, and neutrality is desertion," one critic complained.[24]

Americans became even more upset when, despite the Washington administration's effort to maintain the country's neutral status, English warships began interdicting American merchantmen on the high seas as a means of preventing American trade with France and its colonies.

This insulting behavior forced the Washington administration to take stronger action. In an attempt to mollify the public and seek some solution to the diplomatic impasse, Washington sent Chief Justice of the Supreme Court John Jay to England to negotiate a resolution to the crisis. Although the resulting treaty did little to solve the major issues, it did, at least for the time being, prevent war between the United States and its old nemesis. It did not, however, address the problem of the impressment of American seamen by the English or lead to the recognition of American neutrality on the high seas.

The contest over Jay's treaty was the single most contentious issue during Washington's two terms of office, as the agreement seemed to its critics to be obsequious, insulting and compromising the country's sovereignty. Washington himself even came under partisan attack for his support of the treaty, House members at one point going so far as to break from their custom by refusing to celebrate his birthday. A few critics even called for the president's impeachment.

Thus, although antagonisms over domestic policy profoundly shaped and influenced the course of politics throughout the decade of the 1790s, it was the French Revolution and what ensued in its wake that infused the ongoing domestic political disputes with a polarizing ideology and passion that threatened the future of the country. By 1800 this would escalate into a potentially Union-breaking crisis.

2
THE ORIGINS OF NATIONAL POLITICS IN THE EARLY REPUBLIC

"Our greatest danger is from the contagion of levelism . . . [it] has set the world agog to be all equal to French barbers."
—A Federalist, 1793

I

The reproaches aimed at President George Washington after the ratification of the controversial Jay Treaty, although no indication of meaningful or widespread displeasure with the popular president himself, were nonetheless significant. They were signs of a changing political landscape within the country and government—a mounting divisiveness—that American leaders who came after the popular Washington would be left to grapple with in the years leading up to the election of 1800.

Washington himself, not wanting to seem pressured into leaving office by popular discontent, waited to publicly declare that he would not seek a third term until the publication of his Farewell Address in September 1796. This was based upon Alexander Hamilton's advice that he delay the announcement until a few months before the electors would choose a president in December. Hamilton told Washington that if his plans were left open as far as the public was concerned, the delay would have the advantage of restraining party activity to promote replacement candidates.

There was, however, a general consensus among the leaders of both parties in the late winter and early spring of 1796 that Washington most likely would not seek a third term and that Federalist vice president John Adams and Republican Thomas Jefferson would be the candidates.[1] And these two candidates in the first truly competitive presidential contest in the nation's history would also be pitted against one another once again, of course, in the election of 1800.

Informing and shaping the emerging political culture of the 1790s and both presidential elections were two countervailing, competing, and antithetical political philosophies. How these beliefs played off each other and animated and shaped political battles became the central political narrative of the new republic.

On the one hand, the American Revolution had been the catalyst for moving American society in a more democratic and egalitarian direction. This meant that ordinary citizens had, since the early 1790s, increasingly taken a more active, ongoing role in the oversight of their government. This ferment manifested itself in two ways. First, it spawned the creation of the boisterous and more radical Democratic Republican societies. Second, it caused the two emerging political parties to be more democratic and to start going outside Congress to recruit support and "collect the will of the people."

But underlying this popular spirit was a longstanding belief in classical republicanism, the ideology that had informed the political vision of the country's founders. This philosophy eschewed conflict and partisanship and embraced the notion of a determinable unified public good that could be ascertained by a selfless elite who would govern without regard to personal or sectional interests. James Madison of Virginia captured this sentiment in *Federalist 10* when he argued that representatives of the people in a republic would "refine and enlarge the public views by passing them through the medium of a chosen body of citizens, whose wisdom may best discern the true interest of their country and whose patriotism and love of justice will be least likely to sacrifice it to temporary or partial considerations."[2] In other words, Madison and other founders had faith that the independent, selfless, and virtuous elites who were envisioned as leading the new national government would be unencumbered by local or self-interests and would legislate on behalf of the larger "public interest."

II

This elitist view, however, was challenged as early as 1793 when extraconstitutional Democratic Republican societies began springing up, arguing that the public should play an active oversight role in governmental decision making in a republic. Since the federal government seemed so remote, as many Antifederalists in their campaign against the adoption of the Constitution had argued it would, these societies saw themselves as an invaluable means of educating ordinary citizens about the activities and policies of the government and then helping them voice their opinions through letters, resolutions, and petitions.

One proponent vigorously praised the societies and eloquently articulated their democratic function. "Tell me, if you can," the essayist asserted, "in what manner you communicate information to the mass of people, but by forming them into town meetings or societies. . . . Without such institutions, the public will cannot be determined and government has no solid base." Most citizens, he went on to say, did not have access to information except "in a town meeting or society," but through these "every man may . . . know and judge . . . the conduct of the agent he has entrusted [to represent him] . . . whether he is faithfully served or basely betrayed."[3]

These societies had been formed in response to a growing sense on the part of many Americans that the government under Washington was insensitive to their wishes, especially to their support of revolutionary France. One New York member flatly declared that "he who is an enemy to the French revolution . . . ought not to be intrusted [sic] with the guidance of any part of the machine of government."[4]

Heirs of the Sons of Liberty and Committees of Correspondence that had been established to solicit and enforce support for the American Revolution, these societies quickly grew in number to thirty-five.[5] But while these clubs clearly had American precedents, they were also similar in organization and political purpose to the French revolutionary Jacobin clubs, albeit without the violence. This similarity, along with these societies' displays of support for the French Revolution and their active engagement in the "public sphere" of the United States, caused them to be viewed with suspicion among the supporters of the Washington administration and the more conservative members of American society.[6]

The popularity of the Democratic Republican societies, however, turned out to be short-lived. By 1796 they had virtually disappeared, having been discredited after being charged with fomenting the brief but rancorous western Pennsylvania insurrection against the federal excise tax on whiskey in 1794. Although there was scant evidence that the societies were directly involved in the so-called Whiskey Rebellion,[7] and the majority of the societies condemned the violence associated with it, supporters of the Washington administration and other Americans as well believed they bore some responsibility for the uprising.

In the late fall of 1794 President Washington publicly denounced the societies for their alleged support of the whiskey rebels, saying that he feared them to be linked to French intrigue "to sow sedition [and] poison the minds of the people of this country."[8] His statement reflected a growing concern that the activities of these societies could lead to the same kind of mounting violence and disruption of the civil order that was being experienced in France.

Another critic denounced the societies as arrogantly pretending "sometimes to be the people, and sometimes the guardians, the champions of the people" and as having "more zeal for republican principles than *real* Representatives." In addition, he accused the societies of spreading jealousies and suspicions as well as "fomenting daring outrages against social order and the authority of the laws."[9]

Despite their brief existence, the Democratic Republican societies raised critical questions about the nature of sovereignty and representation in the new republic. Historian Edmund Morgan argues that James Madison "invented a sovereign people" in his proposals at the Constitutional Convention in order to assure the primacy of the national government over the states. But what does it mean that the people are sovereign? The answer, Morgan claims, is that the sovereignty of the people, like representation itself, "is a fiction that cannot survive too close examination or too literal application." "It requires that we believe not only in the existence of something we call people," he asserts, "but also in the capacity of that something to make decisions and to act apart from the elected representatives of particular localities."[10]

Adding to the ambiguity, a number of Americans in the early republic, including the whiskey rebels as well as Jefferson and others, sometimes failed to differentiate between what James Madison and other founders had seen as the two sovereign functions of the people in a republic, the *extraordinary* and the *ordinary*. First, the proclaiming of the Declaration of Independence and the ratifying of the Constitution in 1788 clearly represented *extraordinary* actions exercised by a sovereign people in their constituent, constitution-making role contesting the legitimacy of the constituted authorities. Second, the people in a republic were also expected to exercise *ordinary* electoral duties within the legal framework of the Constitution when they chose representatives to act as their spokesmen.

An appreciation of the distinction between these two roles was considered to be crucial. Madison, in *Federalist 49*, for example, had warned that frequent appeals to the people would "deprive the government of that veneration which time bestows on everything," would disturb the "public tranquility," and would arouse "public passions" by "a frequent reference of constitutional questions to the decision of the whole society." Therefore, it was of great importance, Madison had argued, that while the constitution-making role of the people should be "kept open for certain great and extraordinary occasions," there were "insuperable objections" to constant and frequent appeals to the people.[11]

Thus, in the early republic, there was great uncertainty about the kind of oversight role the "sovereign people" should play in government. Like Madison, most of the elites who composed the membership of the early national government were undoubtedly uneasy with the notion that the people needed to play any ongoing oversight role. Instead, they probably would have agreed with the observer who wrote that the people were only "sovereign on days of their elections." [12]

III

At the same time the Democratic Republican societies were agitating for a more democratic politics, noisily supporting the French revolutionaries and denouncing the policies of the Washington administration, the two loosely drawn and sectionally defined political parties were slowly beginning to emerge. Supporting the Washington administration and Hamilton's financial plan were the Federalists, who also tended to champion England in its war with France. In opposition to Hamilton and the president were the Republicans, including Madison and Jefferson, who identified more closely with the French cause and were somewhat more egalitarian in their outlook.

Both Republicans and Federalists, however, were uneasy with the boisterousness and popular enthusiasm of the Democratic Republican societies. Although most of the societies' members most likely did eventually join the Republican ranks, the Virginia leadership discreetly kept its distance from them in 1793 and during Washington's second term of office. The unabashed egalitarian support for France and radicalism expressed by some of the clubs persuaded Jefferson and Madison that, although they shared many ideas with members of these organizations, they were a liability in national politics.

The Federalists, on the other hand, almost fanatically disagreed with what the societies stood for. Yet, they did begin to learn from them by recognizing the usefulness of attracting and mobilizing a public following. And they responded by starting to organize public activities and events in support of their own cause to compete with those organized by the societies.

The names identifying the two parties were not inadvertently chosen. By calling themselves Republicans, Jefferson and his colleagues meant to convey to themselves and the public that they were devoted to republicanism and representative government—as well as opposed to executive encroachment upon liberty. The Federalists, for their part, adopted the name of those who had supported the ratification of the Constitution, implying that those who opposed them, the Republicans, were disloyal to the new frame of government. And both parties sometimes labeled their opponents as Tories, an attempt to brand their protagonists as somehow un-American and hostile to republicanism and the American Revolution.

This adoption of these party designations, however, did not mean that the participants themselves accepted the idea that they had created political parties. Paradoxically, both Federalists and Republicans condemned *parties* as divisive and factious while nonetheless perceiving *themselves* as the true defenders of the country's "public good," standing up against the disruptive partisanship of their opponents.[13]

Ultimately, competing political parties would be the agencies that would provide public oversight over the role of government in the United States. But in the 1790s, "party" and "faction" were used by most Americans as pejorative terms to defame opponents. For example, Jefferson once wrote that if he "could not go to heaven but with a party," he would choose not to go there at all.[14]

As the radicalism associated with the French Revolution infused ideology and passion into the American schism that had primarily originated with disputes over domestic political policies, the stakes seemed increasingly to involve the very existence of the republic and the Union. Both sides feared that the same drama between revolution and reaction that was taking place in Europe might also be playing out in the United States.[15] So when Jefferson and others saw the success of the American republic as tied to success in France, it terrified the Federalists, who regarded this popular infatuation with France as deluded and dangerous. Their Republican opponents, the Federalists were convinced, were no less than agents of radical revolution who were conspiring to transplant a destabilizing democratic egalitarianism on American soil.

"Our greatest danger is from the contagion of levelism," warned one Federalist, for it "has set the world agog to be all equal to French barbers." He described the Republican opponents of the Washington administration as nothing but "a noisy set of discontented demagogues mak[ing] a rant," while Federalist supporters of the government were composed of "the great body of men of property" who "move slowly but move with sure success."[16]

Confusing as it might seem, most Americans in the early republic—those aligned with both parties—also still held onto the belief that classical republicanism would inform and shape the conduct of the national government, guiding policy deliberations and overcoming petty differences. This was despite the fact that classical republicanism relegated the electorate to a more or less passive role and was thus at odds with the countercurrent in the country characterized by an increasingly democratic public beginning to demand some type of oversight role over the government.

Ironically, the failure in the 1790s of elected officials in the federal government to act in the anticipated selfless, disinterested way did not weaken the appeal of classical republicanism. But it did intensify the divisions between the parties. For as sharply conflicting perceptions of the public good emerged, each side attempted to embrace and define its own understanding of the concept and to equate this understanding with the survival of the republic and the Constitution.

Thus, this sharp and potentially disastrous division over differing conceptions of the public good was a major factor in preventing the acceptance of the legitimacy of political opposition, which in turn accentuated and heightened the gulf between the two parties and kept them from being parties in the modern sense. For, as one scholar has pointed out, one of the "great milestones in the development of democratic institutions" is the "right of an organized opposition to appeal for votes against government in elections."[17]

But this development would only come later, at a time when the country and its institutions were less vulnerable, and when contending groups, no matter how much they might dislike one another, had learned to trust that their opponents would govern within the bounds of the Constitution.

In the early republic, however, opposition to government policies, in many instances, was viewed not as merely opposition to a specific government or administration, but as opposition and disloyalty to the Constitution and the republic. And while Americans would eventually clearly identify government as a temporarily empowered authority operating within the boundaries established by the Constitution, this was a difficult concept to accept in the period immediately after the ratification of the Constitution—and indeed even at times of great crisis in the later history of the country.

In his valedictory address that was based on an earlier draft written by James Madison in 1792 and largely rewritten by Alexander Hamilton in 1796, Washington himself spoke out emphatically against "the danger of parties in the State, with particular reference to the founding of them on geographical discriminations." The "spirit of party" had "baneful effects," he declared. It not only agitated the "community with ill-founded jealousies and false alarms," it also opened the door to corruption and foreign influence.[18]

In rebuttal, William Duane, a Republican editor, condemned Washington's address as being in and of itself flagrantly partisan in its denunciation of political opposition, whether it be from the Republicans or the Democratic Republican societies. Washington's "judgment," he charged, "must have been under the domination of a most domineering prejudice" when he "pronounced an anathema against all combination and association, because a few popular societies of . . . [his] countrymen *dared to assert their opinions in opposition to [him].*"[19]

Despite Washington's admonition and the widely accepted conventional wisdom that "parties" were destructive and detrimental, however, partisanship intensified throughout the decade. So, by the time of the election of 1800, the two parties dominated politics. They organized and ordered the contest and also infused it with ideologies that amplified the differences between them. However, this still did not mean that either party recognized its opponent's legitimacy, or that the participants saw parties as rightfully sharing power in some sort of alternating fashion. Rather, it meant that each of these parties was organized around the belief that it, and it alone, was the interpreter and translator of the wishes of a fictive sovereign people.[20]

IV

Although modern parties did not emerge in the 1790s, efforts by Federalists and Republicans to organize and mobilize grassroots support did. Exasperated by the deep sectional divisions in Congress and the failure to find agreement on fundamental questions, partisans on both sides aggressively turned to the public to legitimize their own conception of the public good.

A key political figure in these endeavors for the Republicans was John Beckley, who had come to Virginia from England in 1769 as a twelve-year-old indentured servant but rose to become a valued Republican factotum nonetheless. Inferior in status and rank to the Virginia gentlemen he served, Beckley was an industrious, intelligent clerk, a plebian who was tireless and creative in orchestrating popular support for the Republicans through his leadership of sophisticated (for the day) canvassing and organizing efforts. Coming first to New York and then in 1789 to the Philadelphia capital to work for the Virginia Republicans, he became the first clerk of the House of Representatives. Later, he helped marshal public opposition to the Jay Treaty, which represented the most significant step in the 1790s toward the popular mobilization of the electorate.

During the presidential election of 1796, Beckley electioneered in Pennsylvania, which had a tradition of popular participation in politics, distributing 30,000 tickets displaying the names of the prominent Pennsylvanians who were listed as Republican electors.[21] Although sometimes anachronistically described as a "party manager" or "campaign manager" by historians, Beckley might have more closely resembled what would later be recognized as a party boss. But there was a fundamental difference. He, like the elites he labored for, viewed politics in the early republic through the lens of the classical republican ideology that celebrated "partnership in virtue among all citizens . . . in the pursuit of the universal good."[22] Thus, Beckley embodied a partisan nonpartisanship.

During the 1796 campaign in Pennsylvania, a Republican address to the people reflected this seemingly contradictory understanding by declaring that Jefferson, "a man of enlightened views, such pure patriotism, such unsullied integrity, and such zeal for human happiness, can alone make our country flourishing, tranquil and happy." Rising above factious interests, he "will be the cement of discordant interests, and of jarring passions—Of no party but the great party of human benefactors, he will allay the heats of our country, heal its divisions, and calm the boisterous elements of political controversy."[23]

This expectation of civic harmony and selfless behavior all working toward the realization of a national public good under the leadership of a virtuous elite was, however, increasingly at odds with the political reality of the 1790s. But signs of this did not discourage men like Beckley or the elite Republican and Federalist leaders themselves. Instead, it caused them to rationalize their partisanship not as a violation of classical republican ideals, but rather as an effort to promote the national public good.

Beckley, for example, asserted in 1800 that the election of Jefferson was a "great national object, in which are involved the peace, liberty & happiness of Country."[24] Therefore, Republican objectives, it was believed, were not narrow, sectional or selfish, but, on the contrary, could be more accurately characterized as congruent with the nation's welfare.

▼

Beckley's activities, however, were just one example of the growing participatory and dynamic politics that developed in the 1790s. As time went on, it became more and more common for Federalists and Republicans to attempt to monopolize patriotic symbols and rhetoric for their own political benefit. As part of this, they increasingly used a variety of activities to recruit, mobilize, and propagandize the public, including banquets, street theater for demonstrations, parades, and festivals. These public celebrations were designed to attract and hold popular support and to give Americans the opportunity to become involved as active rather than passive citizens.

Tributes on Washington's birthday, for example, were used not only to pay homage to the widely beloved president, but to promote support for the Federalists, who represented themselves as defenders of the Constitution and the republic.[25] These Federalist birthday observances as well as other public celebrations, especially on the Fourth of July, became even more blatantly partisan over the years, as supporters of the administration took advantage of these events to exploit the president's great popularity for political advantage.

The Republican opposition was also successful in using Independence Day festivities to gain popular support for their attacks on the Federalists. Indeed, these patriotic celebrations were an important means for the Republicans to reach out to middle- and lower-class Americans and identify their opposition to the Washington administration with the ideals and beliefs of the American Revolution.

Critics of the Federalists also commemorated Bastille Day, July 14, as well as other anniversaries of the French revolutionary armies' military victories. In 1792, the opposition *National Gazette*, for example, asserted that Bastille Day was a very appropriate day to hold a postponed Fourth of July celebration. "On this day," it was argued, "it is expected, there will, in the future, be a general rejoicing in every part of the United States, *by all* who are Friends to the French Revolution, and consequently *real friends* to the revolution in America." And after war broke out between revolutionary France and England, American Francophiles, wearing liberty caps, toasted French victories.[26]

In reporting on a Fourth of July commemoration in Philadelphia in 1793, one newspaper pointedly contrasted the observances of Independence Day and Washington's birthday. "Let slaves toast the birth-days of their masters," it was contended, while "freemen will celebrate that of liberty."

Popular participation in Republican and other anti-administration celebrations swelled during Washington's second term, with the crowds more broadly representative of the general population and reflecting a growing popular opposition to Federalist policies. In Newark, New Jersey, in 1793, for example, some one hundred residents of that city attended an open-air feast that followed a militia parade. In Baltimore the following year, militia volunteers toasted the people as the "fountain of power" while the government served only as the "trustees of the people." This was a clear and eloquent declaration of the democratic belief in the oversight role of the sovereign people in a republic. And in 1795, almost 8 percent of the adult white male population participated in a New York City Fourth of July parade.[27]

Not only were American men politicized by the French Revolution, so were American women, especially in the cities. French women actively participated in a host of public events having to do with the radical upheaval in their country, and American women copied them by involving themselves in similar activities.

Thus, throughout the decade American women hosted salons at which a variety of topics were discussed and also took part in other affairs. In August 1794, in Philadelphia, for instance, women organized an elaborate public ceremony modeled on one that had taken place in Paris almost a year earlier. "Maidens dressed in white and tri-color costumes" paraded, accompanied by music, to the French minister's house to show their support for the French Revolution.[28]

As one historian has noted, "American women used public celebrations of the French cause as an avenue to the political sphere, adopting new clothing and forms of address and engaging in a wider array of public activities." And it was the French model that was the catalyst that "encouraged women to assert their allegiances and expand their participation in public political culture" in the highly charged and polarized public sphere of the 1790s.[29]

3

THE FAILURE OF NATIONAL UNITY

*"Any false, scandalous and malicious writings against the government
. . . with intent to defame . . . or to bring them . . . into contempt or
disrepute" is prohibited.*
—Sedition Act, 1798

I

As Vice President John Adams returned to Philadelphia
to open the congressional session and to preside over the
Senate in December 1796, it was not his duties in the Senate
that preoccupied him. Instead, it was the torment of waiting to hear the results of the presidential election between
himself and Thomas Jefferson. Convinced that he had been
defeated by his Virginia rival, he was overcome by "Cold feelings of unpopularity. Humble reflections. Mortifications.
Humiliation. Plans of future life. Economy. Retrenching ex-
penses. Farming. Returning to the bar, drawing writs, arguing causes, taking clerks." In a brutally frank, personal, and
insightful self-assessment, Adams inconsolably poured out
his heart to his wife, Abigail, confiding that he was "alone
abed, by my fireside, nobody to speak to, pouring [sic] upon
my disgrace and future prospects—this is ugly."[1] Within a
short time, however, his agony ended when he found that
his pessimism had been unwarranted. It was he who had
been victorious.

Unlike Adams, Jefferson had been a reluctant and de-
tached candidate. Having resigned his position as secretary
of state in 1793, Jefferson had given no indication that he
would ever reenter public life. In 1794 he had written James
Madison asserting that he "would not give up . . . [his] own

retirement for the empire of the universe." A few months later he reaffirmed his decision even more emphatically by stating that the question was "forever closed."[2]

Why Jefferson allowed his name to be put forward as the candidate in 1796 by an informal caucus of Republican members of Congress is not entirely clear. One possible explanation for Jefferson's becoming at least passively receptive rather than overtly hostile to returning to public life was that his retirement to Monticello in 1793 had failed to live up to his idealized expectations. A letter to his daughter in 1802 is perhaps revelatory. In it Jefferson reflected on his retirement and offers a possible insight into his changed state of mind in 1796. In his retirement years, his daughter was told, "I remained closely at home, saw none but those who came there, and at length became very sensible of the ill effect it had upon my own mind, [rendering] me unfit for society" and leading "to an [sic] misanthropic state of mind." Happiness, Jefferson advised, "requires that we should continue to mix with the world . . . and every person who retires from free communication with it is severely punished afterwards by the state of mind into which they get."[3] Even as late as September 1796, however, Jefferson's candidacy seemed to be in doubt, prompting the publication of an unsigned letter asserting that the Virginia Republican would, in fact, "serve in the office of President of the United States, if elected."[4]

Once the ballots were counted in December, Adams was shown to have finished with seventy-one electoral votes to Jefferson's sixty-eight. Jefferson's second place finish, under the constitutional provision that pertained until the passage of the Twelfth Amendment in 1804, elevated him to the vice presidency.[5]

A breakdown of the vote reveals a deep sectional split of just the sort that Washington had warned against in his Farewell Address. Adams carried New England, New York, and New Jersey, while only twelve of his seventy-one votes came from states south of Pennsylvania. Jefferson, on the other hand, received fourteen votes from Pennsylvania, with all the rest coming from southern and western states.[6]

Both presidential aspirants, distinguished Whig leaders of the Revolution, had served the country in a number of capacities before the new government was established under the Constitution in 1789. And despite being from different areas of the country and having competed for leadership roles during the Revolution, Adams and Jefferson, while not close friends, had a civil relationship—albeit an edgy one, as each of the men was privately suspicious, critical, and perhaps somewhat jealous of the other.

But the civility between the colleagues would become strained to the breaking point by the stark political differences that damaged their relationship almost beyond repair during Adams's presidency. The estrangement was so complete and severe that it was not until after Jefferson had left his presidency in 1809 that the old patriots would become reconciled and begin a warm and engaging correspondence that would continue until their deaths. As a matter of fact, as one historian has pointed out, the two "exchanged only fourteen letters between 1794 and 1812."[7]

Early on, before Adams and Jefferson would compete against each other for the presidency, the Virginian had offered an unflattering assessment of his colleague's diplomatic skills in Paris working to negotiate a peace treaty to end the American Revolution. Not only was Adams vain, Jefferson wrote, he "hates Franklin, he hates Jay, he hates the French, he hates the English."[8] Although conceding that Adams had a "sound head" and integrity, he went on to damn him with faint praise by adding that at "any rate honesty may be expected even from poisonous weeds."[9]

Jefferson fared no better in a private assessment made by Adams. Despite outward appearances, Adams claimed, at the time of Jefferson's retirement from Washington's cabinet in 1793, Jefferson was consumed by ambition and, in fact, was "as ambitious as Oliver Cromwell." "Jefferson thinks," Adams asserted, that he can "get a reputation of a humble modest man, meek man, wholly without ambition or vanity," and he "may even have deceived himself into this belief." However, he concluded, the real truth was that Jefferson's "soul is poisoned with ambition."[10]

Of the two candidates, Adams (1735–1826) was the older. He was born in Braintree, Massachusetts, a small village on the main road between Plymouth and Boston. Trained as a lawyer after his Harvard education, he then successfully established himself as an honest and effective advocate, winning several high-profile cases. He combined his legal work, however, with the running of his farm in Braintree, which he did with great pleasure and a profound sense of satisfaction. No mere weekend farmer, Adams relied on his farm to provide a critical source of income for his family.

Adams entered public life when he served as a delegate from his native state to the Continental Congress. And, with Benjamin Franklin, Thomas Jefferson, Roger Sherman, and Robert R. Livingston, he was on the drafting committee that produced the Declaration of Independence. Then, at the end of the Revolution in 1783, the Massachusetts native was sent to France to represent his young republic and help negotiate the Treaty of Paris that ended the war. Once peace had been concluded between the United States and England, Adams was dispatched to London to represent his country in the court of the new nation's old adversary.

Over the years, historians have portrayed Adams as a learned, brilliant man, recognizing him as a reader of the classics in Latin and Greek and an avid gentleman scholar who prized learning and had a deep understanding of law, government, and history. And yet at the same time they have seen him as a failed politician who was arrogant, impractical, irascible, ill-tempered, testy, awkward in his relations, rigid in his ideas, frugal to a fault, unforgiving in his personal relationships, and somewhat of a provincial. He has also been described as short and squat, thus not physically imposing, especially in contrast to Jefferson, who was tall, graceful, worldly, and a bit of a dandy and spendthrift.

The charge by Jefferson and other Republicans that Adams was a monarchist has further haunted his reputation, as have the words of Benjamin Franklin portraying him as "always an honest man, often a wise one, but sometimes, and in some things, absolutely out of his senses."[11]

Still, Adams's writings reveal a man, especially in contrast to Jefferson, who was sometimes almost painfully self-reflective and self-aware.[12] And recently, biographer David McCullough has succeeded in humanizing the former president, describing him as flawed and frank in his opinions but brave, courageous, and unswerving in his sense of duty.[13]

A dedicated and loving husband, Adams regarded his wife Abigail (1744–1818) as his most trusted confidante. The other half and equal partner of this remarkable couple, she was the most extraordinary woman of her generation. Had she lived at a time when women were more fully acknowledged as equals in American society, she surely would have had a significant and productive public career. An astute judge of character, she had an unerring and insightful perspective on individuals and public policy—and would often give her husband a frank and honest assessment rather than a more polite and socially acceptable one. She was her husband's chief advisor, and each was the other's best friend. When the two were apart, each felt bereft and incomplete.

Elected as George Washington's vice president for two terms, Adams served in the constitutional yet isolating role of the presiding officer of the Senate. Yet, in 1796, the vice presidency had made him the most logical Federalist candidate to succeed Washington.

Nonetheless, Alexander Hamilton was convinced that Adams was not the best choice to be the nominee. In fact, he had schemed unsuccessfully

President John Adams. His decision in 1799 to conclude a peace treaty with France, although courageous in retrospect, earned him the enmity of Alexander Hamilton and others. It ultimately led to severely splitting the Federalist party. John Adams *by Gilbert Stuart, ca. 1800/1815. Gift of Mrs. Robert Homans. Image courtesy of the Board of Trustees, National Gallery of Art, Washington, D.C.*

to have the man who was chosen to be Adams's vice presidential running mate, Thomas Pinckney of South Carolina, selected as the presidential candidate over Adams. This split between Adams and Hamilton would ultimately cause the fatal schism within the Federalist party that would lead to its downfall. So, while Adams prevailed in the election, he belatedly had to deal with a Hamilton-led rebellion within his own ranks when he assumed the presidency.

One Federalist opponent of Adams summed up the deep misgivings that some Federalists had about the new president in 1797, shortly after he was sworn in. "Mr. Adams," he charged, is "a man of great vanity . . . capricious, of a very moderate share of prudence . . . and of far less real abilities than he believes he possesses." The letter writer gloomily prophesied that this split within the Federalist party would lead to even greater political polarization. "We shall divide under the names of Federalist and Democrat," he warned, "and war as we did under those of Whig and Tory, with the same acrimony."[14] This pessimistic assessment and the harkening back to the terms "Whig and Tory" reflected the writer's view of society as being highly polarized, with each side imagining the worst about its opponent and failing to recognize that both sides did share a consensual loyalty to the Constitution, the Union, and the republic.

Adams himself was deeply resentful of the intrigue to deny him the presidency. "There have been maneuvers and combinations in this election," he wrote Abigail, "that would surprise you." And he pointed to Hamilton as an "active spirit in the Union, who will fill it with his politics wherever he is. . . . [H]e must be attended to, and not suffered to do too much."[15]

II

Perhaps because of the split between the Adams and Hamilton Federalists, there was a shared interest among Adams's supporters and some Republicans immediately after the election to rise above partisanship and work together to form a government of national unity. The new administration of Adams and Jefferson, it was hoped, would rekindle the old collegiality from the days of the Revolution. This show of accord, it was argued, might stop the dangerous spiraling of enmity and dissension that threatened to destroy the republic and instead move the country toward the type of consensual non-partisanship that had been outlined in the Federalist Papers.[16]

One correspondent wrote Hamilton that Adams's supporters believed that it was in the best "interest of the Country to have Mr. Jefferson for vice president rather than Pinckney" because Jefferson would "serve readily under Mr. Adams, and will be influenced by and coincide with him."[17]

Elbridge Gerry, a close friend of Adams and fellow resident of Massachusetts, also looked forward to seeing how the Adams-Jefferson administration might work to heal the growing political bitterness that had characterized the second Washington term. Adams, Gerry envisaged, would serve his two terms as president with Jefferson as his vice president; then, following the established precedent, Jefferson would succeed Adams as chief executive.[18]

Adams himself expressed a measured optimism about the prospect of a harmonious relationship with Jefferson.[19] The two men, Adams claimed, had labored "together in high friendship" since their service together in the Continental Congress, and he fully expected that the Virginian's "ancient friendship, his good sense and general good disposition" would result in a good working rapport between the two even "if not as cordial and uniform a support" as Adams himself had given Washington.[20]

One Federalist noted that after the results of the election had become known, the Republican press was not so scurrilously hostile and that the Republicans were "recommending . . . conciliation of parties." And the *Philadelphia General Advertiser*— the chief Republican newspaper, which had savagely attacked Adams during the fall of 1796—did abruptly change its tune after the election. An Adams presidency would soothe "the irritated public mind" and harmonize "the different parties," it predicted. This would be possible because "ADAMS and JEFFERSON, lately rivals, and competitors for the most distinguished station which a free people can confer, appear in the amiable light of friends. . . . Surely this harmony presages the most happy consequences to our country" and signals an abatement of "THE VIOLENCE OF PARTY."[21]

The potential of an Adams-Jefferson alliance worried Hamilton, who saw it as an impediment to his own domestic and foreign policy objectives. "Our Jacobins [Republicans] say they are well pleased and the Lion and the Lamb are to lie down together," Hamilton gloomily wrote another Federalist. Both Adams's supporters and the Republicans were predicting "a united and a vigorous administration," he said, but even more disturbing, some Federalists were concluding that Jefferson was "not half so ill a man as we have been accustomed to think him."[22]

III

This political honeymoon, however, proved to be only a brief interlude. It ended before it was even consummated. A diplomatic crisis and a quasi-naval war with France immediately captured the energy and attention of the Adams administration and dashed any hope that an Adams-Jefferson coalition would rise above party and sectional antagonisms and govern in a selfless public-spirited manner. In fact, the crisis would go on to consume Adams throughout his presidency.

The first crack in the honeymoon harmony came as a result of a discussion between Adams and Jefferson before the inauguration. Facing dangerously deteriorating relations with France, Adams sought to assemble a diplomatic delegation to travel to France and work to mollify the French as well as forestall any domestic political criticisms. Adams told the Virginian that, while he would like to appoint him as a member of the delegation, he supposed that Jefferson's constitutional duties as vice president would prevent him from accepting such an assignment. Therefore, Adams told Jefferson, he wished to nominate Madison along with Gerry to join the newly appointed Charles Cotesworth Pinckney, who was already in France, as the country's emissaries. And Adams asked Jefferson to investigate Madison's availability.

It was an appointment that was not to be, however. Madison told Jefferson that he would not even consider accepting the post, asserting that his presence as a member of the delegation might result in the Republicans being blamed for any failure that might occur. But Adams also ran into trouble with his own party, finding his cabinet members, all inherited from the Washington administration, to be adamantly opposed to Madison's appointment. In fact, they threatened to resign if Adams went through with the appointment.

So, a short time later, when strolling home with Adams after the two had had dinner with Washington, Jefferson told Adams that Madison would not accept such an appointment. To this news, Jefferson wrote in his diary, Adams responded "that on consultation, some objections to that nomination had been raised which he had not contemplated; and was going on with excuses which evidently embarrassed him, when we came to Fifth street, where our road separated."

Jefferson saw this incident as the turning point in his relations with Adams. From that point on, he said, Adams never brought up the subject again "or ever consulted me as to any measure of government." Jefferson thus concluded that for a short time after the election Adams had forgotten "party sentiment," and had intended "to steer impartially between parties." However, pressures from his cabinet had successfully pressed him to abandon his nonpartisan approach, and afterward he had "returned to his former party views."[23]

Jefferson's account of the incident that caused him and Adams to part ways was corroborated by Adams, who later recalled that following their conversation about Madison he and Jefferson had "parted as good friends as we had always lived; but we consulted very little afterwards." This, Adams said, was the result of the "Party violence," which "soon rendered . . . [cooperation between the two] impracticable, or at least useless, and this party violence was excited by Hamilton more than any other man."[24]

IV

So, it was without a government of national unity, and with a fractious Federalist party, that Adams had to turn his attention to dealing with the rapidly deteriorating relations with France that represented the country's greatest foreign policy challenge since the ratification of the Constitution.

It was the French, angered by the Jay Treaty, who precipitated the crisis. Believing the 1795 agreement to be overly accommodating to England and a signal that the relationship between the former mother country and its old colony was becoming close once again, the French began intercepting and capturing American ships that were trading with France's enemies in the same way that the English had intercepted and captured American vessels. In addition, to underscore their displeasure with the United States, they refused to receive an American minister.

In an effort to resolve the dispute that greeted him upon becoming president, Adams did send three cabinet-approved commissioners to France (Madison not included, of course) to negotiate a treaty of commerce and amity. In addition, wanting to pursue a peaceful course and yet at the same time to prepare for a possible war, Adams also proposed strengthening the navy and army.

Some Federalists saw Adams's recommendations as too tentative and pressed for a declaration of war against France. Hamilton, who no longer was in the cabinet but who nonetheless played a large role behind the scenes as a sort of shadow prime minister, was not willing to go that far. Nevertheless, he was critical of Adams, rallying support for the country to take more dramatic steps than Adams had advocated.

Exacerbating the president's problem with his own party was the earlier decision Adams had made to abide by Washington's request to keep the existing Washington cabinet in place. Members of this group included Secretary of War James McHenry (1753–1816) and Secretary of Treasury Oliver Wolcott, Jr. (1760–1833), both of whom were literally spies for Hamilton. The third major player was Secretary of State Timothy Pickering (1745–1829), who, while perhaps more independent, also was a bitter opponent of Adams. Later, Adams ruefully reflected that keeping the three as part of his administration was one of his worst mistakes: it ended up destroying his presidency. But if he had disagreed with Washington's request, he later lamented, it would have turned "the World upside down." Others, notably Jefferson, recognized Adams's predicament earlier than the president himself did, observing that the Hamiltonians who surrounded Adams were "only a little less hostile to him than to me."[25]

All of the anger directed toward France and the talk about a military buildup outraged the Republicans, who denounced what they believed was ill-advised Federalist-contrived anti-French hysteria being engineered to generate popular support for a war against France. While pretending to defend and support the new republic and the Constitution, they alleged, the Federalists in truth had "secret designs for monarchizing American society and government."[26] As early as June 1797, Jefferson reported that tensions had risen so high in Philadelphia that former friends had been estranged to the point that "men who have been intimate all their lives, cross the streets to avoid meeting, and turn their head another way, lest they should be obliged to touch their hats."[27]

In the midst of this commotion, Jefferson wrote to New Yorker Aaron Burr, who had been his running mate in 1796 (as he would be in 1800). In the letter Burr was told that the president's promise of negotiations was an empty gesture given the militant mood of the administration and its supporters, and that the real intention was to take the country to war against France.

When Washington retired from the presidency, Jefferson went on to say, Jefferson had anticipated that "the natural feeling of the people toward liberty would restore the equilibrium between the Executive and Legislative departments," which had been destroyed by the immense popularity of the president during his two terms in office. Regrettably, however, the French crisis was acting as a surrogate for Washington, Jefferson perceptively observed, and the country was entering a critical point in its history during which its "future character" and "future fortune" were being shaped. If a full-blown war with France were to break out, Burr was told, it would further fuel the anti-French fervor. And this would bring about "what force could not, and . . . we shall, in the end, be driven back to the land from which we launched 20 years ago."[28]

Jefferson's 1797 letter to Burr had at least two political purposes. First, it was an effort by Jefferson to mend fences and reestablish good relations with the New Yorker, who had run fourth among the presidential and vice-presidential candidates in 1796 and had felt betrayed by the Virginians, who had given him only one out of the twenty-one electoral votes that were possible from that state. This Virginia display of suspicion and hostility would be remembered by Burr as events played out in the election of 1800.

Second, it was an attempt to rally his erstwhile ally, for the alliance with the New Yorker was vital to Republican plans for winning the election of 1800, which Jefferson was already beginning to look toward. Adams had won New York's twelve electoral votes in 1796, and it was clear that the Republicans had to maintain their strength in the South and West and to win more votes in the Middle Atlantic states in order to capture the presidency in the next election.

Adams's problems further worsened when the war crisis with France sharply escalated after the American commissioners he had sent were snubbed, the French government refusing to have any official contact with them. Instead, four unofficial French representatives, later scornfully dubbed W, X, Y, and Z by Adams, were sent to meet with the Americans. In these demeaning ex-officio talks in October 1797, the French further insulted the American representatives by rebuffing the American call for negotiations and demanding a bribe of $250,000 for the foreign minister Charles Maurice de Talleyrand and a loan of $10 million to the republic of France.

Dispatches revealing the failed negotiations did not reach the United States until March 1798. But, after consulting with his cabinet, Adams decided against making the inflammatory details of the failed negotiations public at that time or requesting an immediate declaration of war. Instead, in his message to Congress that month, Adams only indicated that the mission had been unsuccessful and called for further strengthening of the nation's defenses.

Once some of the details of the abortive mission began to leak out, however, the more militant Federalists saw it as giving them a real political advantage vis-à-vis the Republicans. It "will afford a glorious opportunity to destroy faction," gloated Senator Theodore Sedgwick of Massachusetts. And in a series of newspaper essays, Hamilton questioned the patriotism of the members of the Republican opposition. They had, he asserted, made "unremitting efforts to justify or excuse the despots of France, to vilify and discredit our own government, of course to destroy its necessary vigor, and to distract the opinions and to dampen the zeal of our citizens," and even worse, "to divert their affections from their own to a foreign country."[29]

Even before the dispatches had reached the United States, Albert Gallatin of Pennsylvania, the Republican leader in the House of Representatives, had predicted the Federalist onslaught. In a letter to his wife in January 1798, he lamented that the Republicans would need to have "fortitude enough to despise the calumnies of the war faction and to do our duty notwithstanding the spirit of our administration and . . . the haughtiness of France." It was necessary to have the perseverance and courage to maintain this course, he explained, even though members of the Republican opposition would almost certainly be "branded with the usual epithets of Jacobins and tools of foreign influence."[30]

A couple of months later, Jefferson expressed his apprehension that it was only a matter of time before the president would ask for a declaration of war against France. And in letters Jefferson wrote to his close Virginia colleagues—James Monroe, soon to become governor of Virginia (1799), and Madison—he recommended an adjournment of Congress to allow passions to cool. This would allow the "Whigs" in Congress to "consult their constituents" and permit "every member to call for the sense of his district by petition or instruction." Such an adjournment would show the "people" which party protected "their safety as well as their rights" and "which is for war and which for peace."[31] It was a strategy that would be discussed again and then implemented after the passage of the Alien and Sedition Acts later that year.

Jefferson's use of the term "Whig" is highly significant, for in 1798 Republicans increasingly saw themselves as heirs of the legacy of the "Whigs" of 1776. Terms such as "Federalists" and "Republicans," he complained, were inadequate to describe the political divisions in the country. Only the older terms, "Whigs" and "Tories," accurately characterized "the distinguishing principles of the two Sects," he claimed.[32] Interestingly, the Federalists also vilified their opponents as Tories, meaning those hated, disloyal American colonists who had supported England and failed to embrace the cause of American independence. Thus, both Republicans and Federalists used the same frame of reference, seeing themselves as protectors of republicanism and the ideals of the Revolution, while reviling their adversaries as untrustworthy and un-American "Tories."

V

Eventually, the Republicans demanded that the letters from the commissioners be made public, which surely must rank among the worst political misjudgments in the nation's history. It certainly underscores the sage advice to "be careful what you wish for."

For after the public was informed about the insolent way the French had treated the American diplomats, wild rumors swept through Philadelphia that gave rise to a sharp upsurge of anti-French feeling and a spiraling war hysteria. Adams himself received three letters about supposed plots to burn down the capital. Fearing the worst, Madison was told by Jefferson, some Philadelphians had "packed their most valuable movables to be ready for transportation."

Amidst this ferocious frenzy of anti-French feeling, it became dangerous to exhibit any pro-French sympathy. Quickly gone from the scene were the tricolored cockade ribbons that Americans had worn proudly and prominently to show their support for the French Revolution. In Morristown, New Jersey, for example, almost "all the little boys" had earlier sported French tricolor ribbons on their hats, while Boston women had worn the French tricolor cockade "upon their caps." But these had been replaced by the black cockade, originally worn by veterans of the American Revolution but which in the late 1790s had come to signify patriotic support for Adams, the Federalists, and what was perceived to be the beleaguered country.

Indeed, not to display the black cockade was to invite trouble in some locations. One New England Republican refused to wear the Federalist emblem, and he and his like-minded colleagues were forced to carry "stiff hickory canes" to ward off attacks. And one Federalist denounced as a traitor anyone who wore the tricolor, suggesting that the names of such "offenders" be published in the newspapers so that they could "be avoided by all Federalists, as if infected with the leprosy or plague." Supporters of France, it was declared, should be objects of public scorn and ridicule, "be hooted by the boys, and . . . finally be obliged to flee to their beloved France, or to meet the doom which traitors deserve, and will e'er long experience."[33]

At one point in early May the tempers and passions ran so high that a riot broke out, with young men who wore the black cockade in sympathy with the Adams administration and with England battling against those sporting the tricolor cockade of France. As a result, Jefferson related, "the city was so filled with confusion from about 6 to 10 o'clock last night that it was dangerous going out." Eventually the "light horse" cavalry had to be called in to subdue the "fray."[34]

All of this anti-French sentiment and nationalistic fervor put the Republicans in a perilous position as they were increasingly portrayed by the Federalists as disloyal, unpatriotic conspirators who were against American independence and republicanism.

Hamilton, of course, welcomed the tumult of the XYZ Affair, as it became known, seeing it as having aroused a "spirit of patriotism" that would crush the Republicans and create a "national unanimity." As a result, he gloated, the Republicans would be scorned and despised, much like "the Tories of our Revolution."[35]

The surge of nationalist sentiment also pleased the president and the first lady, making them unlikely celebrities. The president, reflecting the belligerent public mood, started showing up in public as commander in chief resplendent in full military uniform with a sword at his side. Abigail reported that she was warmly greeted as she went about her social calls in Philadelphia and that "we are wonderfully popular except with [Republican editor Benjamin Franklin] Bache @ C., who in his paper calls the President, old, querulous, bald, blind, crippled, toothless Adams." Both the president and Abigail were in the theater when the singing of "Hail Columbia," the nation's first national anthem, received such an overwhelmingly popular reception that it was repeated six times, with people singing and dancing in the aisles.[36]

Unaccustomed to such attention and admiration, Adams basked in his newfound popularity as patriotic petitions or addresses from citizens across the country poured in. Remarkably, he personally answered them all. "If you have no attachments, or exclusive friendship for any foreign nation, you possess the genuine character of true Americans," he wrote to residents of Bennington County, Vermont. And he praised the sentiments sent to him by the people of Portland, Maine, as "worthy of freemen, and free republicans."

One group of addresses was personally delivered by 1,500 young Federalists who marched to Adams's home in Philadelphia, where the president received them in full military uniform. After listening to members of the group pledge their loyalty to the "religion and the laws," Adams declared that "No prospect or spectacle could excite a stronger sensibility in my bosom than this which now presents itself before me." On their way home, the young men apparently foreswore their adherence to the "laws" by attacking the print shop of Bache.[37]

In a burst of patriotic exuberance, a number of cities raised money to build warships to offer on loan to the government in order to help make it possible for the United States to fight a naval war with France. Newburyport, Massachusetts, for example, constructed a twenty-gun man-of-war, while Philadelphia and New York City each contracted to build two thirty-six-gun frigates.[38]

The ceremonial return to Philadelphia in June 1798 of John Marshall, one of the snubbed commissioners to France, also prompted an outburst of popular and orchestrated anti-French sentiment. Welcomed as a hero, Marshall was greeted by the secretary of state and "all the city cavalry."

This extravagant and jingoistic display of patriotic support for Marshall, and its positive reflection on the Federalist administration, was viewed by Jefferson with a critical and cynical eye. The "bells rung till late in the night, and immense crowds were collected to see and make part of the show, which was circuitously paraded through the streets before he [Marshall] was set down at the city tavern," the vice president wrote Madison.[39]

The same month, tensions were ratcheted up further when it was discovered that Dr. George Logan, a Quaker and Republican, had on his own sailed for France in an independent, but unsuccessful, effort to broker an amicable solution to the impasse between France and the United States. The Federalists reacted to the news by denouncing and demonizing the physician, scientific farmer, founding member of the Democratic Republican societies, and former member of the Pennsylvania legislature. Some even theorized that he had gone to France to raise an army and instruct the French on the best landing sites in the United States. Although well-intentioned, Logan was politically naïve and ended up paying a price for it. In 1799 his name would be affixed to an act that prohibited private citizens from engaging in diplomatic negotiations.

In the eyes of many Federalists, further evidence of a seditious Republican conspiracy surfaced in June 1798 after Bache, the editor of the opposition newspaper *Aurora*, published a letter from the French foreign minister, Talleyrand. Charging the journalist with being involved in a "traitorous correspondence" with the French Directory, one Federalist declared that evidence of a plot was being gathered and information about it would soon be revealed.[40]

VI

The anti-French emotion reached its climax in the summer of 1798, when the Federalist-dominated Congress passed the Alien and Sedition Acts. These repressive laws were ostensibly written to bolster internal security. However, in reality they were blatantly political: aimed at destroying the Republican opposition by suppressing freedoms of speech and the press, and more closely regulating the activities of foreign-born residents, a number of whom had Republican leanings. Many Federalists were certain that the Republican opposition was dangerously deluded at best and seditious and disloyal at the worst. Thus, they deemed the legislation to be essential.

Adams, for one, was convinced "that the profligate spirit of falsehood and malignity" (the problem presumably addressed in the acts) was a "serious" evil bearing a "threatening aspect upon the Union of the States, their Constitution of Government, and the moral character of the Nation."[41] Even long afterward, when reflecting back on the notorious acts that he had signed, he was unrepentant, seeing them as having been necessary defensive measures. "I knew there was need enough of both, and therefore I consented to them," he said.[42]

Passed in the summer of 1798 by the Federalist majority in Congress, the Alien and Sedition Acts were manifestations of the growing anti-French hysteria and the conviction shared by many that efforts to oppose and to criticize the government were treasonable.

Specifically, the three anti-alien acts provided for the registration and surveillance of foreign-born residents and gave the president extensive power to deport those he deemed dangerous to public safety. This targeting of immigrants was motivated by Federalist fears that most of the newcomers, especially those hostile to England, would support the Republican opposition and because of this represented an internal and seditious threat to the security of the United States.

According to one source, there were 5,000 French émigrés in Philadelphia in the 1790s, some having fled from the slave rebellion in Saint-Domingue and others from the reign of terror in France. As a result, the city had French newspapers, booksellers, schools, boardinghouses, and restaurants. So the impression was of a large French presence in the nation's capital. In addition, there were a number of Irish refugees who brought with them a healthy anti-English bias.[43]

Jefferson denounced the anti-alien acts as "worthy of the 8th or 9th century." They have "so alarmed the French who are among us," he informed his Virginia colleagues, that they have chartered a ship that "will sail within about a fortnight for France, with as many as she can carry."[44]

As it turned out, however, Adams ended up only signing deportation orders for three alien French residents, even though Secretary of State Timothy Pickering, who was responsible for enforcing the acts, begged the president to be more aggressive.[45]

The Sedition Act, which passed by a vote of forty-four to forty-one in the House of Representatives, with only four of the "yes" votes coming from Southern representatives, was even more draconian. And, unlike the anti-alien acts, it was vigorously enforced, with seventeen indictments being issued. Aiming at stifling internal dissent, it called for the punishment of those who "unlawfully combine or conspire together, with intent to oppose any measure or measures of the government of the United States . . . or to impede the operation of any law of the United States, or to intimidate . . . any person holding a place or office in or under the government of the United States." Furthermore, the law prohibited "any false, scandalous and malicious writings against the government . . . or either house of the Congress of the United States; or the President . . . with intent to defame . . . or to bring them . . . into contempt or disrepute; or to excite against them . . . the hatred of the good people of the United States." Violators of the statute were made subject to a $5,000 fine and imprisonment for up to five years.[46]

The influence of English actions earlier in the decade to suspend habeas corpus and to pass the Traitorous Correspondence Bill was clearly evident in the American Sedition Act and used to justify its enactment. Federalist Robert Goodloe Harper of South Carolina argued that both England and the United States faced an external enemy [France] that depended on the "internal support" of "domestic traitors."[47] Therefore, he believed that the Sedition Act was entirely appropriate and vital for the preservation of civil order.

Another advocate of the legislation was a Federalist judge in Pennsylvania who made the case for placing curbs on newspapers. If you "give to any set of men the command of the press," he argued in a charge to a grand jury, "you give them the command of the country." The consequences of "unceasing and malignant slander," the judge went on to contend, would be for the country's "wisest and best public officers" to become embittered and "driven from their stations." Their replacements, he feared, "would be obscure, venal, unqualified men—those base enough to write for newspapers or benefit from newspaper writing"—those "without virtue or talents" who could only "rise into consequence . . . by slander."[48]

Among the lawmakers who condemned the Sedition Act was the outspoken Albert Gallatin, the Republican leader in the House of Representatives. Having been born in Switzerland, the Pennsylvania congressman actually was subject to the provisions of the Alien Acts, a situation that some felt may not have been unintentional.[49] "This bill and its supporters suppose," Gallatin accused, "that whoever dislikes the measures of [the] Administration and of a temporary majority in congress, and shall, either by speaking or writing, express his disapprobation and his want of confidence in men now in power, is seditious, is an enemy not of Administration, but of the Constitution, and is liable to punishment."[50]

Gallatin's analysis was confirmed by statements of many Federalists, but perhaps especially those of "Long John" Allen. A six-foot-five-inch Federalist representative from Connecticut, he outdid himself with paroxysms of vituperation in portraying sinister images of a variety of seditious conspiracies.

The Republicans, whom he saw as "hostile to free Governments and genuine liberty," were making false accusations against the Federalists and fomenting "an insurrection against the Government" by insisting that Federalist officeholders "be displaced" by the people.[51]

The emotional statements by both Gallatin and Allen reveal a great deal about the nature of politics in the late 1790s. Because of the lack of a recognized consensus between the contending parties, opposition to the government was regarded by those in power as illegitimate, and not only that, seditious.

The passage of the Alien and Sedition Acts by the Federalists enraged and demoralized the Republicans. The gulf between them and their Federalist foes now seemed almost unbridgeable. It was as if leaders on both sides were the victims of paranoia, looking at their former comrades through hideously distorting spectacles.

Those in the Republican opposition were seen by many government supporters as naïve minions or active agents of France ready to betray the Constitution and the republic. Republicans, for their part, often viewed the Federalists as biding their time until they could repudiate the Revolution, replace the republic with a monarchy, and reestablish a close and dependent relationship between the United States and England.

While political tensions have become superheated and fanatical at several points in the country's history, the newness and the perceived fragility and tentativeness of the Constitution and the republic during the 1790s and the election of 1800 make that period unique. Under such circumstances, the give and take of party politics that would develop in later eras was impossible.

4

THE REPUBLICANS' RESPONSE
THE KENTUCKY AND VIRGINIA
RESOLUTIONS

*"It was not unwise now to estimate the separate mass of Virginia and
North Carolina, with a view to their separate existence."*
—*John Taylor of Caroline, June 1798*

I

After the XYZ Affair, many Federalists and Republicans
expected a formal declaration of war against France. And
initially, after receiving the bad news from his commission
in France, Adams did consider making such a recommendation to Congress. He then had second thoughts. The outspoken Abigail, however, apparently had no such hesitancy.
Despite her husband's decision against recommending war,
she condemned Congress for not taking action, writing her
son when Congress was about to adjourn that "a declaration
of war ought undoubtedly to have been made."[1]

Adams's cabinet was split on the declaration of war question. The most vehement advocate of declaring war on France
and forming an alliance with England was Secretary of State
Timothy Pickering, a holdover from the Washington administration and, more importantly, a friend and supporter of
Hamilton whose disloyalty to Adams was only surpassed by
his ambition, self-righteousness, vindictiveness, and sour,
combative, and generally disagreeable personality. Pickering, like Adams, was from Massachusetts. There he had
compiled a mediocre record of public service prior to joining
the Washington administration in 1795 after the president
had offered the secretary-of-state post to six other candidates
before reluctantly settling on him.

Like other ambitious and ego-driven men, Pickering constantly overestimated his talents and blamed others for his failures. It is hard to imagine anyone less qualified to be America's chief diplomat. Abrasive, unforgiving, and extremely dogmatic, he was the antithesis of what might be expected in a secretary of state; yet he was continued on during the Adams administration until the president in 1800 could not abide his disloyalty and insubordination any longer and summarily dismissed him.

Although he had earlier enthusiastically supported the French Revolution and the execution of the king and queen, Pickering by 1798 had changed his mind and viewed fighting France as vital in the struggle against revolutionary excesses, violence, and civil disorder. However, two other close allies of Hamilton, Secretary of Treasury Oliver Wolcott and Secretary of War James McHenry, opposed declaring war. They preferred the ongoing limited naval war, believing that this would allow more flexibility in any future peace negotiations.[2]

Another holdover from the Washington administration, Wolcott, unlike Pickering, was content to be a detail man rather than an idea one. He took orders well and worked conscientiously under the direction of others. A loyal subordinate to Hamilton in the Treasury Department during Washington's presidency, he was subsequently appointed to be his boss's successor in 1795 and served until he resigned in 1800. Nonetheless, he continued to look to Hamilton for direction.

An immigrant from Ireland, McHenry (1753–1816) was from Maryland, where his family had a successful mercantile business. After serving as a surgeon in the Continental Army, he attracted the attention of Washington and ended up becoming his personal secretary. McHenry's great virtue was his outgoing personality and his ability to make friends. Indeed, even with the distant and correct Washington, McHenry managed in their correspondence to maintain "an affectionate, sometimes even playful tone."

A follower rather than a leader, he deeply admired and venerated both Washington and Hamilton. But, like Pickering, he was far from Washington's first choice to become secretary of war late in his second administration. Nonetheless, similar to Pickering and Wolcott, McHenry continued his service in the cabinet during the Adams administration until he too was fired for incompetence in 1800 after failing miserably to administer the buildup of the army during the war crisis with France. And, along with Pickering and Wolcott, McHenry deceitfully served as a conduit of inside and often secret cabinet information to Hamilton.[3]

Other Federalists outside the cabinet also opposed an immediate declaration of war against France. John Marshall, who had been one of the commissioners in France during the XYZ Affair, resisted the call to arms upon his return to the United States. In response to a committee of New Jersey militia officers urging an immediate declaration of war, Marshall answered that "all honorable means of avoiding war should be essayed before the sword be appealed to."[4]

Despite the differences of opinion within the Adams administration, however, a Federalist-sponsored resolution was introduced into the House of Representatives on July 5, 1798, "to consider the expediency of declaring" war. It was voted down before a roll call vote, with some Federalists and the Republicans voting in the negative. One Federalist opposed it because he believed it would give the Republicans the opportunity "to create, in the popular estimation, a new denomination of parties—those of peace and war." In contrast, a fervent champion of war wrote Washington that a declaration of war was "necessary to enable us to lay our hands on traitors."[5]

II

Before the Federalist-dominated Congress adjourned in the middle of July 1798, it also passed a series of defense measures. In addition to the Alien and Sedition Acts, it approved legislation authorizing the establishment of a Navy Department, increasing the size of the navy, improving harbor defenses, and enlarging the regular army by raising an additional force of twelve regiments of infantry and six troops of light dragoons. In addition, a paper army, referred to as the Provisional Army, was authorized to be organized when and if there was an invasion of the United States by France. And lastly, Congress annulled the treaties between France and the United States, including the Franco-American Alliance of 1778 that had played such a vital role helping the United States win its independence.[6]

The question of who should be the organizer and leader of the expanded army created another divisive problem for the Federalists. Hamilton and a number of his allies had constituted the energy behind the expansion of the army, with the former secretary of treasury eagerly anticipating that he himself would become the de facto commander in chief. It was assumed, or at least hoped, that the retired Washington would agree to be the symbolic and figurehead leader.

However, Adams adamantly opposed Hamilton as the second in command, angrily declaring, in a letter that was probably never sent, that if he agreed to Hamilton's appointment it would be one of the worst decisions of his life, for while he respected "his talents," he questioned "his character."

Instead, Adams was committed to appointing the loyal and trustworthy Henry Knox, former secretary of war and fellow New Englander, to the post. In many ways, Knox was the logical choice because of his seniority and command experience.[7]

Nonetheless, strongly supported by Pickering and McHenry, the politically powerful Hamilton was in a real sense already the country's prime minister without portfolio, in that he commanded the respect and support not only of Adams's cabinet but also of many from the Federalist rank and file. Therefore, in the tug-of-war between Adams and Hamilton over the military post, Adams ultimately had to capitulate and abandon Knox when he found that he was opposed not only by the cabinet, but also by Washington himself, who threatened to resign his symbolic leadership post over the issue. The near-fatal illness of Adams's beloved Abigail at the same time added considerably to the stress on the president.

After the appointment, one of the first chores undertaken by Hamilton and his colleagues was to handpick the officer corps for the fledgling army, and in so doing they deemed political reliability to be a key test, especially since the new force was envisioned, in addition to providing a defense against the French, as sometimes also having a role in subduing the domestic opposition. Hamilton's experience during the Whiskey Rebellion had convinced him that militia forces, as opposed to a federal force, were unreliable in putting down "domestic disorders." Thus, each candidate for a commission was screened, and a comprehensive dossier was completed and circulated to leading Federalists for their evaluations.

Secretary of War McHenry was cautioned by Washington to be wary of "brawlers against Government measures" who "are very desirous of obtaining Commissions." As officers, he warned, they might "divide and contaminate the Army" with their "artful and seditious discourses" and at "a critical moment bring on confusion." It was this heightened distrust of the politics of the candidates that led Hamilton and his associates to reject Adams's efforts to appoint Republicans Aaron Burr and Frederick Augustus Muhlenberg to the rank of brigadier general.[8]

III

Even before the passage of the Sedition Act, Federalists had attempted to use the power of the government to suppress the Republican opposition. Samuel J. Cabell, a Virginia Republican member of the House of Representatives, had been served a presentment by a federal grand jury in Richmond,

Virginia, in the summer of 1797. The presentment accused Cabell of criticizing the Adams administration in his circular letters to his constituents and of distributing "unfounded calumnies against the happy government of the United States" at "a time of real public danger." Cabell's intent, the grand jury charged, was "to separate the people . . . [from the federal government] and to increase or produce a foreign influence, ruinous to the peace, happiness, and independence of these United States."[9]

Cabell denounced the presentment as part of what he saw as "a regular practice of the federal judges to make political discourses to the grand jurors." These judges, he feared, had become "a band of political preachers, instead of a sage body to administer the law" and now seemed "to be making use of their power and influence . . . to control the freedom of opinion."[10]

The case against Cabell was not pursued further. Nonetheless, the presentment was viewed with great foreboding by Jefferson, and the episode did give rise to an important step in the development of Jefferson's opposition strategy. With the Federalists firmly in control of all three branches of the federal government, and likely to remain in control as long as the threat of war remained, Jefferson and his colleagues began to look to the states as the last defensive stronghold against this powerful enemy. There, where they had considerable support, the Republicans reasoned, they could focus their attention on building a strong political base.

In line with this, the vice president proposed to Madison and Monroe that a petition be sent to the Virginia legislature calling for the impeachment of the grand jurors who had issued Cabell's presentment. Monroe argued that the petition should instead be sent to Congress, but Jefferson rejected the suggestion. It would, he believed, increase the power of that "foreign jurisdiction." Jefferson also stressed the extreme importance of the states' retaining "as complete authority as possible over their own citizens."[11]

The upshot of this exchange of views was that Jefferson sent an anonymous petition to the Virginia House of Delegates attacking the grand jury's action, which, he said, struck at the very fundamental right of representation in a republic. Legislators, it was argued, had to be "free from the cognizance or coercion of the co-ordinate branches, Judiciary and Executive." Thus, it was contended, the grand jurors must be impeached for endangering the "safety of the State" and the constitutional rights of its citizens. If the grand jury's action were allowed to stand, it would mean that any communication between a representative and his constituents would be inhibited by fear of criminal prosecution. And this would in effect subjugate the legislative branch to the judiciary. The House of Delegates responded by passing a resolution affirming the principles of Jefferson's petition. The state legislature did not, however, call for any action.[12]

Chief Justice of the Massachusetts Supreme Court Francis Dana perhaps captured the prevailing sentiment among the Federalists and seemed to confirm Jefferson's fears when, in a charge to a jury in 1798, he compared the Republican opposition to the Tories of the American Revolution. And while the comparison was often made by both parties in attempting to slander the reputation of their opponents, in this case Dana argued that even the Tories of the American Revolution were more admirable than the Republicans in that they were adhering to their oath of loyalty to the British empire. However, he saw both the Tories of the Revolution and those Republican "Tories" of the 1790s as alike in that they "marshaled and organized against the government" and were "aided and encouraged by a foreign power."

Ominously, Dana also referred to a 1776 act of the Continental Congress that recommended that local patriot bodies around the country "cause all persons to be disarmed within the United Colonies who are notoriously disaffected to the cause of America."[13] In other words, Dana equated members of the opposition with traitors who could not be trusted with firearms.

After the enactment of the Sedition Act, Federalists became emboldened to move even more vigorously against their domestic enemies, especially opposition newspaper editors. "It is Patriotism to write in favor of our government," the Federalist *Gazette of the United States* proclaimed, and "it is sedition to write against it."[14] Yet the irony is, as historian Jeffrey L. Pasley has pointed out, that the more repressive the Federalists became in suppressing opposition newspapers, the more successful the Republican papers became.[15]

In the long term, Pasley argues, the Sedition Act failed because, rather than suppressing and driving the opposition newspapers out of business, it stimulated a dramatic increase in their numbers and helped create a more politicized press. Despite the fact that the most successful and influential Republican newspapers were prosecuted under the act and many Republican editors were arraigned—with approximately fourteen of them being jailed—eighty-five newspapers championed the Republican cause in 1800, which represented a two-thirds increase from the number before the passage of the act.[16]

The increase in the number of highly partisan newspapers and the key role they would play in 1800, however, are only part of the story. The growing political importance of the printers, who lacked the social status of the elite leadership of both parties, also contributed to the development of a more inclusive, more heterogeneous politics.

Matthew Lyon of Vermont (1750–1822) is a good example, albeit a notorious one, of this new breed of zealous printer-politicians. Lyon had come to the United States from Ireland as an indentured servant in 1765, but, as a shrewd and ambitious businessman, he had achieved a certain amount of success in both business and politics by the early 1790s. Founder of a newspaper to help his own political ambitions, Lyon was elected to Congress as a Republican in 1796. And in early 1798, in the House of Representatives, he stood his ground when Roger Griswold, a Federalist from Connecticut, insulted him over his lowly origins. Lyon spat in his face. When Griswold retaliated on the House floor by beating Lyon with his hickory cane, Lyon grabbed the tongs from the fireplace to defend himself. The two ended up rolling and fighting on the floor of the House until they were pulled apart.[17]

In the summer of 1798, Lyon was arrested and charged with libeling Adams in statements published in his newspaper, the Rutland, Vermont, *Farmers' Library*. Tried and convicted, he was sentenced to four months in prison and a $1,000 fine. Lyon, however, became a martyr for freedom of the press and was re-elected to Congress from his prison cell that same year.[18]

According to Pasley, Lyon and other printers of his social status represented a real menace to the Federalists. "By giving non-gentlemen the ability to influence public opinion and electoral politics," he asserts, "partisan newspapers possessed the potential to overturn the social and ethnic hierarchy as the organizing principles of political life."[19]

Nonetheless, the failure of the Sedition Law to restrain Republican criticism of the government can be seen only in retrospect. Neither Federalists nor Republicans in 1798, 1799, and 1800 knew what the impact of this law would be. And the fact remains that the 1798 Sedition Act stands today as one of the most flagrant violations ever of American civil liberties as guaranteed by the Constitution, ranking with other shameful government excesses, including the internment of Japanese during World War II and the McCarthy hearings of the 1950s.

IV

With the Federalists vigorously attacking their legitimacy, the Republicans needed to find a way to survive as an opposition. The question on their minds was this: what strategies could be employed to withstand the Federalist onslaught and gain power in the presidential election of 1800?

In the weeks immediately prior to the passage of the Alien and Sedition Acts, some Republican leaders, notably James Monroe and James Madison, had urged that the opposition should keep a low profile. They seemed confident that the Federalists' excesses would eventually lead to their downfall. The only hope "is that . . . violence by defeating itself may save the Country," Madison had asserted.

Monroe carried this logic to an almost ludicrous conclusion, arguing that the Federalists be allowed to "fight on, plunge our country inevitably in a war with France, intimidate and traduce the republican party and promote civil discord at home as they are doing." These actions, he maintained, would surely be self-defeating, for they were not "the way to merit or preserve the esteem of the good people of this country." Thus, Monroe cautioned Southern Republicans to avoid criticizing the Federalist representatives from the Eastern states. To do so, he warned, would convince the public that the political division in the country was a sectional one rather than one of principle.[20]

It is difficult to know how widely Madison's and Monroe's sentiments were shared among Republicans. But, for whatever reason, a number of Republican congressmen did leave Philadelphia in the weeks before the passage of the Alien and Sedition Acts. Jefferson wrote Madison in April 1798 that "[William Branch] Giles, [John] Clopton and [Samuel J.] Cabell" were gone. A Federalist happily confirmed Giles's departure, reporting that the Virginian had "gone home with a broken heart and ruined constitution." He also stated that "Edward Livingston has been home for several weeks and I see no symptoms of his return," and that, while "Gallatin continues to clog the wheels of government," he has not "sufficient strength to stop its motion."[21]

A more extreme strategy of last resort was also discussed in June 1798 in an exchange of letters between Jefferson and his more radical Virginia colleague, John Taylor of Caroline (1753–1824),[22] an alumnus of William and Mary College, a successful lawyer, and a planter acknowledged to be the era's foremost advocate of scientific agriculture. Taylor also was active as a public servant. A veteran of the American Revolution, he served for eight years in the Virginia legislature, 1779–1781, 1783–1785, and 1796–1800. Although Taylor, along with Patrick Henry, had ardently opposed the ratification of the Constitution in 1787–1788, he later served in the Senate of the new federal government (1792–1794, 1803, and 1822–1824).

Despite Taylor's many accomplishments and record of public service, however, his historical reputation rests primarily on his prominence as the most systematic Republican theoretician of his time. In his challenging and often extremely dense political and philosophical writings, he championed states' rights and relentlessly criticized Hamilton's financial plan.

In 1798, when he was serving in the Virginia House of Delegates and deeply concerned about protecting liberty and Southern interests, Taylor had insisted to Jefferson that secession from the Union had to be part of any discussion of opposition strategy, claiming that "it was not unwise now to estimate the separate mass of Virginia and North Carolina, with a view to their separate existence."[23]

Although Jefferson himself was soon to entertain secession as a possible tactic, he was initially shocked by Taylor's extremism. In those weeks before the passage of the Alien and Sedition Acts, Jefferson had continued to hope that congressional Republicans would be able to restrain the worst excesses of the Federalists. Any discussion of disunion, he feared, might alienate potential non-Southern Republican support.

Taylor had thus been told in response that the "cunning of Hamilton" and the fame and reputation of Washington had been the chief factors leading to the consolidation of power by those who were anti-republican. This, however, was "not the natural state," Jefferson had assured Taylor, for the Federalists' assaults on the Constitution, as well as their policies that had led to higher taxes and possible war, would cause their repudiation. Then, Jefferson predicted, the New England–dominated Federalists would "ever be the minority."[24]

In his reply to Jefferson, Taylor protested that his earlier letter had been misinterpreted. All that he had desired, he claimed, was the "perfection, and not the scission of the union." He then, however, did rebut the vice president on several points, calling the Republican idea to allow the anti-republicanism of the Federalists "to run through its natural course" a dangerous one that would only aggravate the problem. If "the mass of our citizens are now republican, will submission to anti-republican measures, increase that mass?" he pointedly asked.

Taylor's remedies included democratizing the electorate and officeholding by extending the suffrage and "rotation in office." In addition, however, he recommended "a new mode of abrogating law" that would require laws to be renewed periodically and not enacted in perpetuity. And finally, in what was to become the ideological foundation for the Virginia and Kentucky resolutions passed later that year, he insisted that state governments had the "right . . . to expound," or interpret, the Constitution. But if this were to be "insufficient, the people in state conventions, are incontrovertibly the contracting parties, and . . . may proceed by orderly steps to attain the object" by exercising their sovereign right to change the Constitution.[25]

Distraught by the passage of the Alien and Sedition Acts in July 1798, and beleaguered by the growing anti-French hysteria and the determination of the Federalists to eliminate their political opposition, Jefferson and other Republicans began to agree with Taylor that more radical action was needed. Thus, in order to protect the very survival of the opposition and to prevent what they saw as further Federalist usurpation of power, they began to pursue a state and local opposition strategy focused on building a strong political base in the states where they had considerable support, especially in the South and West, where Republicans held majorities in the legislatures. This development of a state-oriented opposition carried with it the strong implication that unless the Federalists moderated their policies, state secession and the breakup of the Union might be the opposition's only viable option.

Republicans, especially in Virginia, believed that a crisis point had been reached and that in order to save the Union and republicanism, the states must be strengthened politically and militarily so that they could, if need be, become bastions of safety from illegal and repressive federal actions.

For instance, an associate of Burr in New York wrote Monroe that he and Burr were going to Albany to meet with Republican legislators. It was "highly important, at this moment and will be more so every day, to pay particular attention to the State Legislatures, and to get into them men of respectability," he advised, for "if any good can be expected it must be through their means."[26] And Jefferson promised a correspondent that Virginia would be a safe asylum from the "delusion" that had produced the Alien and Sedition Acts, for Virginians were "sufficiently on their guard" to assure that the "laws of the land, administered by upright judges, would protect you from any exercise of power unauthorized by the Constitution of the United States."[27]

Looking back at this time, Jefferson explained years later that "leading republicans in Congress," after finding themselves "no use there," determined "to retire from that field, take a stand in their state legislatures, and endeavor there to arrest" the growth of Federalist hegemony.[28]

V

The Kentucky and Virginia resolutions of 1798 were the embodiment of the Republicans' defiant ideological and constitutional challenge to the Federalists' aggrandizement of political power, and the tangible evidence of a shift in opposition strategy. And the most militant expression of the doctrine of state interposition was Jefferson's draft of the Kentucky Resolutions. Initially, these resolutions were intended to be put forward in North Carolina, but Federalist gains there in the election of 1798 made that option risky. So, instead, Jefferson's draft was given to John Breckinridge of Kentucky to introduce in his state's legislature.

In his draft that was to become the template for the Kentucky Resolutions, Jefferson asserted that the national government, which had been created by a "compact" between the states, had been granted "certain definite powers" by the Constitution. It was the states, he claimed, that held "the residuary mass of rights to their own self-government." Consequently, when the general government arrogated "undelegated powers, its acts are unauthoritative, void, and of no force." Furthermore, Jefferson argued, it was neither logical nor constitutional for the federal government to be the "final judge of the extent of the powers delegated to itself." Congress, for instance, was not a party to the compact, he pointed out. It was "merely" its "creature."

There was a significant difference, Jefferson maintained, between the general government's violation of *delegated powers* and the usurpation of *undelegated powers*.

A remedy for the first would be to replace those responsible through the electoral process. However, for the second, "where powers are assumed which have not been delegated, a nullification of the act is the rightful remedy."[29] Since the Alien and Sedition Acts clearly represented such an unconstitutional exercise of federal power, Jefferson appealed to the states to join "in declaring these acts void, and of no force" and to thus prevent "these acts [and] any others of the General Government not plainly and intentionally authorized by the Constitution," from being "exercised within their respective territories." In order for this to be executed, he recommended that a "committee of conference and correspondence" be created to send out the resolutions to the other states along with the assurance that the backers of the resolutions were supportive and loyal to the Union and "sincerely anxious for its preservation."[30] This proposed revival of the extralegal committees of correspondence of the American Revolution in order to bypass the Federalist-controlled federal government revealed how perilous Jefferson believed the crisis to be.

In forwarding his resolutions to Madison, Jefferson declared in an accompanying note that "we should distinctly affirm all the important principles they contain, so as to hold to that ground in the future, and leave the matter in such a train as that we may not be committed absolutely to push the matter to extremities, and yet may be free to push as far as events will render prudent."

John Taylor of Caroline received the same message. But, in addition, he was warned against doing anything "which should commit us further."

The future must be open, Taylor was advised, "to shape . . . measures or no measures by the events which may happen." Still, in conclusion, Jefferson also reaffirmed his belief that the preservation of liberty rested with the state governments that were the "very *best in the world*, without exception or comparison," while "our general government has swallowed more of the public liberty than even that of England."[31]

John Breckinridge introduced the resolutions in the Kentucky legislature, but, in an effort to make Jefferson's draft more compatible with many of the county resolutions that had been submitted to the legislature, he made some major changes. Instead of advancing Jefferson's argument that Congress was a creature of the constitutional compact between the states, Breckinridge's version appealed to Congress itself to repeal the Alien and Sedition Acts rather than to the states to take action. Even more importantly, the finished draft made no mention of Jefferson's claim that each state had the right to nullify usurpatious federal laws.[32] The result was that the Kentucky legislature passed the resolutions in late November 1798, then forwarded them to the other states as well as to Kentucky's members in Congress.

Virginia was next to consider the nullification of the Alien and Sedition Acts. Upon reading Madison's initial draft of that state's resolutions, however, Jefferson was disappointed in their mild and weak language. Republicans, he feared, were too timid to take a bold and principled stand against the Federalists' abuse of power and were overly concerned about Northern opinion. Virginia should be more confrontational in its language, he insisted. Instead of asking the other states "to cooperate in the annulment" of the Alien and Sedition Acts, Virginia should request that the other states "concur with this commonwealth in declaring . . . that the said acts are, and were *ab initio*, null, void and of no force, or effect."[33] Virginia should then proceed in a courageous, confident, and forthright manner to meet the extraordinary threat offered by the Federalist-controlled general government, he strongly advised.

John Taylor of Caroline introduced the resolutions containing Jefferson's more radical language in the Virginia legislature, where they were met with a fierce Federalist response that played on white Southern males' fear of sexual violence by slaves against white women.

If the Alien Acts were to be nullified, the Federalists contended, the door would be unwittingly opened to chaos and disorder, as outside revolutionaries would have more freedom to enter Virginia and foment slave insurrections.[34] One Federalist legislator in particular graphically and shockingly imagined what might then ensue. "The inexorable and blood-thirsty negro would be careless of the father's groans," he warned, while "wives and daughters ... with naked bosoms, outstretched hands and disheveled hair" would be ripped away "to gratify the brutal passion of a ruthless negro, who would the next moment murder the object of his lust."[35]

In addition to pursuing this line of attack, the Federalists charged the Republicans with hypocrisy for having earlier, in 1792, supported a Virginia sedition act.[36]

Madison, uneasy with Jefferson's more radical language, told his colleague that logically there should be a distinction made between the power of the state and that of the legislature. If, for example, a state "is clearly the ultimate Judge of infractions, it does not follow that the ... [legislature] is the legitimate organ," since a convention initiated by the sovereign people "was the organ by which the compact was made."[37] Ultimately, the Jefferson draft was amended to restore Madison's less militant language, removing any unilateral action by Virginia and appealing to the other states to join Virginia in a collective condemnation of the Alien and Sedition Acts. With that modification, the resolutions were passed in December 1798, by a vote of one hundred to sixty-three.[38]

Disappointed with the dilution of the original resolutions before the Virginia legislature, Taylor told Jefferson that he had expected that once the Alien and Sedition Acts had been declared null and void the resulting crisis between the state and national governments would have forced the calling of "the people in convention as the only referee." The assembling of such a convention with unlimited powers to amend or dissolve the structure of the federal government, Taylor argued, would, as a strategy of last resort, have been a means for the public to appeal over the heads of the government after all normal electoral remedies had failed. Jefferson's opposition to this "ultimate effort," however, doomed what Taylor had envisioned.[39]

As 1798 ended, then, the Republicans were on the defensive and searching for an effective response to what they considered to be the dangerous usurpation of power by the Federalists. Grave and crucial questions had been raised, and there was a pressing need for them to be addressed and resolved. How would the other states respond to the Kentucky and Virginia resolutions? What would the Federalists do? Would the Republicans be able to survive as a functional and effective opposition? Finally, lurking just below the surface but constantly worrisome was the unthinkable possibility that military force would be used to resolve the crisis.

Earlier in the year, a close friend and classmate of Jefferson's at William and Mary, John Page (1744–1808), had explored the nature of party divisions in a revealing letter to Jefferson. The Republican congressman from Virginia, whose analysis reflected the thinking of most, if not all, his Republican colleagues, had cast the conflict in larger, more general, ideological terms. It was a conflict, he argued, between the virtuous and the corrupt. The United States, as well as most countries, had a "pure patriotic Party" that contended against the corrupt, narrowly partisan and selfish interests that plotted against the "Liberty and true Interests of the people." Such a "patriotic Party" of the "truly virtuous" (the Republicans, of course) was essential "in a free State to preserve its Freedom" and to thwart "the wicked designs of the Enemies of the Doctrine of Equality and the Rights of Man," he said.[40]

Thus, Page ardently believed that the Republicans had a duty to educate and awaken the people to their republican responsibilities in order to maintain a free government. Lamenting the "Abolition of the Republican and Democratic Societies," whose end had resulted in the "rapid Propagation of anglo-monarchical" and "aristocratical Principles among us," Page contended that had the societies continued to exist and "boldly done their Duty . . . the People would have learned their Rights, and understood their interests."[41]

But while Page could make the argument that the Republicans were that "patriotic Party," the Federalists also believed that they warranted that designation. Under those circumstances, when both Federalists and Republicans embraced such exclusionary, self-righteous views of themselves, the danger that violence might be used to solve political differences increased exponentially.

5

THE FEDERALIST COUNTERATTACK
THE ELECTION OF 1798

"Nothing can save us from an anglo-monarchical-aristocratic-military government."
—*John Taylor of Caroline, April 1799*[1]

I

The success or failure of the Kentucky and Virginia resolutions depended on how they were received throughout the rest of the country. So, after transmitting them to the other states, the Republicans awaited the verdicts in apprehensive anticipation.

The results could hardly have been more disheartening. State after state north of the Potomac River condemned the resolutions, while Southern and Western states were remarkably silent. In Massachusetts one Republican newspaper editor was even prosecuted and jailed for defending the resolutions, the judge calling the "positions" embodied in them "monstrous" during the journalist's sentencing. The appraisal was consistent with the Federalist contention that opposition to state or federal government policies was a crime.[2]

A Federalist newspaper in New Hampshire denounced the resolutions as nothing short of a threat to use the force of arms against the federal government, while the Vermont legislature took issue with the logic of the resolutions, especially the Kentucky Resolutions. The Articles of Confederation, the Vermont Federalists argued, were "formed by the state Legislatures, but the present Constitution of the United States was derived from an [sic] higher authority." That higher authority was the "people of the United States."[3]

Thus, a resolution passed by a state legislature had no power to affect a national law.

In New York, one hapless Republican gave only tepid support to the resolutions. In "cases of dangerous encroachments and innovations on the rights and sovereignty of the State Legislatures," he argued, the states were obliged to "mark and proclaim such innovations." However, because of the "necessity of preserving harmony between the national and state governments," he believed that it was neither "expedient" nor "proper" to adopt the Kentucky and Virginia resolutions.[4]

The Maryland legislature determined that the resolutions were asking the states to do something that was not lawful, mirroring a criticism that had been offered earlier by Madison. "No state government by a Legislative act is competent to declare an act of the Federal Government unconstitutional and void," the legislature proclaimed.[5] Republicans in the other Southern states, fearful of being labeled disunionists, were also reluctant to take action. While most of the Southern Republicans probably did agree with the sentiments expressed in the resolutions, they were not willing to face the political consequences of supporting their colleagues in Kentucky and Virginia.

Aghast by the response, the Republican leadership scrambled to assure their critics that the resolutions had not threatened disunion. In Kentucky, George Nicholas published a pamphlet in 1799 clarifying, he hoped, what his state's position was. Kentuckians would obey laws that were impolitic, but constitutional, he said. However, they would ignore laws that were both unconstitutional and impolitic. At the same time, however, he pledged rather vaguely and perhaps intentionally unclearly, that Kentucky contemplated "no means of opposition, even to . . . unconstitutional acts," but instead would "appeal to the *real laws* of our country."[6]

Madison had, from the beginning, been apprehensive about the resolutions, especially the radicalism of Jefferson's early draft of the Kentucky Resolutions. And by early 1799, Jefferson himself seems also to have become convinced that his earlier, more radical, stance had been counterproductive and that there was now a need for more moderation. He admitted to Madison that the South now had to temper its opposition and follow a course of "firmness . . . but a passive firmness" since "anything rash or threatening might check the favorable dispositions of these middle States, and rally them again around the measures which are ruining us." Thus, it was essential, Jefferson argued, that nothing should be done by the Southern-based opposition to jeopardize the potential future support of Pennsylvania and New York in the presidential election of 1800.[7]

On the other hand, John Taylor of Caroline, true to form, denounced the temporizing and timidity of the Republicans in their refusal to rally around the call for nullifying the Alien and Sedition Acts. The checks and balances of the Constitution, he maintained, had failed to curb the power of the federal government. The result of this, he worried, was that "the southern states must lose their capital and commerce . . . that America is destined to war—standing armies—and oppressive taxation, by which the power of the few . . . will be matured into an irresistible scourge of human happiness." Liberty can only be secured, he argued, when the people had "as much political strength as may be consistent with good order and social happiness."[8]

Therefore, Taylor urged, the Republicans had to renounce their "inert" and passive model of politics. Rather than waiting for the public to renounce the excesses of the Federalists, it was essential that the Republicans educate and mobilize the people "by something that they can understand," namely the imminent danger of the imposition of an "anglo-monarchical-aristocratic-military government." Indeed, if this were not done, Taylor cautioned, the public mind would be "cultivated, deceived, solicited and corrupted by strenuous efforts" of the Federalists.[9]

One of Jefferson's more optimistic expectations—that the Federalists' tax on land to fund the defense buildup would lead to their downfall, and thus the "tax-gatherer" would be the "doctor which will cure the disease"—was also challenged by Taylor. Gently chiding his fellow Virginian, Taylor suggested that "this doctor is now under the protection of an army and navy" and "may safely administer what doses he pleases."[10]

II

Taylor was surprisingly prescient. Hamilton and his Federalist associates had for some time been deeply suspicious of Virginia and its Southern and Western allies, and the passage of the Kentucky and Virginia resolutions had convinced many in this circle that the Southern-led Republicans were indeed moving toward some kind of armed confrontation with the federal government. Thus, the Kentucky and Virginia resolutions were seen as treasonable.

Theodore Sedgwick, a Massachusetts Federalist, condemned the documents as "little short of a declaration of war."[11] And a few months later Secretary of State Timothy Pickering raised the apprehension level by reporting a rumor that Virginia Republican William Branch Giles had declared "that he desired that the Union of the States might be severed."[12]

Seeming to substantiate the rumors and worst fears of the Federalists were reports that Virginia was accumulating arms in preparation for a violent confrontation between the state and the Federalist-controlled national government. And, indeed, the Virginia legislature in the 1798–1799 session did pass, in addition to the Virginia Resolutions, bills to reorganize the militia, purchase additional arms, build an armory in Richmond, and raise taxes by 25 percent.

One Virginia Federalist warned Hamilton that his state wanted "Nothing short of DISUNION, and the heads of JOHN ADAMS, and ALEXANDER HAMILTON. . . . Take care of yourself." A few days later the Virginian further reported that money originally intended for the building of a penitentiary in his state might be diverted for the purchase of arms. He saw this as evidence that the state could be preparing for civil war. In that event, Hamilton's correspondent said, he was volunteering for service in the federal army.[13]

The accuracy of these suspicions seemed to be confirmed in a shocking letter written by John Nicholas, a member of a prominent Republican family in Virginia. Renouncing the Republicans, he corroborated the rumors, claiming that the state was storing arms in Richmond to support a rebellion. Nicholas's accusations, however, were widely and vigorously denied by Republicans, including his own close relatives, who urged him to change his name so as not to disgrace the rest of the family.[14]

Others, however, echoed Nicholas's charges, including a Federalist from North Carolina who reported that a friend who had been traveling in Virginia had told him that the Virginians "were determined upon the overthrow of the General Government and if no other measure would effect it, that they would risk it upon the chance of war." Another Federalist worriedly reported that Virginia was readying "its militia [to be] as formidable as possible" and building up "its arsenals and magazines."[15]

Years later some Republicans admitted that the Virginians had indeed been amassing arms in preparation for defending themselves in the event of a possible armed conflict. William Branch Giles, a member of the Virginia legislature during the 1798–1799 session, recalled how "successful" the defensive actions had been. Measures to protect the freedom of debate, to arm the militia with the purchase of "5,000 stands of arms" and to build an armory were passed and, according to Giles, "saved the union."[16]

As rumors of Republican perfidy circulated around the country early in 1799, the Republicans in Kentucky and Virginia saw themselves as in a particularly vulnerable and precarious position. And, because of this, they attempted to walk a tightrope between defending themselves against a perceived usurpatious federal government and not appearing to be acting irresponsibly. Their objective was to chart a course that would solemnly rebuke and challenge the Federalists and also intimate that secession from the Union was a step that might be taken as a desperate last resort. At the same time, however, they wanted to assure their fellow countrymen that they would not jeopardize the Union by any reckless and impetuous actions.[17]

Thus, the early months of 1799 were stressful ones for the new nation. Not only did public anxiety remain high because of the ongoing quasi-naval war with France that some feared, rather fantastically, might even lead to a French invasion of the United States—and one that would be welcomed by disaffected foreigners and members of the opposition—but Americans were also being rocked by reports and rumors warning of a possible breakup of the Union and civil war.

Two polar opposite reactions were expressed by the Federalists. While some found the militancy of the Republicans alarming, others realized that it could be used as a means of justifying a Federalist move to crush their adversaries.

Hamilton was in the camp that saw the situation as providing a unique opportunity, and he hastened to seize the moment by recommending the establishment of a "special Committee," presumably a congressional one, to respond to the Kentucky and Virginia resolutions. And he also suggested exactly what the conclusions this committee should come to. The committee should, he said, affirm the constitutionality of the Alien and Sedition Acts, condemn the resolutions as destructive to the Constitution, and denounce Kentucky and Virginia for conspiring "to overturn the government." Its members should also declare, Hamilton said, that there was "full evidence . . . of a regular conspiracy to overturn the government" as well as of Southerners seditiously encouraging France "to decline accommodation [with the United States] and proceed in hostility."

This indictment of the two states should then be followed, Hamilton advised, by the strengthening of the regular army forces. And once the army had been readied, it should "be drawn toward Virginia . . . and then measures be taken to act upon the laws and put Virginia to the Test of resistance." It would be important, he emphasized, to use the regular army rather than a militia force, which could not be counted upon to subdue a *refractory and powerful state.*"[18]

Later in 1799 Hamilton expounded on more aggressive actions that might be taken to crush the Virginia-led opposition, explaining that extraordinary threats called for extraordinary steps. The federal judiciary should be strengthened, he said, and supplementary laws enacted to penalize "incendiary and seditious practices" in order "to preserve confidence in the officers of the general government, by preserving their reputations from malicious and unfounded slanders." Most drastic was Hamilton's proposal to amend the Constitution so that "the great states" might be subdivided. It was a step that Hamilton described as "indispensable [to the] security of the general government, and with it of the Union," in order to reduce Virginia's influence and power. [19]

Hamilton's radical recommendations, however, were not heeded by the Adams administration and other Federalists. But had the national government thus attempted to fragment Virginia into several smaller states and/ or move a federal army to the state's borders, it almost certainly would have resulted in a scission of the Union as well as a civil war in 1799.

III

Coming on the heels of the Virginia and Kentucky resolutions and their challenge to federal authority, a rebellion in eastern Pennsylvania in 1799 aggravated and amplified the Federalists' sense that the national government and the Union were on perilous ground.[20] At a time when there was already much talk of sedition, civil war, and even vast interconnected conspiracies, the Fries Rebellion seemed to be the missing piece of evidence—the Rosetta stone—that served to confirm the Federalists' most terrifying fears.

To the Republicans the revolt was a cautionary note. Already politically exposed by the Kentucky and Virginia resolutions, the leaders of the opposition recognized that any linkage or sign of support for the Fries Rebellion would be politically disastrous, corroborating in the minds of their opponents and others in the American electorate the charge that Republicans were conspiring to break up the Union and overthrow the federal government. Jefferson had been worried earlier about a possible "insurrection" in Pennsylvania, fearing that "Nothing could be so fatal," for anything "like force would check the progress of the public opinion & rally them round the government." "This is not," Jefferson emphasized, "the kind of opposition the American people will permit." If force could be avoided, he said, then the people would halt the "evil propensities of the government, by the constitutional means of election & petition."[21]

Fries Rebellion was not a spontaneous action. Indeed, it was the culmination of months-long simmering anger and frustration among the followers of the German Lutheran and German Reformed churches in the eastern area of the state. Specifically, these churchgoers were outraged at the federal government for its Direct Tax Act of 1798. That legislation had put a levy on lands, homes, and slaves and established a system dividing each state into districts in order for federal assessors to assess and keep records on the sizes of homes, the building materials used in their construction, and the sizes and numbers of their windows.

The tax infuriated these Pennsylvanians for a variety of reasons, one being that it was particularly oppressive on small farmers, who had little or no cash to use for payment. But the tax was also detested because it was seen as being levied to support an unpopular Federalist-controlled central government that had passed the Sedition Act and now was being used to expand and mobilize the federal military.

The conflict that was to become known as Fries Rebellion began when local residents protested the hated tax by aggressively thwarting the property assessors (largely Quakers and Moravians) from doing their jobs, with the result that seventeen of the protestors were jailed. Then, shortly afterward, local auctioneer and militia captain John Fries rallied to his neighbors' support by organizing and leading a militia force nearly 400 strong to nearby Bethlehem, Pennsylvania, to force the release of the rebels being held there.[22] As part of the militia effort and protest, the insurgents also condemned the tax, the Alien and Sedition Acts, Congress, President Adams, the Constitution, "and all the friends to government because they are all tories."[23] After a standoff in Bethlehem between the U.S. marshal, who had custody of the jailed rebels, and the increasingly drunken and unruly Fries-led militia force, the prisoners were released without bloodshed or violence.[24]

When the news of the rescue reached the eastern seaboard, however, the Federalist press inveighed in a full-throated denunciation about the seditious conspiracy against the government by protesters that were perceived as French sympathizers. The *New York Daily Advertiser* alleged that the "*mania insurrection*" was prompted by "Jacobin Resolves, and the inflammatory and seditious movements of the French Party in the United States."[25] And Secretary of Treasury Oliver Wolcott told Adams that the insurgency had resulted from "misrepresentations of the measures of government, in seditious pamphlets and newspapers, and in letters from popular characters."[26]

The near-hysteria that characterized the Federalist response to the rebellion was further fueled by a fear of and disdain for the foreign-language speaking and culturally distinctive German rebel force. One Federalist called the Germans "ignorant, bigoted, numerous and united," while another referred to them as stupid, ignorant, ugly, and "to the Irish what the negroes of the south are to their drivers."[27]

Adams and his administration condemned the freeing of prisoners as treasonable and, even though there was no evidence of any further disturbance, called for a military expedition to restore order and bring those involved in the rebellion to justice. Hamilton, working through his acolyte, Secretary of War James McHenry, worried that a federal response with "inadequate force" might magnify "a riot into an insurrection." Therefore, the government, he urged, "ought to appear like a *Hercules,* and inspire respect by the display of strength."[28]

A force of 600 regular army soldiers and 320 volunteer and militia cavalry, supported by 2,000 Pennsylvania and New Jersey militia, was sent to the area to arrest the rebels, protect the tax collectors, and prevent future disruptions. Although most of the rebels fled to avoid capture, Fries and more than ninety others were imprisoned and indicted on charges ranging from treason to sedition. Then, in order to intimidate the local population with the overpowering strength of the army, parades and formal reviews of the troops were conducted to drive the point home.

In the end, however, after lengthy judicial proceedings, only Fries and two colleagues were found to be guilty of treason and sentenced to be hanged.

IV

With all the animosity and suspicion swirling around the country in 1798 and 1799, both the Republicans and the Federalists looked to voters for vindication in the 1798–1799 elections for state offices as well as for representatives to be sent to the Sixth Congress. Members of both parties knew these contests would set the stage for the upcoming presidential election of 1800.

Total success in the races seems to have been the goal (and perhaps the expectation) of the Federalists, whose fortunes in the wake of the impressive show of military force in Pennsylvania seemed to be at their zenith. This objective was reflected in the insistence by one of the party's adherents that it was "not sufficient . . . [to] content ourselves with victory" unless it were "followed up until every germ of faction be destroyed." [29]

For their part the Republicans desperately wanted evidence that the voters were as incensed as they were about the passage of the Alien and Sedition Acts and that they supported their strategy to withdraw from the national scene and concentrate on building up areas of strength in some Southern states.

Unbeknownst to the participants at this time, of course, was the crucial role that those who were elected to the Sixth Congress would play in the 1800 presidential election. Ultimately, it would be that group of representatives who would end up with the responsibility of electing the next president.

An important Federalist tactic in the elections was to exploit the popularity of Southern public men, especially Washington, Patrick Henry, John Marshall, and General Daniel Morgan from Virginia, in an effort to mobilize support in areas of Republican strength.

Hamilton, who had long been concerned about the sectional nature of the political conflict, urged the retired Washington to use his influence and prominence to counter the "Opposition-Faction" that had assumed "so much a Geographical complexion."[30] And following up on Hamilton's suggestion, Washington did indeed work to persuade Patrick Henry (1736–1799) to stand for election to the Virginia General Assembly.

Henry, whose "give me liberty or give me death" oration had been one of the most memorable and stirring calls for independence during the Revolutionary era, was still one of the most popular men in Virginia. But his career after the Revolution made him difficult to categorize politically. Virginia's first governor after independence, serving from 1776 to 1779 and from 1784 to 1786, he later became a passionate Antifederalist who had used his oratorical skills in a losing effort to get Virginia to reject the new Constitution. He also was influential in getting the Bill of Rights adopted.

Although distrusted by Jefferson and Madison, Henry, like them, had opposed much of the Federalist policy during the Washington administration. Nonetheless, he had ended his uneasy association with the Republicans by opposing their efforts to scuttle the Jay Treaty. He later also opposed the Virginia Resolutions. In both cases, Henry thought the Republicans were going too far and feared "disunion" and the "baneful effects of faction."[31] Responding to Washington's entreaties, Henry did decide to run for a seat in the General Assembly. Both Henry and Washington, however, were dead by the end of the year.

John Marshall (1755–1835), whose popularity was significantly enhanced by the near-hero status he gained by standing up against the insulting behavior of the French during the XYZ Affair, was nominated for a seat in the House of Representatives, a candidacy that offered the Federalists their best opportunity at winning an additional seat there. A captain during the American Revolution, Marshall had served numerous terms in the Virginia House of Delegates after the war and was one of the leaders urging ratification of the Constitution at the Virginia convention. Although having little formal education, he had become one of the foremost lawyers in Richmond through his sharp analytical mind and natural eloquence.

Of all the Virginia Federalists, Marshall was one of the few with a truly national, rather than local, vision. He struck an independent note when he informed the public that he did not support the Alien and Sedition Acts and would have voted against them had he been in Congress. The acts, he contended, were "useless" and created "unnecessary discontents and jealousies at a time when our very existence as a nation, may depend on our union." At the same time, however, he condemned faction (meaning Republicans) and the dangerous French influence in the country. And with his fellow Federalists, he shared an abiding devotion to Washington and a fear that Republican factionalism and devotion to France would lead to civil war and social chaos.[32]

Marshall's willingness to stand for election to Congress greatly pleased the Federalists. One claimed that Marshall "would become a most powerful auxiliary to the cause of order and good government."[33] Another lauded him as "highly and deservedly respected by the friends of the Government from the South." He would, he said, "give a tone to the federal politics South of the Susquehanna"; and "we can do nothing without him."[34]

For their side, the Republicans charged Marshall with harboring a deep and abiding affinity for the English monarchical system. He was supported, it was alleged, by those who were "partisans of Great Britain and the inveterate enemies of independence." And Marshall himself, it was contended, was one of those "who have long endeavored to restore us to the abject condition of the British colonies."[35]

Marshall's opponent was Republican incumbent John Clopton, who had served in both the Fourth and Fifth Congresses during which time he had condemned the Alien and Sedition Acts and vowed to oppose any attempts by the government to bring the United States under England's sphere of influence, while promising to support France as long as it did not compromise America's interests. At one point, however, he was accused of the crime of calling President Adams "a traitor to the United States." The charges were dropped, but only after Secretary of State Timothy Pickering had instituted prosecution proceedings against him for sedition.[36]

Even though he did not run for reelection, General Daniel Morgan, a Revolutionary War hero and Federalist member of Congress from Virginia from 1797 to 1799, was active in the campaign, using his popular standing in the community to denounce the Republicans and the Virginia Resolutions. It "is a dreadful melancholy truth," he charged, "that we have a considerable party among ourselves, who, instead of supporting and rendering respectable our government, would divide and distract it. . . ." "The crisis," he warned voters, has arrived, and "You are now to determine whether you will support your nation" or allow the Republicans to reduce the United States by their support of France "to a state of Tributary vassalage."[37]

The Virginia Republicans, like the Federalists, saw the 1799 election as an important opportunity to preserve and even increase their dominance in the state by electing well-known Republican figures to positions of responsibility and power. John Taylor of Caroline, in anticipation of a hostile confrontation between Virginia and its allies and the Federalist-controlled federal government, urged that James Monroe be put forward for the governorship of the state, as eventually he was. It was of "immense importance," Taylor argued, to have a "decided character at the head of one government" for "the influence it will have upon public opinion." Furthermore, as Jefferson was reminded by his colleague, the Virginia governor exercised considerable and significant power, including "the important one of commanding the militia." And the Republicans needed to be more attentive "to the consequences of having a tory first magistrate and military commander of the state."[38]

Madison, who had retired from Congress in 1797, was successfully recruited by Taylor to stand for the Virginia legislature. Calling Madison "the hope of Republicans throughout the union," Taylor stressed that his candidacy was even more important because of the great possibility that Henry's election to the Virginia legislature as a champion of Federalism might so dispirit the republicans that they might fall "easy prey to the enemies of liberty." "Save your country," Taylor begged Madison, for Virginia was at a critical point and "at the next assembly it will take a permanent form which will fix the fate of America."[39]

Jefferson, as well as other Republicans, added their voices to the appeal that Madison run for a legislative post. It was crucial, one supporter said, that the state government be in the hands of the Republicans so that "*wise* and *firm* State measures" would be able to keep "the general government within the just limits of the Constitution."[40]

v

The results of the 1798–1799 elections both stunned and dismayed the Republicans and overjoyed the Federalists, who made serious inroads in areas where Republicans were assumed to be dominant. Nationally, the Federalists increased their control in the House of Representatives from a majority ranging from six to eleven in the Fifth Congress to a majority of around twenty in the Sixth.[41] But most troubling for the Republicans was the erosion of support for Republicans in their Southern base. For much to the Republicans' chagrin and distress, the Federalists were able to elect twenty-two congressmen to the Republicans' fifteen in the congressional elections in that section of the country.

In line with this, the Federalists scored some impressive gains in Virginia. Although the Republicans did manage to capture eleven House seats, the Federalists doubled their representation from four to eight. Among the Federalist victors stood Marshall, who edged out Clopton after receiving a late public endorsement by the widely admired Henry, who had earlier seen himself as above the partisan fray.[42]

The news about Virginia especially shocked Jefferson, who lamented that "the Virginia congressional elections have astounded everyone . . . how long we can hold our ground I do not know."[43] In that presumed Republican stronghold, the statewide congressional vote totals in 1799 show the state to have been closely divided, with the Republicans winning 12,915 votes (or 52 percent) to the Federalists' 11,888 (or 48 percent).[44]

The Federalists also gained representatives in the Virginia House of Delegates, including Patrick Henry. Madison, however, did win his seat. And Monroe was also elected governor by the legislature in a vote of one hundred eleven to forty-four over his Federalist opponent. He thus served as chief magistrate of the state during the critical years from 1799 to 1802.[45]

Congressional results in other Southern states were equally alarming to Jefferson, with the Federalists capturing five out of ten seats in North Carolina. Even more worrisome to the Republicans, the total vote from that state's ten districts showed a healthy Federalist majority of 17,904 to 10,142.[46] The timing of this state election, however, perhaps had an important influence on the outcome. It was held in the late summer of 1798, closely following the passage of the Alien and Sedition Acts and the accompanying anti-French frenzy. Another factor in the increased strength of Federalism in the state was the anti-French sentiment within the large German population in the Piedmont that most likely came in reaction to the French incursions on German soil in the late 1790s.[47]

Anti-French sentiment was also important in South Carolina, where the Federalists gained five out of the six seats in the House of Representatives in an election held in October 1798. The sole Republican winner, and an incumbent, was a transplanted Virginian, Thomas Sumter, the brigadier general who had commanded the South Carolina militia during the American Revolution and who had later become an opponent to the ratification of the Constitution.

The news of the failure of the negotiations with France received the spring before the election, and the subsequent talk of war, had deeply alarmed South Carolinians. Some private citizens there even contributed their own funds to provide for the state's defense against a possible French invasion. Indicative of the tenor of the electoral contest in the state is a widely circulated campaign letter that was written by prominent Federalist Edward Rutledge. Warning that the French made a practice of attacking vulnerable nations "where the people are divided," the letter appealed to South Carolinians to defend "the Constitution & Government of our own Country." If this were done, the letter promised, the French would "have no reason to expect a successful attack." However, it cautioned, if Federalist congressmen who supported firm measures against France were defeated in the election, it would be a strong signal "that the People in this State Disapprove of those Measures of Congress."[48]

In Georgia, two new Federalist congressmen were elected. This represented a net gain for the Federalists, but the new members wore their political affiliation lightly; once in Philadelphia, they voted consistently with the Republicans. The statewide vote was 3,495 for the Federalists to 2,697 for the Republicans.[49]

Maryland gave the Republicans one additional member of the House of Representatives as compared to what they had in 1796. The Federalists in the balloting for House members, however, recorded 14,458 statewide votes to the Republicans' 10,718 and retained a five-to-three lead in the number of representatives. One observer in Baltimore noted that the electioneering was intense: "Wherever I went, the ensuing election for Representatives to congress seemed to take up the entire thoughts of the People, and party spirit rages everywhere with great violence. . . . In this Town and County parties are beyond anything ever before known."[50]

Despite the losses in the South, the vote in the Western states was solidly Republican, with Kentucky electing two Republicans to Congress and Tennessee choosing a Republican for its sole seat.

And the Republicans did make some gains in the Middle Atlantic States. In New Jersey, for example, the Republicans picked up three of the five members of the House of Representatives, compared to no seats in 1798. And in New York the Republicans elected six to House seats, compared to the Federalists' four, which reversed the 1798 total of six Federalists and four Republicans. The Federalists in Pennsylvania lost two congressional positions, which meant that the Republicans there ended up with a nine-to-five majority.[51]

As expected, the Federalists swept the congressional elections in New England, carrying all the House seats except one in Vermont and three in Massachusetts.

Thus, on the eve of the election of 1800, the shocked and disappointed Republicans were looking for answers. From the time of the passage of the Alien and Sedition Acts in 1798, they had counted on remaining strong, and even on gaining strength, in certain citadels and sanctuaries of support in the South, especially in Virginia and North Carolina. And now to see major cracks in the foundation of those defensive bastions raised fundamental questions about the Republicans' ability to survive the Federalist onslaught.

The Federalists, however, were thrilled at the results, especially their increased support in the South. Washington wrote Marshall of his "infinite pleasure" in receiving the news of his election. Marshall was also advised to be "content," for "the tide is turning; the current [in Virginia] will soon run strong in your favor."[52]

6

EARLY CRACKS IN THE FEDERALIST HEGEMONY, 1799–1800

The "whole system of the American government seems to me to be tottering to its foundations . . . I much doubt their power of maintaining internal tranquility."
—Lord William Grenville, February 1800

I

The year 1799 began with the Federalists enjoying near hegemonic control of the federal government. The Federalist victories in the congressional elections in 1798 (and those to come in 1799) were dispiriting to the Republicans, who saw them as ominous precursors of what might be expected in the presidential election in 1800 between the presumed candidates, Adams and Jefferson.

The quasi-naval war with France showed no signs of abating, reinforcing the justification for the Federalist grand designs to strengthen the army and demonize and ultimately destroy the domestic opposition. And the Republican opposition itself seemed to be in retreat, withdrawing to certain local enclaves of support.

Domestic as well as diplomatic events, however, were on the verge of transforming the political landscape, and this would have a major impact on the election of 1800.

In February 1799, Adams, in one of the bravest actions of his long public career, decided to reach out to the French.[1] After receiving encouraging news from several sources during the fall of 1798 and early winter of 1799, Adams had become convinced that the French government was ready to begin negotiations to end the hostilities between the two countries. Thus, he nominated William Vans Murray, who

had been serving as the U.S. minister to the Hague, to be the minister pleni-
potentiary to France.

Adams must have been ecstatic with the intelligence. Having been humil-
iated by supporters of Washington and Hamilton, and forced to accept Hamilton as the second in command of the army, Adams suddenly found himself
in a newly empowered position. Although Fries Rebellion, which erupted at
about the same time, gave some legitimacy to the call for an enhanced army,
the prospect for peace with France ended the main rationale for the force.
With no French enemy, there would be no need for an expanded military.
And consequently, there would be no need for the unpopular taxes and rev-
enues used to support the augmentation of the nation's armed forces. With
a certain smugness, he wrote McHenry that at "present there is no more
prospect of seeing a French army here than there is in heaven."[2]

An important influence on Adams's decision to reopen negotiations with
France came from Elbridge Gerry, his old, trusted friend and fellow Feder-
alist, who had returned from France in the fall of 1798 declaring that the
French government wanted peace.

The fiercely independent public man from Massachusetts had compiled
a distinguished public record early on as a signer of both the Declaration of
Independence and Articles of Confederation and, later, as a delegate to the
Constitutional Convention. However, he had refused to support the Constitution in the end because it lacked a bill of rights. Subsequent to that, having
been elected to Congress, Gerry had become an enthusiastic defender of
Hamilton's financial plan.

Then, after serving two terms in the House of Representatives, he had
accompanied John Marshall and Charles Cotesworth Pinckney to France in
1797 in the effort to negotiate an end to the crisis between France and the
United States. Following the ill-fated XYZ Affair, however, Gerry had chosen
not to return immediately to the United States with Marshall and Pinckney.
Instead, in spite of the insulting behavior on the part of the French, he had
remained in France in hopes of reaching some accord. This action had infuriated some Federalists, and his eventual return in the fall of 1798 bringing
news of the possibility of a diplomatic settlement between the two countries
aroused further hostility. Shortly after his meeting with Adams, Gerry reported that he had been ignored and shunned by Boston society and that a
mob had shouted abuse at him outside his home in Cambridge.

It was not only the messenger that drew the ire of Hamilton and his
Federalist allies, but the president himself as well. One wrote Hamilton
denouncing Adams's decision to send another mission to France, claiming

that "Had the foulest heart and ablest head in the world, been permitted to select the most embarrassing and ruinous measure, perhaps it would have been precisely the one [reopening negotiations with France], which has been adopted." Secretary of State Timothy Pickering declared that Adams must be "suffering the torments of the damned."[3] Another critic wished that on his trip back to Quincy, Adams would fall from his horse and break his neck.

Just a few days before Adams nominated Murray to undertake the diplomatic mission, Theodore Sedgwick had reported to Hamilton about a disturbing meeting that he had had with the president. Virginia was no threat to the federal government, Adams had declared, but "if you must have an army I will give it to you, but remember it will make the government more unpopular" than any of its acts. The American people, the president had maintained, had been patient with "the burden of taxes," but this patience might not last.[4]

Senate Federalists rebuffed Adams's nomination of Murray, fearing that he, even though a Federalist, could not be trusted with negotiating with France. Adams balked, threatening to resign if a new mission to France were rejected—an action that, of course, would have given the presidency to Vice President Jefferson. Ultimately, however, Adams was forced to accept a negotiating commission of three members: Murray, Chief Justice Oliver Ellsworth, and Patrick Henry. Later, Henry, who was in ill health, was replaced by the Federalist governor of North Carolina, William Davie.

The departure of the commission was delayed, however, until after Adams received further assurances that the American representatives would be greeted by the French with the respect due to diplomats from a sovereign nation and would not be subjected to the humiliating treatment their predecessors had suffered during the XYZ Affair.

Robert Liston, Great Britain's minister to the United States, reported to his superiors in London of the factional fighting among the Federalists. Despite this, the "federal party," Liston reported, "have felt the necessity of temporary forbearance, and seem determined, for the sake of the Country, to continue to give the Chief Magistrate [Adams] their support." Some of Liston's dispatches, however, drew a more somber picture, implying that Adams was in his dotage and that the breakup of the Union was possible.

These reports describing the lack of stability in the government of the United States caused considerable concern in London. The "whole system of the American government seems to me to be tottering to its foundations," one of Liston's superiors in the Foreign Office wrote, "and so far from being able to enforce upon the country good faith towards foreign powers, I much doubt their power of maintaining internal tranquility."[5]

Relations between Adams and the Hamilton faction of Federalists grew steadily worse. Full of distrust and animosity toward Adams, Hamilton and his followers feared that Federalism was being irrevocably damaged by the capricious and unreliable president. To them he seemed bent on destroying the newly authorized army, an institution that they believed was essential to protect the country against foreign threats as well as from the seditious actions of Virginia and its allies.

To say that Hamilton was heavily invested in the creation of this army would be an understatement. After Adams had been forced to accept him as Washington's second in command, the former secretary of treasury had thrown himself into the organizing and equipping of the embryonic military force with an almost obsessive zeal. From the outset it had been obvious to all that Hamilton would be the de facto commander, given Washington's age and reluctance to take on day-to-day management duties. And Hamilton reveled in his new role. There was no detail that escaped his eye: the design of the uniforms, the choice of sidearms for the various ranks, the organization of the various units, and the vetting of candidates for the officer corps through the certification of their political reliability.

Hamilton's conception of the role of the army he was building was a dramatically expanded one. It went far beyond simply defending the country from possible French attacks and quelling domestic disturbances. Along with some other Federalist leaders, he saw the force as the active instrument of a new, more grandiose, more aggressive, more imperialistic foreign policy.

In cooperation with the British navy, the army was envisioned as having a part in the liberation of Spanish Latin America and thus in preventing the French from gaining a foothold there. A Venezuelan, Sebastian Francisco de Miranda, first outlined this scheme to an eager and receptive Rufus King in London in 1798. King, the U.S. minister to England at the time, then excitedly relayed the information to Hamilton. In response, Hamilton wrote that he was "glad" that the United States would "furnish the whole land force necessary." His assumption, he said, was that the command of the force "would very naturally fall upon me—and I hope I should disappoint no favourable anticipation."[6]

Adams, however, seemed to show little or no interest in the project, which caused King to implore Hamilton to "attend to the very interesting subject. . . . Providence seems to have prepared the way. . . . Our children will reproach us if we neglect our duty."[7]

And Hamilton in late 1798 and early 1799 did attempt to push ahead for a formal declaration of war against France, recognizing that this would be essential for the grand scheme to proceed. The first step after a declaration of war, he argued, would be to secure for the United States the Spanish territories of Florida and Louisiana. This was crucial because of the risk that these Spanish territories might fall into the hands of the more formidable French. This preemptive attack, Hamilton emphasized, would be in harmony with the Miranda plan "to detach South America from Spain which is the only Channel, though [sic] which the riches of *Mexico* and *Peru* are conveyed to France."[8]

Hamilton's work on creating an army with himself at the helm was clearly more than a desire on his part to strengthen the hand of the federal government against domestic and foreign enemies. Rather, it seems to have been the fulfillment of some deep-seated personal aspiration. Leading the army would be his avenue to distinction and power, even adulation and glory, goals that drove him throughout his life.

Hamilton had been born out of wedlock in the West Indies to a mother who had been jailed earlier as an adulteress. Then, she and Hamilton had later been abandoned by Hamilton's father, a bankrupt businessman. And Hamilton's extraordinary ambition and striving for distinction and success seems to have been driven, at least in part, by his shame over his background of poverty and disgrace.

Not only was Hamilton brilliant, he was a man of prodigious energy and industry and capable of an enormous output of work. During the campaign to ratify the new Constitution, for example, he wrote fifty-one well-reasoned, well-researched Federalist Papers, which amounted to about two a week— many more than his co-contributors, James Madison and John Jay. And his private papers exhibit a wide-ranging intelligence and familiarity with classical history and international law as well as a passion for detail, whether pertaining to the most minute financial accounts of the Treasury Department or to the technical particulars of organizing an army.[9]

The notorious and legendary diplomat, Charles Maurice de Talleyrand, who brilliantly served and survived various French regimes for a half a century, awarded Hamilton high marks as a political figure. "Napoleon, Pitt, and Hamilton" were the greatest political leaders of the era, according to Talleyrand, and of the three, he "would without hesitation give the first place to Hamilton."[10]

Adams and his wife Abigail undoubtedly recognized the qualities of Hamilton that drew Talleyrand's praise. But both were deeply troubled by the New Yorker's incessant ambition. They were worried about what they considered to be his insatiable appetite for power, and apprehensive that Hamilton saw the army as the instrument through which he could satisfy this appetite. Adams heard an alarming rumor that a plot existed to first elevate Hamilton to be commander in chief of the army and then to "appoint him general over the President."[11] In line with this, Adams informed a friend that he "thought Hamilton and a party were endeavoring to get an army on foot to give Hamilton the command of it, and thus to proclaim a regal government and place Hamilton as the head of it, and prepare the way for a province of Great Britain."

Abigail echoed her husband's trepidations. She worried that Hamilton "would . . . become a second Bonaparte."[12] Certainly, the example of Napoleon Bonaparte was fresh in the minds of the Adamses and others as the French general moved toward seizing political power in France: so this was not just an idle fear.

II

After Adams had negotiated with the Federalist caucus about sending a commission to France, he left Philadelphia for seven months. This was, according to one historian, the major turning point of his administration.[13] Deeply concerned about his frail and bedridden Abigail, he returned to Massachusetts to be with her. And, at home, he stayed somewhat isolated from the government, which had fled from Philadelphia to Trenton, New Jersey, in order to escape the yellow fever epidemic—an evacuation that caused many thousand people to leave the capital. By the end of the epidemic, more than 3,000 people had perished, including the mayor of the city, four of the president's servants, and the two leading editors of the political presses, Benjamin Franklin Bache of the Republican *Aurora* and John Fenno of the Federalist *Gazette of the United States.*[14]

Although Adams kept in contact with his subordinates, this extended leave from the center of government weakened his authority and provoked even greater hostility from Hamilton and his supporters. One Federalist complained to Rufus King that Adams was governing "by fits and starts—without the advice of his friends around him—nay without even consulting them." Another wrote King that the president seemed to be practicing the "pitiful politics of Gerry," which had "been reprobated by 9/10ths of the good Federalists and by a good majority of the people."[15] It was not only Gerry's decision to remain in France to negotiate after the XYZ Affair that had infuriated many Federalists; but even more dangerous from their perspective was his nonpartisanship and moderation. Thus Gerry's conduct and politics were seen by the anti-Adams Federalists as threatening to Federalism, and, as such, threatening to the welfare of the country.

Adams's absence from the center of government continued into the summer of 1799, emboldening his critics to become increasingly vocal in their condemnation. Hamilton, frustrated by the prospect of peace and the consequent dismantling of the army, implored the Cabinet to assume more responsibility, since Adams was so blatantly disregarding his presidential duties. A mark of Hamilton's desperation was his effort to persuade Washington to come out of retirement and seek a third term of office in 1800.[16]

For their part, Adams's supporters cautioned the president that the "public sentiment is very much against your being so much away from the seat of government." Furthermore, "your real friends wish you to be with your officers, because the public impression is that the government will be better conducted." And any further delay, Adams was advised, would help fuel a plot against his presidency by his opponents.[17] Benjamin Stoddert, the secretary of the navy and a cabinet member loyal to Adams, pleaded for the president to come to the temporary seat of government in Trenton. "Artful and designing men might make such use of your absence" to upset the negotiations for peace, Adams was told, and "make your next election less honorable than it would otherwise be."[18]

In early August Adams received French assurances in a letter from Talleyrand that American diplomats would be accorded the respect due envoys from any sovereign nation. Also immeasurably strengthening the prospect for peace was the long-rumored news, now confirmed, of the stunning defeat of the French fleet by England's Lord Horatio Nelson in the Battle of the Nile a year earlier. And with that news, any concern whatsoever about a French invasion of the United States also vanished. Peace was in the offing.

Nonetheless, Adams was receiving reports that Secretary of State Pickering and others were urging the delay of the envoys' departure. This news of the Cabinet's obstructive behavior finally did bring Adams out of the seclusion of his home and to Trenton to rejoin the government. Once there, he confronted his secretary of state. While maintaining that he remained wary of French intentions, Adams declared the French would "find, as long as I am in office, candor, integrity, and, as far as there can be any confidence and safety, a pacific and friendly disposition." "In this spirit I shall pursue the negotiations, and I expect the cooperation of the heads of departments," the president sternly admonished Pickering.[19]

Hamilton, seeking to have the mission to France delayed or suspended, also had a contentious meeting with Adams in Trenton, where he lectured the president as if he were a schoolboy about the realities of European affairs. Hamilton's style and tone were condescending and "most peremptory and even Swaggering," according to Adams, and showed so little understanding of France and Great Britain that the president pitied "the little man." "Never in my life," he asserted, "did I hear a man talk more like a fool" or an "impertinent ignoramus." Dismissing Hamilton's arguments, the president ordered the immediate departure of the American commissioners to France.[20]

Hamilton and his Federalist allies felt betrayed by Adams's action, which would, they lamented, inevitably lead to the defeat of Federalism and also produce "a temporary reign of *American Jacobinism*."[21] This constant use of the terms "Jacobin" or "Jacobinism" by the Federalists to characterize their Republican opponents offers a useful insight into their state of mind at the end of the eighteenth century. First of all, it was an emotionally laden epithet associating the violence and chaos of the French Revolution with the Republicans. But it was not merely a propaganda trick to discredit the opponents for popular advantage. It was more significant and sincere than that. Most Federalists ardently believed that the Republicans had a naïve and dangerous attachment to France. Thus, an accession of the Republicans to power in the election of 1800, they were convinced, would threaten the safety and stability and even the continued existence of the republic.

III

Although the 1798 and 1799 election results left the Republicans reeling, especially because of their disappointing showing in the South, Jefferson's refrain throughout 1799 was that the Republicans had time on their side and that an awakened public would eventually repudiate the excesses of the Federalists. High taxes and a standing army, Jefferson argued, would arouse the American people to embrace their true republican principles, which were being flagrantly violated by the Federalists.

What was needed, Jefferson believed, was for the Republicans to publicly and forcefully restate their principles, "principles already advanced by Virginia and Kentucky." Those resolutions should not "be yielded in silence," he said. Thus, it was necessary for additional resolutions that would clarify, amplify, and answer the criticisms of the original ones to be adopted. When the American people understood "their attachment to those very rights which we are now vindicating," he was confident, they would, "before it shall be too late, rally with us round the true principles of our federal compact." The "rights" of the states to defend themselves from "palpable violations of the constitutional compact by the Federal government" had to be safeguarded. And it was imperative that any new resolutions express "in affectionate and conciliatory language our warm attachment to union with our sister-states, and to the instrument and principles by which we are united."

Jefferson also suggested that the new resolutions make clear that Virginia and Kentucky were not "disposed to make every measure of error or wrong a cause of scission" and were "willing to sacrifice to . . . [the Union] every thing except those rights of self government the securing of which was the object of that [our] compact." Thus, the Virginians and Kentuckians, Jefferson said, must indicate that they are willing "to wait with patience till those passions and delusions [that led to the passage of the Alien and Sedition Acts] shall have passed."[22]

Jefferson's conciliatory language was meant to reassure critics of the original Kentucky and Virginia resolutions that neither state was anxious to take any final and fateful step toward secession. Nonetheless, Jefferson did want to include in the new resolutions a more radical warning about the *possibility* of secession. And in his most extreme statement on the subject, he proposed that if Kentucky and Virginia were to be disappointed in their expectations, they would "sever . . . [themselves] from that union we so much value, rather than give up the rights of self government which we have reserved, and in which alone we see liberty, safety and happiness."[23]

Madison, whose more cautious manner reined in Jefferson's impetuousness many times during their long friendship and political partnership, urged moderation. Apparently Madison's advice was taken, for in a letter a couple of weeks later Jefferson asserted that "we should never think of separation but for repeated and enormous violations, so these, when they occur, will be cause enough themselves."[24]

Both Kentucky and Virginia legislatures adopted new resolutions in an effort to counter the criticism of their original ones and to renew their attack on the Alien and Sedition Acts. Kentucky pledged its "attachment to the Union" but declared that "a nullification of those acts by the States to be the rightful remedy."[25] Madison's Virginia Report of 1800 reiterated the 1798 condemnation of centralized governmental power, warning that the Union could be endangered by an excess of federal power that could transform "the republican system of the United States to a monarchy." Denying that the earlier resolutions had advanced disunion, Madison asserted that the objective had been to stimulate discussion and provoke "reflection."[26]

Made public at the same time as Washington's death in December 1799, the second set of Kentucky Resolutions apparently caused little public notice, overshadowed by the passing of the revered first president. Because Kentucky did not send out the 1799 Resolutions to legislatures in other states, as they had done with the first resolutions, there were no legislative responses to them, either. Apparently, the Virginia Resolutions also received little attention, with Jefferson in Philadelphia complaining as late as February 1800, that he had not even seen the final copy as approved.[27]

IV

As the presidential election of 1800 drew near, both Federalists and Republicans took stock of their relative political strengths in comparison with the previous election. Jefferson, the presumed 1800 Republican candidate, had lost the 1796 contest to Adams, the presumed 1800 Federalist candidate, by a vote of seventy-one to sixty-eight in the Electoral College. Adams had swept New England with its thirty-nine votes. The Middle Atlantic States of New York, New Jersey, Pennsylvania, and Delaware had split their votes, twenty-three for Adams and fourteen for Jefferson. However, Jefferson's only votes from that section had come from Pennsylvania, with Adams carrying the rest of the region. Jefferson and the Republicans had won the Southern states of Maryland, Virginia, North Carolina, South Carolina, and Georgia by the large margin of forty-seven to nine. The only Federalist votes cast in that section were seven from Maryland and one each from Virginia and North Carolina. Both Western states, Tennessee and Kentucky, awarded their electoral votes, seven in all, to Jefferson.[28]

For the Federalists to be successful in the 1800 presidential contest, then, they needed to retain their 1796 base and hold onto or extend the inroads they had made in the South in the 1798 and 1799 state and congressional elections. On the other hand, for the Republicans to win, they had to stop or reverse Federalist advances in the South, to gain votes in the Middle States, and possibly even to break the Federalist domination of New England.

While the Republicans had some hope of making political gains in New England and the Federalists had some hope of expanding on their 1798 and 1799 victories in the South, the Middle States provided the most promise for both parties.

Some early indications seemed favorable for the Republicans. In the fall of 1799, the Republican, Thomas McKean (1734–1817), had defeated Federalist senator James Ross for the governorship of Pennsylvania by a vote of 38,036 to 32,643. And his victory had rested, in no small part, on his strong showing in the counties where the Fries Rebellion had been centered.

McKean's margin reflected a 20.7 percent increase in the Republican vote from the congressional returns of a year earlier. The Federalists also showed a vote increase, but one of only 8 percent.[29]

But there were disturbing signs for the Republicans in Pennsylvania as well. The Federalists had maintained control of the state senate and had refused to pass an election law defining whether the electoral votes for the 1800 presidential election would be determined by the legislature or by popular vote, raising the possibility that Pennsylvania would cast no electoral votes at all in the next fall's presidential election.[30] This would be catastrophic for the Republicans, since they had received fourteen out of fifteen of the state's electoral votes in 1796.

In addition to McKean's win in the Keystone State, several other electoral victories the same year also inspired Republican optimism. Republicans had gained control of the New Jersey legislature, and Matthew Lyon, the editor who had been convicted under the Sedition Act, had won reelection from his jail cell as a Republican member of the House of Representatives from Vermont.[31]

The uncertain status of Pennsylvania's electoral votes in 1800 made the spring contest for control of the legislature in New York even more essential for the Republicans if they hoped to win the presidency. And the key to victory in New York was Aaron Burr (1756–1836).

Described as a frail, slight man with delicate health, Burr had been only twenty years old at the time of the Declaration of Independence. Nonetheless, he had served in the Continental Army until he was forced by ill health to resign in 1779 at the rank of lieutenant colonel. During his service he had fought with General Benedict Arnold in the arduous campaign to take Quebec and was later involved in the Battle of Monmouth. By all accounts he was a good officer, who, while being a strict disciplinarian, was popular with the soldiers under his command.

Burr was from a distinguished family. His father, the Reverend Aaron Burr, had served as the second president of the College of New Jersey, the school that later became Princeton University. And his mother, Esther Edwards Burr, was the daughter of one of the most renowned theologians of the eighteenth century, Jonathan Edwards. The young Burr, however, was orphaned before he was three years of age and raised by an uncle. Entering Princeton at the tender age of thirteen, he graduated with honors in 1772.

After leaving the army, Burr read law and was admitted to the New York bar in 1782. But, while he enjoyed a certain success as a studious, attentive lawyer with a legal style that was *"persuasive* and *imaginative,"* he apparently considered legal work "laborious" as well as boring and unchallenging.[32]

Entering politics, Burr served in the New York Assembly in 1784–1785 and was appointed by Governor George Clinton to be attorney general of New York in 1789. In 1791 he was elected to national office as one of New York's two U.S. senators. While in the Senate, Burr allied himself with James Monroe, and, along with John Taylor of Caroline, led the opposition to Washington's naming of John Jay to be envoy to England, arguing that the appointment of the chief justice to conduct this executive-branch duty was a violation of the constitutional separation of powers. After this losing effort, Burr nonetheless remained close to Monroe, who in 1797 asked him to serve as his intermediary in a bitter dispute he was having with Hamilton that for a while appeared to be heading toward a duel. Cooler heads prevailed, and there was no duel, although Hamilton did have "a habit of engaging in affairs of honor." In the years from 1779 to 1804 he was the challenger or the recipient of a challenge a dozen times.[33]

Despite his youth and his paucity of experience relative to many of his contemporaries, Burr in 1796 had come highly recommended to the Virginia Republican leadership by some of his fellow New Yorkers. One of several Republican vice presidential possibilities, Burr had been singled out to be on the ticket that year even though some regarded him as "unsettled in his politics" and even feared that he might "go over to the other side."[34] This wariness about Burr's fidelity, as well as concerns about his scheming and plotting, haunted him throughout his adult life. He was, as many contemporaries believed, a man less than he appeared to be, driven by obvious self-interest in an age when it was not seemly for a public man to be so clearly in the grip of personal ambition.

As Jefferson's running mate in 1796, Burr had finished a poor fourth, behind Adams, Jefferson, and Thomas Pinckney. But it was the insulting behavior of the Virginia Republicans, who indicated their distrust of Burr by giving him only one out of a possible twenty-one electoral votes in that contest, that deeply offended him. Nonetheless, while this betrayal created resentment and not a small amount of bitterness, Burr had continued to work incessantly and relentlessly for the Republican cause.

Later, after he had left the Senate in 1797, Burr won a seat in the New York State Assembly. At about the same time, he reached out to the Virginia Republicans in an effort to repair his strained relationships with them. In addition to corresponding with Jefferson about politics, Burr accompanied the vice president and Albert Gallatin when the two went to welcome James Monroe on his return home from France, where he had been serving as U.S. minister.[35]

As a member of the New York Assembly for the second time (1798–1799), Burr quickly made his mark as an influential Republican leader and gifted political strategist. Along with his fellow Republicans, Burr promoted a popular legislative program that supported internal improvements, lower and more equitable taxes, and debtor relief. Despite this, however, he was defeated for reelection in 1799. One Federalist opponent noted that his loss was fortunate for the Federalists, for Burr, who had already "done a great deal toward revolutionizing the state," might have converted all of New York to Republicanism.[36]

Out of public office, Burr threw himself into laying the groundwork for the future Republican takeover of the state by turning his energies toward capturing the New York Assembly for the Republicans in the crucial spring election of 1800—crucial because under state law, the combined vote of those elected to the New York Assembly and Senate would determine the state's electoral vote in the upcoming presidential election.

In the past, the state had been a bastion of Federalist strength, especially in New York City. In 1799 the Federalists had swept the elections in the city, with their entire slate gaining an average majority of 900 votes. Thus, if the Republicans were to turn things around, they had to do well in New York City.[37] The key to victory would be winning the city's thirteen Assembly contests. And Jefferson was well aware of this, writing Monroe that "all depended on the city election."[38]

Burr recognized that in order to be victorious, he and his Republican colleagues had to gain the loyalty of the commercial classes as well as the entrepreneurial-minded master craftsmen and mechanics. But it was the more numerous lower-class mechanics and journeymen, those making up the petit bourgeoisie, whose support would be most essential for a Republican victory.

Burr's masterstroke in winning the election for the Republicans was to put forth a slate of notables as candidates for the Assembly. These well-known figures, as Burr correctly foresaw, would command recognition and support from the electorate. Among others, they included George Clinton, who had served six terms as governor, and General Horatio Gates, a hero from the Revolution. Also on the slate were members from each of the three Republican factions in the state: the Clintonians, the Livingstons, and the Burrites.

The names of these prominent contenders, however, were held in confidence until the Federalists had announced their slate of candidates. Then, when the Federalist list was revealed as "two grocers, a ship chandler, a baker, a potter, a bookseller, a mason, and a shoemaker," the Republicans were overjoyed.[39] In that age of deferential democracy, when political elites expected and won deference from ordinary citizens, the Republicans had a great advantage by fielding a list of prominent public figures who had been celebrated for their leadership roles in the past.

In addition, Burr's frenetic, but also disciplined, approach to the campaign, along with his studious attention to detail, made him an enormously effective and ahead-of-his-time political organizer. One colleague reported that during the election campaign Burr had held "open house for nearly two months, and Committees were kept in session day and night at his house. Refreshments were always on the table and mattresses for temporary repose in the rooms. Reports were received hourly from sub-committees, and in short, no means left unemployed."[40]

During the three-day balloting period, both sides, Burr's and Hamilton's, played active, almost frenzied, roles, sometimes debating one another at various polling places or addressing groups of voters. One Federalist worker complained that he had "not eaten dinner for three days and have been constantly upon my legs from 7 in the morning till 7 in the afternoon."[41] Burr, himself, it was said, spent ten hours at a polling place during the last day of voting.

In the end it was Burr's efforts that paid off. The Republicans won a stunning victory, capturing all thirteen of the seats from the city. This meant that the Republicans would have enough votes in the state legislature, combining those in both the Assembly and the Senate, to control the selection of electors the following November. One Republican was so astonished by the victory that he believed that it must have been the result of "the Intervention of a Supreme Power and our friend Burr the agent."[42]

By accomplishing the sweep, the Republicans had successfully cultivated support from the lower classes, who had been alienated by the Federalists' elitist bias, often expressed in contemptuous terms, against the poorer members of society. The Sixth and Seventh Wards, two of the poorest in the city, for example, gave the Republicans a win of more than 65 percent of their votes.[43]

In the aftermath of the New York election, Abigail Adams, in a surprisingly emotionless and resigned comment to a friend, reported that it "is generally supposed that N York would be the balance" in the upcoming presidential election of 1800. Republicans understandably greeted the news more enthusiastically, with one from Virginia proclaiming, "The Republic is safe. . . . The [Federalist] party are in rage & despair."[44]

Hamilton and other New York Federalists, however, were not as ready as Abigail Adams to concede defeat. For Hamilton's part, he proposed a daring and dangerous scheme, claiming that a civil war would be "preferable to having Jefferson for President." In a letter, Hamilton pleaded with Federalist governor John Jay to convene the Federalist lame duck legislature to change the mode of selecting electors to a district election system that would "insure a Majority of votes in the U States for Federal Candidates." He urged Jay not to "be overscrupulous . . . by a strict adherence to ordinary laws," for the Federalist defeat had raised the issue of "public safety." Drastic measures must be taken to deal with the desperate and perilous circumstances. "Scruples of delicacy and propriety," Hamilton urged, "ought not to hinder the taking of a *legal* or *constitutional* step, to prevent an *Atheist* in Religion and a *Fanatic* in politics from getting possession of the State."[45]

Jay wisely rejected Hamilton's radical suggestion. The Federalists had put into place the plan to allow the state legislature to choose the electors, and any change that would circumvent the authority of the newly elected Republican legislature would have had, most likely, severe political repercussions. It would have been regarded for what it was, a reckless Federalist effort to subvert the will of the electorate as expressed in the election.[46] And, if executed, Hamilton's plan surely would have moved the already tense country closer to some violent confrontation.

Earlier the same year, Senator James Ross, a Federalist from Pennsylvania, had made an equally daring proposal that would have virtually guaranteed a Federalist victory in the approaching presidential contest. What the failed 1799 Federalist candidate for governor of Pennsylvania had recommended was bypassing the constitutional provisions for counting the electoral votes by empowering Congress to set up a commission of thirteen members—six from the House of Representatives, six from the Senate, and the chief justice of the Supreme Court—and giving it absolute power to count the votes. Since the Federalists controlled both houses, the commission was, according to one historian, guaranteed to be virtually "an adjunct of the Federalist party." Examining each electoral vote, the commission was to have the power to decide whether the vote was legitimate or illegitimate, to tally the votes as they determined them, and to report who had been elected president. The proposed law also provided that the commission's findings would not be subject to appeal. A disagreement between the Federalist-controlled House of Representatives and the Federalist-controlled Senate, however, killed any chance for the measure to be enacted. The opposition of Virginia Federalist representative John Marshall was apparently a major factor in defeating the Ross Bill in the House.[47]

William Duane, who was Benjamin Franklin Bache's successor as Republican editor of the *Aurora* after Bache had fallen victim to the yellow fever, became legally entangled in the controversy over the Ross Bill for unlawfully obtaining a copy of it and printing and criticizing it before it had been made public. Since the proceedings of the Senate were secret and privileged, Duane was charged with "false, scandalous, and malicious assertions" that demeaned the reputation of the Senate.

The Federalists then made every exertion to try, convict, imprison, and perhaps even deport Duane, who, while born in the United States, had spent a number of years with his mother in Ireland and was thus subject to prosecution under both the Sedition and the Alien laws.

Duane and his paper, the *Aurora*, President Adams was told by Secretary of State Timothy Pickering, were responsible for "an uninterrupted stream of slander on the American government." Furthermore, Pickering described the editor as a treacherous alien who was particularly dangerous since he was a captain of a militia company who would "oppose the authority of the government; and in case of a war and invasion by the French" betray his country.

Adams needed no encouragement to go after Duane. Infuriated by the journalist's criticism of the government as well as by the mocking ridicule that had been directed against him personally, Adams sputtered, "Is there anything evil in the regions of actuality or possibility, that the Aurora has not suggested of me?" Pickering was warned that if any prosecutor did "not think this paper libelous," he was "not fit for his office." Duane, however, avoided almost certain incarceration by going into hiding until Congress adjourned. [48]

Thus, Hamilton's scheme to short-circuit the legally established mode of electing electors in New York, Senator Ross's dangerous and risky attempt to rig the electoral votes to assure a Federalist victory, and the Adams administration's efforts to punish a Republican editor all failed. Still, they stand as important indicators of just how desperate the Federalists were to retain power in 1800.

By the end of 1800 and the beginning of 1801, however, the Federalists would be faced with deciding just how far they were willing to go in preventing a Republican presidency.

7

ADAMS VERSUS HAMILTON
THE SPLIT BECOMES
UNBRIDGEABLE

Unity alone <u>can possibly save us from the fangs of Jefferson.</u>
—Alexander Hamilton, May 1800

I

The news of the Republicans' stunning victory in New York had an almost tsunami-like effect on the Federalists. It portended a catastrophe in the making. The first political good news for the Republicans since before the XYZ Affair, it forecast a better-than-even chance that Jefferson might win the fall's presidential election.

But the most immediate impact of the New York election on the Federalists was that it stoked long-simmering intra-party suspicions and hatreds. Earlier in the year, before the balloting in New York, Hamilton had meditated on the dilemma that he and the anti-Adams faction faced. Should they risk "a serious schism by an attempt to change" presidential candidates, Hamilton asked, or should they "annihilate themselves and hazard their cause by continuing to uphold those who suspect and hate them?" The first course, he warned, might have the most dangerous consequences, since divisions in the Federalist ranks might empower the factious Virginians—who were "more violent than ever." Indeed, the Virginians, he asserted, "possessed completely all the powers of the local government" and were "resolved to possess those of the nation, by the most dangerous combinations." Failing this, he predicted ominously, they would "resort to the employment of physical force" to seize national political power.[1]

Following in the wake of the New York elections were the congressional party caucuses to choose the nominees for president and vice president. Hamilton, although disappointed by Jay's refusal to overturn New York's legislative elections and change the state's presidential electoral selection system, did maneuver to get South Carolinian Charles Cotesworth Pinckney (1745–1825) on the ticket with the detested Adams.

Pinckney was a distinguished South Carolina Revolutionary War leader who had helped draft his state's 1776 constitution and had then vigorously advocated the adoption of the federal Constitution. As a member of the ill-fated diplomatic mission that resulted in the infamous XYZ Affair, he had become known for his alleged defiant response, "No, no, not a sixpence," to the French emissaries' demands for a bribe and a loan. It was a memorable, defiant, patriotic phrase that endeared him to his countrymen. Later he would run, unsuccessfully, as the Federalist candidate for president in 1804 and 1808.

Members of the caucus did follow Hamilton's recommendation of Pinckney, but, importantly, they did not distinguish between the South Carolinian and Adams in terms of who was to be the presidential candidate. This, of course, did not go unnoticed by Adams.

This failure to differentiate between the two candidates as to which office each was being nominated for made it possible, although unlikely, that Pinckney might be elected president over Adams. In 1796, Hamilton had attempted to promote Charles Coatesworth Pinckney's brother, Federalist vice presidental candidate Thomas Pinckney, as a replacement for Adams, but had failed. In 1800, however, given the surprising strength of the Federalists in the South in the elections of 1798 and 1799, and given Adams's unpopularity among many Federalists, the chances of a Hamilton-engineered scheme to bypass Adams being successful had substantially improved. Nonetheless, the country at large—both Republicans and Federalists—assumed that Adams was the presidential candidate of his party.

Theodore Sedgwick, Federalist speaker of the U.S. House of Representatives from 1799 to 1801 and one of Hamilton's close associates, lamented the Federalists' predicament. The decision to reopen negotiations with France, he asserted, had estranged Adams from his "best friends" and had split the Federalists between pro- and anti-Adams factions. However, the caucus decision to support Adams had to be followed, or "otherwise we cannot escape the fangs of Jefferson."

It is noteworthy how closely the words in Sedgwick's letter followed Hamilton's of a week earlier. The Federalists must remain united, Hamilton had written, for that alone "can possibly save us from the fangs of *Jefferson*." This is just one of many instances in which Hamilton's comments or instructions were relayed almost word for word by other prominent Federalist leaders and indicative of how much influence the New Yorker had over them.[2]

The Republicans had a much easier time choosing their presidential candidate in caucus. Jefferson's nomination, as had been assumed, was unanimous. Burr's renomination as the vice presidential candidate, however, was a different matter. Certainly Burr's reputation as a skilled politician had been immeasurably enhanced by the Republican victory in New York. However, questions remained about his reliability. Former New York governor George Clinton should be preferred, Madison was told by one of his correspondents, because "he would be more acceptable to New York and New Jersey than anyone else."[3]

Albert Gallatin (1761–1849), the Swiss-born Pennsylvania Republican leader in the House of Representatives who had become the Republican leader and spokesman in 1797 after Madison had left Congress, was entrusted by the Virginians to discreetly investigate the New York political situation through conversations with his father-in-law, New Yorker James Nicholson. Gallatin, however, could hardly be called an objective source. In 1793 he had been elected to the U.S. Senate by the Pennsylvania legislature only to see his membership immediately challenged by the Federalists, who had claimed that Gallatin was a foreigner and had caustically pointed out that "ancient Republics made it death for an alien to intermeddle in their policies." It was Burr as senator from New York at the time who had led a spirited defense of Gallatin, although the Pennsylvanian was eventually denied his senate seat by the Federalist-dominated Senate. Furthermore, Gallatin's father-in-law—the source of much of his information about New York politics—was a close personal friend of Burr's.[4]

Gallatin, who often discussed political questions with his wife in his letters, wrote her that the "serious question" was, "Who is to be our Vice President—Clinton or Burr?"[5] Nicholson, after interviewing both Clinton and Burr, answered that question by recommending Burr, whose "generalship, perseverance, industry, & execution [of the New York Assembly campaign] exceeds all description, so that I think I can say he deserves any thing and every thing of his country."[6] Furthermore, Clinton was seen as a reluctant candidate, having told Nicholson that he would resign after the election.

Burr, still stinging from the lack of electoral support in the South in 1796, had complained to Nicholson that he had been "ill-used by Virginia and North Carolina." But "if assurances can be given that the Southern States will act fairly," he would accept the vice presidential nomination.

After Gallatin relayed this intelligence back to the Republican congressional caucus, Burr was unanimously nominated as the vice presidential candidate. But, unlike the Federalists, the Republicans clearly designated which of the two men was their *presidential* candidate—Jefferson.[7]

Gallatin's key role in these crucial negotiations reflected the confidence that the Virginia leadership placed in him. Earlier a member of the Pennsylvania constitutional convention and state legislature, the resident of western Pennsylvania had played a critical role in attempting to moderate western violence against the whiskey tax. Elected to the House of Representatives in 1795, he was the congressman primarily responsible for the creation of the Ways and Means Committee, Congress's first standing committee.

But in addition to his strengths as a legislator and negotiator, Gallatin had mastered public finance and thus was able to perform an extensive analysis of the Federalist financial program. His conclusion, unlike Hamilton's, was that the public debt was not a blessing, but a curse. Later, he would serve in the Jefferson and Madison administrations as secretary of the treasury.

The spring political fireworks surrounding the New York election and Federalist caucus were not over, however. Acting swiftly on the heels of the congressional caucuses, Adams fired two disloyal members of his cabinet. This seemed to many in the anti-Adams, pro-Hamilton Federalist camp to be the last straw. It simply confirmed in their minds that the president was untrustworthy, treacherous, and deceitful. It even raised questions about his sanity.

The firings were actions that Adams should have taken earlier. Both men owed their allegiance to Hamilton and had been open conduits of confidential cabinet information back to the New Yorker, information that was often used against Adams. Finally, however, angered by the slight during the Federalist caucus and deeply pessimistic over his chances for reelection after the New York election, Adams did take out his fury and frustration on the unfaithful pair, Timothy Pickering, secretary of state, and James McHenry, secretary of war.

McHenry was given a monumental tongue-lashing by the president, who charged that the secretary of war was not only disloyal but also incompetent. But it was Hamilton, whom Adams held responsible for the defeat in New York, who was the object of much of Adams's wrath and vitriol. The New Yorker, Adams raged, was the "greatest intrigant in the World . . . a man devoid of every moral principle—a Bastard, and as much a foreigner as Gallatin." Jefferson was an "infinitely better" and "wiser" man, and, if he should become president, Adams "would rather be Vice President under him, or even Minister Resident at the Hague, than indebted to such a being as Hamilton for the Presidency."[8] Shocked and bewildered, McHenry went

Albert Gallatin. A Pennsylvanian, he led the Republicans in the House of Representatives as they discussed various strategies to ensure Thomas Jefferson's election in 1801. Albert Gallatin by James Sharples (the Elder), ca. 1796. Gift of Miss Josephine L. Stevens, 1908. 08.144. Image copyright © The Metropolitan Museum of Art / Art Resource, NY.

away believing that Adams was "actually insane," for this could be the only explanation for such extraordinary behavior.[9]

Given an opportunity to resign, the arrogant and spiteful Pickering defiantly refused—so Adams summarily dismissed him as well. Abigail Adams surely was too kind to the surly and churlish Pickering when she described him as a man "whose manners are forbidding, whose temper is sour and whose resentments are implacable."[10]

The split between Adams and his Federalist critics became an unbridgeable chasm later the same month when Adams suddenly announced his decision to pardon Fries, the Pennsylvania rebellion leader, and his two colleagues, all of whom had earlier been sentenced to death for their roles in the insurrection. Against the advice of his cabinet and advisers, Adams issued his pardon fewer than forty-eight hours before the scheduled executions. Even more than the dismissals of Pickering and McHenry, the pardons convinced a number of Federalists that Adams was no longer a viable candidate and could not be supported for the presidency.[11]

The sacked Pickering, always willing to believe the worst about Adams, was further convinced that the president's behavior proved evidence of a conspiracy. By firing his cabinet *and* pardoning the Fries conspirators, Pickering charged, Adams was attempting to gain favor with the Republicans and win the vice presidency under Jefferson. After the pardons, the former secretary of state avowed, "I can believe Mr. Adams capable of anything to promote his personal views." It is this *"new system of politics"* that *"*can alone account for the astonishing act . . . of *grace* to the Jacobins."[12]

Adams's irrational behavior, Pickering declared, was endangering the "cause of federalism (which we consider to be the cause of our country)" to the extent that the Federalists would "be as little or as less in jeopardy under Mr. Jefferson than under Mr. Adams." And since Adams had forfeited his position of trust and responsibility within Federalism, it was essential, Pickering maintained, that "we . . . all strive to place General Pinckney in the chair."[13] This belief was widely shared by other Adams-haters in the Hamilton wing of the Federalist party, who had become convinced that Adams's reelection would be as ruinous to the Federalists as a Jefferson victory.

Pickering's claim that Adams and Jefferson were conspiring to run together on a kind of unity ticket was reported elsewhere at that time, but there is no evidence to substantiate such an assertion. And, although it cannot be said for certain, Pickering's rumor may well have had its origin in McHenry's account of his firing and Adams's claim that he would rather be vice president under Jefferson than obligated to Hamilton for his election.

Nevertheless, a Federalist paper in Trenton, New Jersey, did publicly contend in early June that the two erstwhile opponents had colluded together "to produce a *common interest*, which shall place them again in the seats of magistery, and produce a neutralization of the two great contending parties."[14] But even Hamilton—who considered Adams "more mad than I ever thought him and I shall soon be led to say as wicked as he is mad"—dismissed the rumors.[15] The rumors were vigorously denied by the Republican press as well.

But perhaps more was made of the matter than should have been because a number of Americans in 1800 hoped for the emergence of a nonpartisan national politics. This was, of course, a goal that had been briefly entertained in 1797 after Adams and Jefferson had been elected president and vice president. It was an unrealized aspiration in 1797, as it was to be in 1800, but there was strong public sentiment supporting the idea of a national unity government that would bring an end to what was perceived as a corrosive and destructive partisanship threatening the very existence of the republic.

II

In the midst of the political turmoil and unrest surrounding the presidential election in 1800, the capital was in the process of being moved from Philadelphia to Washington, and that also elevated the nation's tension level. It required a tremendous leap of faith. Philadelphia, the second largest city in the country, was viewed as a sophisticated and cosmopolitan urban center.[16] Despite the grand dreams of its planners, Washington was not much more than a collection of shacks in a swamplike setting that was a breeding ground for mosquitoes. The contrast with Philadelphia could not have been greater. Nearby Georgetown and Alexandria were the closest settlements, and they were only villages.

President Adams had signed an order in May 1800 to begin the government's move to the outpost on the Potomac River, a relocation that would take nearly a year in all. The plan called for the infrastructure of the government (clerks, messengers, subcabinet functionaries, employees of the Congress) to move in the summer, with the president, vice president, and members of Congress to follow in November.

Just the first stage of the move proved to be an immense undertaking. Office furniture, equipment, books, and files had to be shipped, and nearly 500 people, including women and children, had to be moved. Making matters more difficult, much of the projected construction was unfinished. There were neither churches nor schools. Only one of the public buildings and a few private homes had been completed.[17] As a result most members of the government were obliged to live in the seven or eight boarding houses, and the only services or amenities available to them were those provided by "a tailor shop, a shoemaker, a printer, a washerwoman, a grocer, a stationer, a dry-goods establishment and an oyster house."[18]

In short, Washington in 1800 was seen by many as a place barely fit for human habitation. It was an unhealthy location in an unbearable climate, with "large naked ugly buildings" and fences that were "unfit for a decent barnyard." The food, some complained, was often "hog and hominy grits," and largely inedible.[19]

Unlike other members of the government, Adams did have his own residence, although Abigail found the executive mansion far from comfortable, or even suitable. Its shabbiness made its occupants "an object of ridicule with some and of pity with others," she groused. Only six of the thirty rooms were plastered, she reported, and "not a single apartment finished." The main staircase to the second floor was not completed, and the "great unfinished audience room" for affairs of state was converted by Abigail into a room to hang wet laundry.

Nor did conditions much improve for a long time. The ceiling of the audience room fell down at one point. And the great room, ostensibly for state entertaining, was not ready for use until the administration of John Quincy Adams, and even then it was not completely plastered. It would be eight years before a staircase to the second floor would be built.[20] Even so, the president's home, known as "The Palace" in the early years, was the only place for amusement. Otherwise, the denizens of Washington "lived like bears."[21]

One Philadelphia editor probably expressed the dismay and dejection of a number of his fellow burghers, who undoubtedly felt like abandoned lovers. Washington "is in reality neither town nor village," he wrote spitefully. Rather, "it may be compared to a country seat where state sportsmen may run horses and fight cocks; kill time." Nonetheless, there "sits the President . . . like a pelican in the wilderness, or a sparrow upon the housetop."[22]

A few government workers decided to quit their jobs and stay in Philadelphia rather than move to "the half-finished village on the banks of the Potomac." One disenchanted new Washington resident wrote a friend back in Philadelphia urging him to stay there. If he did decide to relocate, he was advised not to bring his family. Supplies were in short supply and expensive, he said, with "the people who tended the markets . . . [being] the neediest and poorest under heaven."[23]

The sight of the new capital had to be disheartening. Stumps of fallen trees and piles of cleared brush, as well as poorly marked, barely passable roads and half-finished buildings, dominated the landscape. Tropical humid heat and mosquitoes added to the misery and discomfort that Washington residents had to endure in the summer. After heavy rains the roads would become impassable, with the result that many carriages had to be pulled from the mire. One cabinet member wrote that, returning from an evening visit, it "was a mercy that we all got home with whole bones." Our "carriage . . . was overset, the harness broken . . . and at the Treasury Office corner we were obligated to get out of the carriage in the mud." At that point, "I called out the guard of the Treasury Office and borrowed a lantern." Even in better weather it took three hours of travel to make the round trip from Capitol Hill to Georgetown, he said, describing the area between Capitol Hill and the site of the President's House[24] as "wet and marshy ground covered with weeds . . . where sportsmen [hunted] . . . where cattle formed paths in zigzag courses . . . and where fishermen often took their spoil, especially at full tide." [25]

Even seven years after the move to the capital, a congressman fell from his horse halfway between the executive mansion and Capitol Hill and had a frightening experience. He described himself as "a man almost bruised to death, on a dark, cold night, in the heart of the capital of the United States, out of sight or hearing of human habitation."[26]

Such was the disdain for Washington by most of its official residents in 1800 and for years to come that there was a serious question about whether the city should be rebuilt after the British burned and destroyed it during the War of 1812. A vote to abandon and not rebuild came within nine votes of passing in the House of Representatives. The question was debated in the Senate for more than three months. And it was only after local bankers offered a loan to rebuild the city that it was decided that the government should remain there.[27]

Washington, then, on the eve of the electoral crisis of 1800–1801, was a raw, remote, isolated, parochial Southern backwater, a "Federal City" that Gallatin wrote his wife was "hated by every member of Congress without exception of persons or parties."[28] And this remoteness, with the consequent difficulty in communicating between the capital and other parts of the country, exacerbated the growing political anxieties. The scarcity of housing and lack of other amenities meant that politicians found themselves in a kind of unrelieved pressure-cooker atmosphere in which politics was the be-all and end-all of their lives without the diversions that might be found in a larger, more mature city. This led one public man to complain that he was "brutalized and stupefied ... from hearing nothing but politics from morning to night and from continual confinement."[29] As a result, every rumor, no matter how fanciful, seems to have been exaggerated, magnified, distorted—and then often accepted as fact.

III

Immediately following the Federalist electoral disaster in New York and at the time of the caucuses to choose candidates for the presidency and vice presidency, Hamilton had argued that the Federalists had to remain united to escape the "fangs of Jefferson."[30] In the aftermath of Adams's firing of Pickering and McHenry, however, he had a change of heart.

In a letter to Pickering, Hamilton asserted that "*most* of the *influential men* of ... [the Federalist party] consider ... [Adams] as a very *unfit* and *incapable* character." Furthermore, Pickering was told, Hamilton had made up his mind that he would "never more be responsible for [Adams] by my direct support, even though the consequence should be the election of *Jefferson.*" "If we must have an *enemy* at the head of the government," Hamilton insisted, "let it be one whom we can oppose, and for whom we are not responsible, who will not involve our party in the disgrace of his foolish and bad measures." Both Adams and Jefferson "will sink" the government, and whoever controls the presidency shall "sink with it, and the advantage will all be on the side of his adversaries." Thus, it was necessary for the Federalists to rally around their principles and disavow their support for "a weak and perverse man." The only hope for the Federalists, he concluded, was for them to support Charles Cotesworth Pinckney for president instead.[31]

Hamilton most likely realized that it would be a long shot to get Pinckney elected. But desperate situations called for desperate measures. And he did have a strategy. First, he would work to ensure that Adams and Pinckney both received the full complement of electoral votes in the Federalist stronghold of New England. Four years earlier, eighteen New England Adams electors had refused to support the Federalist vice presidential candidate, Charles Cotesworth Pinckney's brother, Thomas. If New England could be counted on to share its votes equally between Adams and Pinckney, then southern Federalists, especially in South Carolina, where the legislature chose the electors, would hold the election in their hands. And assuming that the South Carolina electors would cast their two votes for Jefferson and Pinckney, it was likely Pinckney, a native South Carolinian, would emerge the winner. But if South Carolina cast its votes equally for Pinckney and Adams, the election would likely end in a tie in the Electoral College and then go to the House of Representatives for resolution. And if the election were thrown into the Federalist-dominated House of Representatives, Hamilton reasoned, a discredited Adams would lose to Pinckney.[32]

In his first step to implement his plan, Hamilton made a trip to New England in June. Ostensibly, his travel had to do with a military inspection visit, but in reality it was to campaign against Adams and to attempt to win votes for Pinckney. Hamilton was not altogether pleased with what he found, however. Although "the greater number of strong-minded men" supported Pinckney over Adams, he said, "in the body of . . . people there is a strong personal attachment to that gentleman [Adams], and most of the leaders of the second class are so anxious for his election that it will be difficult to convince them otherwise." One New England Federalist who heard Hamilton speak was unimpressed. "Electioneering topics were his principal theme," he reported, but in "his mode of handling them, he did not appear to be the great general which his talents designate him." Thus, unconvinced by Hamilton, the Federalist declared that he was "decidedly for the re-election of Mr. Adams."[33]

The shrewd Abigail Adams saw through Hamilton's deception. The New Yorker, she charged, was endeavoring to unseat her husband at the top of the Federalist ticket and replace him with Pinckney because he knew "that he cannot Sway" the president "or carry such measures as he wishes." She feared that Hamilton was conniving "to make a stalking Horse of the President" in an effort to "bring in a military man" to the presidency. Pinckney, she concluded, "may or may not be a good Man," but she would prefer a "vote for mr. [sic] Jefferson."[34]

Adams's youngest son, Thomas Boylston Adams, reported similar news. The Federalists "have split," he wrote. "Some are resolved to abandon the present leader while some abide by him and resolve to see it out with the Anti's [Republicans]." The plan of those who wanted to abandon Adams, he explained, was to run "Gen'l Pinckney . . . as V.P. in several of the Eastern States and as President in the Southern, which according to some calculations will put him into the chair."[35]

A number of prominent Federalists endorsed Hamilton's plan. The "object is to keep an *anti* out, and get a federal President in," Fisher Ames wrote, "and . . . the only way to do it, is by voting for General Pinckney, at the risk . . . of excluding Mr. A."[36] George Cabot was even more positive, claiming that Pinckney would unite "*the true men* . . . under the banner of the Constitution."[37]

The major sin of the president, according to the Federalists close to Hamilton, was that his egotistical and capricious behavior was destined to destroy the Federalist system that was a delicate balance of harmony between men, principles, and institutions as established under Washington. In 1800, Ames maintained, there were actually three parties. One, the Republicans or Jacobins, "abhor[ed] restraint," while the second, the anti-Adams Federalists, "from principle, habit, or property," embraced restraint. Adams and his followers made up the third party, "whose caprices and weaknesses have been . . . often blindly used to weaken our party to animate the other."[38]

Oliver Wolcott responded to Ames in a long and thoughtful letter analyzing the political situation in the country from his perspective as an opponent of Adams and Jefferson. Like Ames and Hamilton, Wolcott was dismayed by Adams's "revolutionary, violent, and vindictive" temper of mind, his "passions and selfishness," and his "pride and interest." And, like the other two, he feared that a second term for Adams would fundamentally compromise the underlying principles of the Federalist hegemony. Adams had been "elected by a joint effort of the federal party, under an expectation that he would maintain their system," Wolcott asserted, but Adams had betrayed the trust and "subverted the power and influence of the federalists," thus demonstrating "himself unfit to be their head." "Incapable of adhering to any political system," Adams could not be counted upon to protect the "characters of individuals and the interests of the federal party," he lamented.[39]

Jefferson fared no better in Wolcott's analysis, for he, like Adams, would "refuse to consult and pursue the advice of able and virtuous men." By "able and virtuous men," Wolcott obviously meant the Federalist anti-Adams elites who he believed governed from an independent perspective, above partisanship and personal interest. Administrations led by either Adams or Jefferson would be too weak to control violent factions, and these would subvert "the government by rendering it contemptible in the eyes of both parties."

And while he saw it as likely that Jefferson would be elected, Wolcott urged that the Federalists retain their principles, assuring that "in a short time" they would regain their influence. This was essential, he concluded, for if "we resort to temporary expedients, and permit the opinion to prevail that the two parties are equally influenced by personal and sinister motives, and that neither are in fact directed by system and principles, we may soon bid adieu to the constitution, and to the hope of maintaining internal peace or free government in our country."[40] In other words, he saw the elite-dominated politics of deference being threatened by increasingly raucous, increasingly democratic contests for leadership, and he did not approve.

Wolcott's general argument would have been accepted by most public men of the era. When they discussed the "party" of their opponents, they generally meant a fractious body of self-interested and highly partisan men who ignored the "public good" and promoted sectional or other highly divisive interests. In contrast, they saw their own "party" as nonpartisan and personifying the general will and common good of all society. Thus, to the Federalists a Jefferson victory would be an aberration, but most likely a temporary one, because only the principles embodied by the Federalists guaranteed the future security and prosperity of the nation.

John Adams made an argument similar to that of his Federalist critics, but came to a different conclusion. He and his supporters, he believed, embraced a nonpartisanship that was "founded in principle and system," while his opponents (Hamilton and friends) were driven by "private interests and passions." An "honest party will never exclude talents, and virtues, and qualities eminently useful to the public, merely on account of a difference in opinion," he argued, while a "factious man will exclude every man alike, saint or sinner, who will not be a blind, passive tool." Thus, Hamilton and his supporters were driven, Adams believed, by a passionate, unthinking, selfish, obsessive, and destructive factionalism, while he and his supporters constituted a Bolingbroke-like party of patriots dedicated to the public good.[41]

To a political culture dedicated to an anti-party nonpartisanship, the election of 1800 must have seemed an aberration. Vicious personal attacks, portents of doom and disaster if one or another of the opponents were to be elected, and scurrilous rumors of betrayal and intrigue pervaded every aspect of the contest.

Yet the combatants sincerely regarded themselves as above partisanship. And ironically, it was this belief that became the catalyst for the polarization. For if members of one party deeply and sincerely believed that they, and they alone, represented the public good and were the true guardians of the principles of the American Revolution and protectors of the Constitution and the Union, they could not tolerate any opposition to their custodianship. It would threaten the very existence of the republic.

IV

Active presidential campaigning by the candidates was not to become part of American politics until late in the nineteenth or early in the twentieth century. Although the 1858 contest between Abraham Lincoln and Stephen

Douglas, during which the candidates traveled around Illinois debating one another, has often been mentioned as representing a more modern style of campaign, that was for a U.S. Senate seat, not for the presidency. Democrat William Jennings Bryan, who ran for the presidency against Republican William McKinley in 1896, did travel to twenty-seven states and make 600 speeches, but it was a losing effort, as his opponent, who waged a "front porch" campaign sitting at home and entertaining thousands of supporters, defeated him. It was not until the 1912 presidential contest involving Republican William Howard Taft, Democrat Woodrow Wilson, and Bull Moose nominee Teddy Roosevelt that candidates actively waged campaigns.[42]

Thus, in 1800 Adams and Jefferson for the most part maintained a high-minded public indifference and detachment to the presidential campaign.

Adams, however, in his trip to inspect the Washington construction in late May and June 1800, did take the opportunity to make a number of speeches defending his administration. In Lancaster, Pennsylvania, for instance, he was warmly received by public officials before going on to Fredericksburg, Maryland. And the citizens of Alexandria, Virginia, welcomed him as a guest of honor as part of their celebration of the establishment of the new capital across the Potomac. There, the president reflected on the prosperity of the upper South and how the heroes of the Revolution who had risked lives and fortunes to fight for independence must be well satisfied with the present prosperity and contentment of the country. On his return north, Adams visited Annapolis and Baltimore as well as a number of smaller towns, celebrating the country's independence as the great achievement of the Revolutionary generation of leaders. In Baltimore, he urged the citizens to vote for candidates with "integrity of heart."[43]

The Federalist *Gazette of the United States* boasted that the "very affectionate reception and respectable addresses which have everywhere met our venerable and vigilant President has [sic] greatly increased the malignity of the Jacobins." However, the Republican *Aurora* gleefully pointed out that Adams was ignored in Newark by discontented Federalists.[44]

Once back in Massachusetts, Adams sought to blunt Hamilton's efforts to derail his candidacy, sarcastically observing in a private overheard aside that, if the New Yorker had been given his way, "it would have taken a second army to disband the first one."[45] Then, upon returning to his home in Quincy, Adams mainly concerned himself with the ongoing negotiations with France until he traveled to Washington to establish his new home there in October.

One historian has concluded that in taking to the "stump in defense of his record," Adams became "the first presidential candidate in history to carry his appeal directly to the people."[46] While this is probably true, it did not establish a precedent.

Jefferson played virtually no publicly visible role in the campaign. Nonetheless, he corresponded with the Republican press from time to time and occasionally urged Madison and others to take up their pens and do battle with the Federalists on one topic or another. He also wrote letters to influential political figures in key states to enlist support. Recognizing, for example, that the Republicans needed votes from states outside of the South and West, Jefferson made an effort to weaken the hold the Federalists had in New England by writing a series of letters to public men from that section whom he saw as sympathetic. These included Gerry, the Massachusetts Federalist who would shortly become a Republican, and two Republicans— Gideon Granger, from Connecticut, and Sam Adams, the old Massachusetts Revolutionary patriot.

In these letters Jefferson expressed his hope that the Federalist-induced "delusion" in New England was fading and laid out principles that he professed would govern his and other Republicans' actions should he be elected.

Echoing George Washington's Farewell Address, Jefferson declared that in order to avoid foreign entanglements he was "for free commerce with all nations; political connections with none." In addition, reacting to Hamilton's efforts to build a large army, he stated that the militia should be the primary defensive force and that the navy's main task should be to protect the nation's harbors and coast. And, defending himself against charges that he would compromise the security of the United States by naïvely supporting the French, Jefferson explained that while he supported France's aspirations to establish a stable, free, and orderly republic, he was not insensitive to "the atrocious depredations . . . [the French] have committed on our commerce." The "first object of my heart is my own country," he assured his correspondents.

To counterbalance the Federalists' governing philosophy, Jefferson contended that the state governments had to continue to play a major role, for the United States was "too large to have all its affairs directed by a single government." And he and the Republicans, he promised, would work to restore the essential constitutional balance between the federal government and the states. Professing himself against enlarging the federal government or increasing the debt, he also, in one of his most oft-quoted phrases, proclaimed, "I am for a government rigorously frugal and simple."

In addition, Jefferson told the New Englanders that he and the Republicans would strive to protect certain essential freedoms guaranteed by the Bill of Rights, such as those of religion and the press, and the right to trial by jury. Condemning the Federalist-backed Sedition Law, Jefferson declared that freedom of speech to criticize the government was essential and denounced "all violations of the constitution to silence by force and not by reason the complaints or criticisms, just or unjust, of our citizens against the conduct of their agents."

If New England persisted in opposing "freedom of religion, freedom of the press, trial by jury and . . . economical government," Jefferson added pointedly, the future of the country would be jeopardized. The federal government, the Virginian argued, would "never be harmonious and solid, while so respectable a portion of its citizens support principles which go directly to a change of the federal constitution, to sink the state governments, consolidate them into one, and to monarchize that."[47]

v

Both Jefferson and Adams were attacked mercilessly in the newspapers during the summer and fall of 1800. Jefferson, it was charged, was a Jacobin, a Francophile, and a libertine unfit and unreliable to defend his country against France. A civil war would surely follow if he were to be elected. He was, some went so far as alleging, an immoral and godless man who would order the confiscation of Bibles. Even George Washington's widow, Martha, seemed to be caught up in the frenzy of the campaign when she told a visiting clergyman that Jefferson was "one of the most detestable of mankind."[48]

Many of the charges published against Jefferson had been made before. The accusation that he was an atheist was often used in New England in print as well as from the pulpit. One Connecticut Federalist asked: "Do you believe in the strangest of all paradoxes—that a spendthrift, a libertine, or an atheist is qualified to make your laws and govern you and your posterity?"[49] The Virginian's wartime record as governor was also attacked as one of "pusillanimity" and "uninspiring patriotism," with readers being reminded of Jefferson's ignominious retreat ahead of the British forces.[50]

But perhaps the most serious of the allegations was that Jefferson was a radical Jacobin who put the interests of revolutionary France ahead of the interests of his own country. Jefferson and the Republicans, it was claimed, were "artful and ambitious demagogues" who led "discontented hotheads," "democratic blockhead[s]," and "cold-hearted Jacobin[s]." Republican rule, it was predicted, would result in the same kind of social chaos and bloodshed that characterized the French Revolution. Furthermore, it would lead to war with England and the ruin of American commerce.[51]

Federalists also used the argument that any political change would be dangerous and disruptive. A Delaware Federalist, for example, wrote that the twelfth year of government under the Constitution and the Federalists had been "as free and republican as it was the first year." But "if the Jeffersonians wish more republicanism," he warned, "what must it result in? Not in the freedom of equal laws, which is true republicanism, but in the licentiousness of anarchy."[52]

Adams suffered similar abuse with charges that he was incompetent, "quite mad," and a monarchist and warmonger. The Alien and Sedition Acts, voters were reminded, were stark examples of Adams's treachery and his willingness to violate American civil liberties. One Republican editor challenged his readers: "If you have not virtue enough to stem the current, determine to be slaves at once."[53]

Adams's running mate Charles Cotesworth Pinckney was attacked as a man of "limited talents" with a "temper illy suited to the exalted station" of chief executive. Not only was Pinckney thought to be too sympathetic to England, probably due to his early schooling there, he was seen as a toady of Hamilton's. Like Abigail Adams, many also feared that he would become a stalking horse permitting "Caesar [meaning Hamilton] to govern."[54]

Hamilton himself was not spared by the Republicans. His support for "the establishment of a permanent executive" and a stronger national government at the expense of the states at the Constitutional Convention was condemned. One Republican editor told his readers that if Hamilton's proposals had been accepted, Americans would be bowing before "the throne of a powerful and almost absolute monarch."[55]

Perhaps the most outrageously partisan and bitterly vituperative writer was James Thomson Callender (1758–1803), who, born in Scotland, came to the United States in the 1790s and quickly made a name for himself as a scurrilous essayist. Fleeing Philadelphia for Virginia in 1798, apparently to escape prosecution under the Sedition Law, Callender developed an uneasy relationship with the Virginia Republican elite. While a writer for the *Richmond Enquirer*, the master of defamatory and vindictive prose made a series of attacks on the Adams administration, assailing the president himself as a "repulsive pedant," a "gross hypocrite," and a "hideous hermaphroditical character which has neither the force and firmness of a man, nor the gentleness and sensibility of a woman." How was it, Callender asked, that the United States had degraded itself by choosing as president "a wretch whose soul came blasted from the hand of nature, of a wretch that has neither the science of a magistrate, the politeness of a courtier, nor the courage of a man?"

Virginia, however, did not turn out to be the safe haven Callender had expected. In the spring of 1800 he was charged, convicted, and sentenced to nine months in jail for his criticism of Adams.[56] Later, angered by the lack of support coming to him from the Republicans, Callender turned his vitriol on Jefferson with accusations about the Virginian's fathering of a child with his slave, Sally Hemings.[57]

Although hardly in the same league with Callender as a master of outrageously caustic writing, William Duane was nonetheless more influential as a critic of the Adams administration and a journalist substantially more important in the development of a Republican opposition press. As editor of the *Aurora*, the intrepid Duane published a number of stories in the summer of 1800 exposing suspected Federalist malfeasance in office. In these articles a close ally of Hamilton's, Federalist Speaker of the House of Representatives Jonathan Dayton, was charged with using his official position to profit from land speculation. And Dayton and several other leading Federalists, including Pickering and Secretary of Treasury Oliver Wolcott, were accused of mishandling public funds that had been entrusted to their keeping. Wolcott, it was alleged in a piece that ran under the headline "PUBLIC PLUNDER," had failed to supervise funds that had been allocated to various public officials for public use. Instead, according to Duane, these public monies had been appropriated by these officials for their own private use and speculation.

These men "in their princely estates," Duane charged, had corrupted and "mistaken the true meaning of *oaths* . . . *public obligations* . . . the *intent of laws*" and "the nature of republican government." Therefore, how can "honest men, real Americans, devoted to liberty, virtue, and national independence," place any confidence in them, "their adherents, or supporters"?[58]

In October 1800, the *Aurora* published a graphic comparison of the supposed differences between the Federalists and Republicans. The Republicans, it was claimed, wanted to restore the "Principles of the *Revolution*," to allay "the fever of domestic feuds . . . by the force of reason and rectitude," to decrease public debt and reduce taxes, to refrain from meddling in European affairs, and to promote liberty of the press and "free enquiry into public character and our constitution charter." The Federalists, on the other hand, it was charged, had encouraged the "reign of terror created by false alarms," promoted a war fever, and increased the public debt and taxes.[59]

One writer for the Federalist *Connecticut Courant* saw in Duane's *Aurora* the hub of a Jacobin network of conspiracy, pointing out that stories that appeared in the paper were reprinted by other Republican newspapers throughout the country. "Whatever appeared" in the *Aurora*, it was claimed by the *Courant*, "was faithfully copied . . . and in this way the main sentiments" were circulated around the country to newspapers that faithfully followed the lead of the *Aurora*, and created "a perfect union of opinion . . . on every important subject."[60]

While the charge of conspiracy was partisan exaggeration, the Federalist critic did accurately portray the political importance of Duane and the *Aurora*, and the development of an informal network of Republican newspapers. And although it is impossible to gauge exactly how effective the shrill and vituperative partisan press was in attracting or repelling voters, this growth of opposition newspapers, often savagely critiquing the Federalists, did represent an important phase in the creation of a more democratic politics.[61]

Another indication of a more democratic politics in 1800 was the indictment of the older deferential, elitist politics in Connecticut by Republican Abraham Bishop, the clerk of the state's Superior Court. Proudly styled "the land of steady habits" by the Federalists, Connecticut had changed little since the American Revolution, he scornfully argued. It had continued to be controlled, he said, by a political and hereditary elite supported by the established church.

A statement made by a Connecticut Federalist congressman at the time corroborated Bishop's observation, although not his conclusions. "In this state," the congressman declared, "no instance has ever been known where a person has appeared as a public candidate, and solicited the suffrages of the freeman, for place in the legislature." "Should any person have the effrontery or folly to make such an attempt," he insisted, that candidate would be met with "the general contempt and indignation of the people."[62]

For Bishop, these traditional political practices were destructive and posed a major problem in the election of 1800, since the people of Connecticut had transferred their habit of blindly supporting their elite leaders for state offices to the national sphere as well. Furthermore, foreign policy crises that stirred emotional and unthinking patriotism, he argued, were cleverly being used tactically by the "great, wise, and rich men" who "well understand the art of inflaming the public mind" to gain public support.

The Federalists' use of patriotic symbols and rhetoric associated with the nation's independence, and their identification of themselves as defenders and keepers of the faith, were also denounced by Bishop, who instead saw the opponents to the Republicans as "well-fed, well-dressed, chariot-rolling, caucus-keeping, levee-revelling federalists." Striking back, the Federalists accused Bishop of the "base art of electioneering," which they said destroyed "the purity of elections."[63]

Bishop's critique of the Federalists and their criticism of him, then, clearly represented a widening political fault line. The older, deferential politics embraced by most public men of the "better sort" throughout the decade of the 1790s was being challenged. Just beginning to emerge was a more democratic politics that would dominate the political life of the nation in the decades after 1800.[64]

8

TIE VOTE
THE ELECTORAL COLLEGE IN 1800

Adams has "great and intrinsic defects in his character, which
unfit him for the office of chief magistrate."
—Alexander Hamilton, October 1800

I

The already high political tensions in the summer of 1800
were further aggravated in late August by an event seemingly
unrelated to, but nonetheless having a major impact on, the
presidential election. That month an attempted slave insurrection in Virginia created a climate of terror, not only in Virginia but throughout the slave South. It served as a powerful
and horrifying reminder of just how vulnerable Southern
whites were to their large slave populations. Furthermore,
this threat of a slave conspiracy revealed how politically exposed the Southern Republicans were to condemnations by
the Federalists, who saw the insurrection as the direct, but
unintended, result of bondsmen being incited by the Republicans' lofty rhetoric about liberty and natural rights and their
embracement of French revolutionary ideas.

The insurrection had been planned and organized over
a period of several months by a slave named Gabriel, who
lived near Richmond. A skilled blacksmith, who could read
and write and whose master hired him out to work for others, Gabriel enjoyed a certain amount of status and standing
as well as freedom of movement in the community.

The scheme was for the conspirators to arm themselves
with homemade weapons, march to the state's arsenal in
Richmond and capture arms there, and then massacre
whites and incite a general revolt. The hope was that the

uprising would attract not only the support of slaves, but also that of lower-class whites.

On the night of the intended revolt, however, a heavy rainstorm made travel in and out of Richmond virtually impossible, thus foiling the plans of the insurrectionists. In addition, authorities had been alerted to the uprising by two slave informants. Ultimately, Gabriel and twenty-six of his followers were executed. Others involved in the planned insurrection escaped the noose but were sentenced to "transportation" to the Deep South, where they faced even harsher working conditions.[1]

But the failure of the plot did not put an end to its effects. The South's white population lived in constant fear of slave insurrections, and the news of the violent plan further exacerbated those fears. Fresh in the memories of Southerners were the graphic and vivid reports given by the white refugees from the sugar island of Saint-Domingue in the Caribbean. They told of the terrible slaughter that had accompanied the slave rebellion in that French colony.

Jefferson himself was rarely free from a pervasive unease and apprehension that the South was teetering on the brink of a racial bloodbath. In 1793, after the Saint-Domingue rebels, under the leadership of Toussaint-Louverture, had gained control of the island colony, Jefferson had postulated "that all the West India Islands . . . [would] remain in the hands of the people of colour, & a total expulsion of the whites sooner or later . . . [would] take place." Furthermore, Jefferson had not been sanguine that the violence and revolution could be contained there. It would only be a matter of time before such racial and class conflict would afflict the southern United States, he stressed. "It is high time," he warned, "we should foresee the bloody scenes which our children certainly and possibly ourselves" south of the Potomac River will "have to wade through, & try to avert them."[2] Later, Jefferson pessimistically cautioned that "if something is not done, and soon done, . . . we shall be the murderers of our own children. . . ." The "revolutionary storm," he warned, "now sweeping the globe, will be upon us."[3]

The exposure of Gabriel's plan presented the Federalists with an opportunity to make political capital by attributing the conspiracy to the Republicans' emphasis on liberty and natural rights and convincing Southerners that they would be more secure under a Federalist administration that stressed discipline of the senses and social order. And the Federalists moved to take advantage of the opening.

The insurrection, the Federalist *Gazette of the United States* declared, "*appears to be organized on the true French plan.*" And this alone should persuade

Southerners to support General Pinckney, whose "military skill and approved bravery . . . must be particularly valuable to his countrymen at this moment."[4] A Virginia Federalist was even more outspoken in his criticism of the Republicans, charging that "this dreadful conspiracy originates with some vile French Jacobins, aided and abetted by some of our own profligate and abandoned democrats," whose doctrines of "liberty and equality have brought the evil upon us . . . [which] cannot fail of producing either a general insurrection, or a general emancipation."[5] The Virginians were now experiencing "the happy effects of liberty and equality," a friend of Hamilton's derisively wrote.[6]

This public sentiment was also voiced privately by the Federalists. In a letter to the president's son, John Quincy Adams, William Vans Murray, the U.S. minister to the Hague and a member of the delegation appointed by Adams to go to France in 1799, observed that there were "motives sufficiently obvious, independent of Jacobinism, to account for an insurrection of the slaves; but I doubt not that the eternal clamor about liberty in Virginia and South Carolina both, has matured the event which has happened."

But the younger Adams was advised that the events in Virginia did have a positive side. Referring to the Virginia Resolutions, Murray reminded that "a year or so earlier" Virginia Republicans had discussed "a separation from the Union" and had advanced the plans to the point of restocking the state arsenal with arms and enacting a "rigid collection of extra taxes" to pay for the arms buildup. This state particularism and defiant, bordering on seditious, opposition to the Federalist administration, however, would now be tempered and mitigated, he predicted. The threat of a slave insurrection would serve as a powerful antidote to the militancy of the Republican opposition, convincing all but the most factious that the power and military might of the federal government would be necessary for their survival.[7]

The Federalist charge that the Virginia Republicans had unwittingly been catalysts for the insurrection by their use of the language of natural rights and liberty was not that far off the mark. The highly combustible mixture of revolutionary ideas, black resentment, and white working-class animosity and bitterness combined to further aggravate the already volatile political environment. Furthermore, there was evidence that two shadowy figures, one a Frenchman, might have been involved in the Gabriel conspiracy. This information, according to one historian, was so potentially devastating to the Republicans because of their friendship toward France that Governor James Monroe chose to suppress it.[8]

Gabriel's Rebellion could hardly have come at a worse time for those

Virginians consumed by the approach of what they perceived as the transformative election of 1800. They were already engaged in what they saw as a climactic battle with the Federalists—a battle that, if lost, might jeopardize individual liberties, diminish the power of the states in a federated republic, and even cause the Union to disintegrate. Now the news of Gabriel's conspiracy was heightening their already profound sense of vulnerability. Their defensive citadel had almost been breached, and their state refuge protecting them from the aggressive Federalist general government had been threatened from within by a slave uprising. Thus, on the eve of the election of 1800, Virginia Republicans and their Southern allies felt besieged.

II

The shock and horror that greeted the news of Gabriel's Rebellion was soon matched, however, by the astonishment that was produced by the publication of a fifty-four page vitriolic and venomous pamphlet written by Hamilton. Attacking Adams's character, personality, and performance as president, this bombshell, entitled *A letter from Alexander Hamilton, Concerning the Public Conduct and Character of John Adams, Esq., President of the United States*, appeared in late October and fueled the escalating internecine battle within the Federalist party.

Some of Hamilton's closest friends and colleagues had been deeply apprehensive about his plan to attack Adams so publicly, arguing that if he persisted in publishing the incendiary pamphlet, it should be written anonymously.[9] But that advice was disregarded.

At the time of the American Revolution, Hamilton wrote in the document, he had had "high veneration for Mr. ADAMS," but with "subsequent experience" he had concluded that Adams was "eccentric; propitious neither to the regular display of sound judgment, nor to steady perseverance in a systematic plan of conduct." Furthermore, Adams was a man with "a vanity without bounds, and a jealousy capable of discoloring every object."

Adams, Hamilton charged, did "not possess the talents adapted to the *administration* of government." There were "great and intrinsic defects in his character, which unfit him for the office of chief magistrate." Although not calling Adams mad or insane, Hamilton implied as much by citing the president's "disgusting egotism . . . distempered jealousy, and . . . ungovernable indiscretion of temper." Adams's "ill humors and jealousies" have "divided and distracted the supporters of the government" and have "furnished deadly weapons to its enemies by unfounded accusations."

Perhaps the most serious of Adams's failings, according to Hamilton, was that he had undermined, and perhaps destroyed, the foundations of the federal government as put in place by Washington. "New government, constructed on free principles," Hamilton perceptively observed, "is always weak and must stand in need of the props of a firm and good administration, till time shall have rendered its authority venerable, and fortified it by the habits of obedience." But there was a real danger that the new American government "might totter, if not fall, under . . . [Adams's] future auspices."

And in a gesture of support for Pinckney at the expense of Adams, Hamilton likened the South Carolinian to Washington. Pinckney was, Hamilton argued, "distinguished," mild and amiable in his manners, and a man known for "the rectitude and purity of his words, and the soundness and correctness of his understanding, accompanied by a habitual discretion and self-command, which has often occasioned a parallel to be drawn between him and the venerated WASHINGTON."

Hamilton's extraordinary pamphlet concluded with a fervent defense of himself against Adams's libel of him "as a man destitute of every moral principle" and a member of the "British faction." He was stunned, he said, "to have to combat a slander so vile, after having sacrificed the interests of his family to the service of th[is] country, in counsel and in the field."[10]

The attack on Adams by Hamilton both confounded and enraged his fellow Federalists. Connecticut's Noah Webster denounced Hamilton in another pamphlet as extremely disloyal. Addressing Hamilton directly, he wrote that if Jefferson were to be elected, "the fault will lie at your door and . . . your conduct on this occasion will be discerned little short of insanity." The Republicans, on the other hand, were elated, Madison assuring Jefferson that Hamilton's missive virtually assured a Republican victory. "I rejoice with you that Republicanism is likely to be so *completely* triumphant," he exulted.[11] And Republican editors saw to it that Hamilton's words were reprinted far and wide in newspapers sympathetic to the Republican cause.

The Republican *Aurora* gloated that the "pulsation given to the body politic, by *Hamilton's* precious letter, is felt from one end of the union to the other," for there has never been "a publication so strange in its structure, more destructive in its purposed end." Not only had the *Letter* "thrown much false glare on the character of Mr. Adams," the paper asserted, it had also revealed "the real character and designs of the writer and his partisans."[12]

What drove Hamilton, especially under his own name, to take such an extreme and risky step as publishing a document that was destined to alienate a number of Federalists as well as perhaps doom Adams's chances to hold on to the presidency? Historians have differed in their answers to this question. Some have concluded that the pamphlet "revealed that [Hamilton] had become an inept politician," while others have argued that Hamilton's strategy was to destroy Adams's chances for reelection and pave the way for a Jefferson victory. This would have allowed Hamilton and his friends to pick up the pieces and later rebuild the Federalist party. Still others have maintained that Hamilton's actions were part of a very shrewd and calculated maneuver to have Pinckney elected president or at a minimum to create a tie vote in the Electoral College, forcing the House of Representatives to decide the election.[13]

There is no doubt that Hamilton hoped Pinckney would be elected president. But, if the motive behind the pamphlet was to win support for Pinckney, it surely was a major miscalculation, because its publication severely damaged and weakened Hamilton's reputation and power among the Federalists.

Clearly, Hamilton had disliked and distrusted Adams since he had assumed the presidency in 1797. But subsequent acrimonious disagreements over the building of the army and Hamilton's role in it, as well as the United States' relationship with France, had driven him to despise the New Englander. The ensuing May firing of cabinet members McHenry and Pickering, both staunch allies and stooges of Hamilton, coupled with the pardoning by Adams of the condemned Fries Rebellion leaders, had also intensified Hamilton's profound sense that Adams was a traitor to the Federalist cause and to him personally.

But the last straw came when Adams questioned the New Yorker's patriotism by speaking of "the existence of a *British Faction*" in the country, with the clear implication that Hamilton was the leader of it. This had provoked an extraordinarily intemperate, excessive, and out-of-character public outburst by Hamilton. Demanding an explanation from Adams, but receiving none, Hamilton decided to write his *Letter* publicly excoriating the president.

Most likely, then, Hamilton's decision to write the pamphlet was driven by a deeply felt fury to strike back at his hated antagonist, who not only had insulted him but who also had destroyed his ambitious and grandiose vision for the United States to play a major imperial role in teaming with England in the reordering of the Spanish empire in the Western Hemisphere. The newly constituted army with Hamilton at its head was to have been the instrument for the fulfillment of this grand plan that Hamilton had counted on to be the basis for his achieving glory and building a legacy to leave to his country.

But while the revenge motive was important, Hamilton was also, most likely, suffering a severe crisis of self-doubt and despondency. From the end of 1799 down to the publication of the attack on Adams in October 1800, Hamilton had endured a number of wrenching setbacks, the most important of which was Washington's death.

Hamilton's contemporaries, especially earlier, had described Hamilton as an affable man with an easy charm and broad-ranging intelligence. His brilliance dazzled. But, even earlier, he was also viewed as someone who could be tempestuous, turbulent, headstrong, and lacking in patience with those who disagreed with him.

An even more private side of Hamilton, however, reveals a dark and more brooding personality. Immediately after the end of the American Revolution, Hamilton flirted with supporting a conspiracy of army officers to use the army to force the Articles of Confederation government to accede to their demands for payment of back pay and lifetime pensions. The conspiracy, if successful, would have amounted to a military coup over civilian government. Chastised by Washington, Hamilton reflected that he often felt "a mortification, which it would be impolitic to express, that sets my passions at variance with my reason." And in a letter to his best friend, he offered a surprising and profoundly heartrending lament: "I hate Congress—I hate the army—I hate the world—I hate myself."[14]

Washington's death at the end of 1799 hit Hamilton particularly hard. The news, Hamilton said, filled his heart with sadness and bitterness. "Perhaps no man in this community has equal cause with myself to deplore the loss," Hamilton grieved. "I have been much indebted to the kindness of the General, and he was an *Aegis very essential to me*."[15] "Aegis," as defined in the eighteenth century and as used by Hamilton in this context, meant a "shield or defensive armour,"[16] and the metaphor captures the enormous significance of Hamilton's relationship with Washington. For with Washington's death Hamilton lost an advisor, father figure, and advocate. Washington was the final arbiter, the court of last resort of the republic—such was the immensity of his reputation and influence. And while Washington lived, Hamilton felt secure in knowing he had a powerful champion who could be appealed to for support. Washington was Hamilton's anchor.

Hamilton, then—with the death of Washington, the acrimonious battle and break with Adams, and the loss of his army and his command—simply lost his moorings.

At the time of Gabriel's Rebellion and Hamilton's public denunciation of Adams, the selection of the electors who would vote in the 1800 presidential election was well underway. It took place over nine months, beginning in March and continuing through the end of November, with each state having its own timetable and voting arrangements.[17] It was not until 1845 that Congress set the Tuesday after the first Monday in November as the uniform date for electing presidential electors.[18]

The election of 1800 was actually less democratic than the 1796 contest had been. In 1796, for example, presidential electors had been chosen by popular vote in eight states, some candidates running on statewide tickets, others on district ones. The state legislatures had chosen the electors in seven states; and in one state, Tennessee, electors had been selected by a complicated arrangement involving the state legislature, counties and districts.[19]

By 1800, however, only five states allowed popular election of presidential electors, either by general statewide ticket or district balloting. Four states—Maryland, Virginia, North Carolina, and Kentucky—continued in their practice of letting voters choose the electors, and they were joined by Rhode Island, which had run against the undemocratic current and adopted the popular election method for 1800. Four states, however—Massachusetts, New Hampshire, Pennsylvania, and Georgia—moved from choosing their electors by popular election in 1796 to choosing them by legislative vote in 1800. Legislatures in Connecticut, New York, New Jersey, Delaware, South Carolina, and Vermont chose their electors in both elections, and Tennessee continued its practice of selecting electors by its complex system.[20]

Despite the efforts of Republicans to make inroads into New England's earlier solid support for the Federalists, and the Federalist split between the anti-Adams and pro-Adams forces, the result in that section of the country in 1800 was similar to what it had been in 1796—a big win for the Federalists.

In New Hampshire and Massachusetts, Republican gains in state spring elections had worried Federalists, who feared that this trend might carry over to the presidential election. Thus, New Hampshire, having in 1796 elected its electors by general ticket, changed to having the Federalist-dominated legislature make the choice in 1800. This had the desired result, with that state's six electoral votes going to Adams.

Massachusetts Federalists changed that state's method of selecting electors

from a district-by-district popular vote in 1796 to a selection by the state legislature in 1800. This was clearly a political move by the Federalists there to
preserve an undisputed hold on the electoral vote. For in the race for seats in
the legislature, Republicans had garnered a very respectable 44.5 percent of
the total vote. Had the old district scheme been continued, it almost certainly
would have meant that some Republican electors would have been chosen.
But in Massachusetts, as in New Hampshire, the Federalist-controlled legislature delivered unanimous support for Adams—sixteen votes.

Federalists also dominated Vermont and Connecticut, with their legislatures awarding all their votes to Adams: four from Vermont and nine from
Connecticut. Finally, in Rhode Island, despite its change to a more democratic selection process and despite the fact that the Republicans had won
two state elections earlier in the year, Rhode Islanders voted 2,345 to 2,149
for Adams, giving him four votes.[21]

Thus, in spite of their apparently bitter internal divisions, the Federalists
swept New England. And there is some evidence that Hamilton's denunciation of Adams, rather than rallying Federalists around Pinckney as their
presidential candidate, backfired by creating considerable sympathy for the
president and isolating Hamilton.

Notwithstanding the outward appearance of New England's overwhelming Federalist partisanship, there were also signs that this partisanship was
often confusing and ambiguous. In Massachusetts, Elbridge Gerry supported Adams for president, but ran unsuccessfully for governor as a Republican, thus reflecting his hope for a kind of latitudinarian politics embracing
both Federalists and Republicans. In other New England states, there were
attempts to obscure the differences between the two parties, at least in the
names they went by. Republicans in Rhode Island, for example, called themselves Republican-Federalists. It was so confusing for some that one "Connecticut farmer," probably speaking for a number of his fellow citizens,
protested that he wished that "we might reject the words, *federal, anti-federal,
democrat, aristocrat, Jacobin*, etc., and go back to our old language Whig and
Tory."[22]

It is significant that the "Connecticut farmer" framed the division in
1800 in such terms as "Whig and Tory," referring, as they did, to the polarized politics of the American Revolution. The division between Whig
and Tory was fundamental: it separated those who were in support of the
Revolution and independence from those who were opposed, preferring to
remain British subjects. Under these circumstances, with such deepseated
and elemental political divisions, there can be no resolution until one side

becomes victorious and hegemonic. Thus, accommodation and compromise are impossible.

The Middle Atlantic states had been expected to play a critical role, if not *the* critical role, in electing a president in 1800. They had been strongly in Adams's camp in 1796, when he had received twenty-three votes from the region, including twelve from New York, seven from New Jersey, one from Pennsylvania, and three from Delaware. Jefferson had received votes only from Pennsylvania, fourteen.[23]

The Republican victory in New York in May 1800, of course, represented a great turnaround there and gave control of the state legislature to the Republicans, thus guaranteeing that all of New York's twelve electoral votes would be cast for Jefferson. This was highly ironic, since prior to the legislative elections the Republicans had proposed that the electors be selected by district, which they had calculated would give them an opportunity to win at least some electoral votes from Republican-dominated districts. The Federalists had defeated the proposal, and the state had thus retained the winner-take-all selection of the electors by the legislature. This represented a misjudgment by both parties but a catastrophic one for the Federalists, who ended up robbing themselves of a significant number of electoral votes, since they polled more than half the overall popular vote in the election, 24,607 to 22,539, even though they ended up winning fewer seats in the state legislature and in Congress.[24]

After the Republican victory in New York, the major question mark was Pennsylvania: there was a distinct possibility that that state might not cast any votes at all for president. The Pennsylvania legislature had adjourned in January 1800 without resolving a dispute between the Federalist-controlled Senate and the Republican-controlled House of Representatives over the method for choosing the state's electors.

A few months earlier, the Republicans had won a significant victory in Pennsylvania by electing Judge Thomas McKean governor. His margin of victory over his Federalist opponent, 38,036 to 32,643, had come from the Fries Rebellion area of the state. Smarting from their gubernatorial defeat but still in control of the state senate, the Federalists had then been able to block any attempt to pass legislation governing the selection of electors, thus creating an impasse. The Federalists hoped that a strategy of preventing Pennsylvania from casting any electoral votes might mitigate the loss of New York. Ultimately, however, a last-minute compromise was worked out in the late fall of 1800, and the Pennsylvania legislature divided the state's votes between the two sides, with eight going to Jefferson and seven to Adams.[25]

Significantly, however, a comparison of the 1799 vote for governor with the 1800 vote for Congress and the state legislature showed a precipitous falling-off of the Federalist vote in the state. While in 1799 the Federalists had polled 32,643, in 1800 they got only 19,706, a drop of almost 13,000. Republican candidates in 1800 for the legislature and Congress garnered 35,867 votes, a modest decline from 1799, but still a significantly higher number than the Federalists tallied.[26] If this popular vote had been expressed by the people in a general election—the way the electors had been chosen by the state in 1796—the Republicans most likely would have captured all fifteen of Pennsylvania's electoral votes.

In New Jersey, where in both 1796 and 1800 electors were selected by legislative action, the Republicans hoped to win the state's electoral votes even though they had all gone to the Federalists in 1796. In 1800, however, the Republicans were better organized and expected to be more successful. A Republican campaign publication appealed to the voters, reminding them: "Knowing as we do, that the men who shall be returned to the next Legislature will . . . chuse the Electors . . . we ought to give our suffrages for those characters in nomination, who will vote for Electors that will join in placing at the head of the American Government, men who have distinguished themselves. . . . Such men are THOMAS JEFFERSON and AARON BURR."[27] Despite a dramatic increase in turnout, however, Republican efforts failed and the state gave all of its seven votes to Adams. Like the parties in some of the other states, the New Jersey Federalists had perhaps confused the issue by calling themselves Federalist-Republican.[28]

Delaware, as expected, gave its three votes to Adams, with the Federalist-controlled legislature outvoting the Republicans more than two-to-one (twenty to nine).[29]

The South and West had been strongholds of Republicanism in 1796. That year, Adams had gotten only nine of his seventy-one electoral votes from those two sections, seven from Maryland and one each from Virginia and North Carolina. But Federalists hoped that in 1800, with Charles Cotesworth Pinckney of South Carolina on the ticket, their appeal would be stronger. A number of anti-Adams Federalists even hoped that Pinckney's attraction to Southerners might be enough to win the presidency for the South Carolinian.

The Republicans needed to maintain their hegemony in the South and West and believed that Georgia and the western states of Kentucky and Tennessee were safely Republican. The results of the congressional elections of 1798 and 1799 in some of the southern states, however, had been shocking, with the Federalists winning twenty-two seats to the Republicans' fifteen.[30] Federalists had increased their numbers in the Virginia delegation in the House of Representatives from four to eight, while they had picked up five out of eleven House seats in North Carolina and five of six in South Carolina. Thus, going into the election of 1800, Republicans were determined to roll back these inroads the Federalists had made in the South.

In Virginia, one of the five states that chose electors by popular vote, Republicans worked to nullify Federalist gains in their state by changing the method of the popular voting. In 1796, the electors had been chosen in district elections, with Jefferson winning all of the contests except one. By 1800, however, with the impressive Federalist political gains the previous year in mind, the Republican-dominated legislature changed the rules, and electors were chosen by a winner-take-all general ticket. The intention was to negate pockets of Federalist strength within the state.

In addition, the Republicans selected an impressive array of notables with considerable popular appeal to be electors, including George Wythe, Edmund Randolph, and James Madison. This was especially important because Virginians voted *viva voce* (or orally), giving the advantage to well-known candidates, and the Federalists had difficulty in matching the prominence of the Republican candidates with their slate of electors. Evidence of the Federalist desperation with the Republican tactics was the designation of their slate as "The American Republican Ticket" and their bitter complaints about the change in the mode of electing electors. The new system was rigged "to exclude *one third* at least of the citizens of Virginia from a vote for the President of the United States," the Federalists grumbled.[31]

Not leaving anything to chance, the Virginia Republicans also set up an elaborate campaign structure that included a central committee in Richmond and committees in every county of the state in order "to communicate useful information to the people relative to the election" and "to repel every effort which may be made to injure either the ticket in general or to remove any prejudice which may be attempted to be raised against any person on that ticket." Also, Monroe's election as governor was a powerful factor in the Republicans' favor, in that he could "form a center around which our interest can rally."[32]

The Republican efforts paid off, and Jefferson won all twenty-one electoral votes from Virginia.

A comparison of fragmentary Virginia returns from the balloting in the 1799 congressional and 1800 presidential elections from select counties indicates that the total Federalist vote declined in the state in the year between the elections. In addition, a comparison of sixty-two select counties in

Virginia in 1800 shows a 28.6 percent decline in *overall* voting as compared to the 1799 totals. This decline, in part, may have been a function of a sense that voting in a winner-take-all general election in a strong Republican state like Virginia was a futile effort.[33]

Maryland had given Adams seven out of its eleven electoral votes in 1796, making it the only Southern state to award Adams more than a single vote. Thus, one of the most discussed issues in the election of 1800 was how the state should choose its electors. The prevailing system of popular election by district was up for debate. As was true in other states, it boiled down to the partisan question of how best to get one party's candidates elected over those of the rival party. "We deem it a sacred duty," four Federalist candidates for the state assembly avowed, "to pursue every *proper and constitutional* measure to elect John Adams president of the United States."[34] But despite the discussion of changing the mode of election, the district system was retained.

Campaigning around the state was boisterous and spirited, leading one historian to conclude that "in no other state were the methods of campaigning so advanced." Any large gathering, such as a "horse race—a cock fight—or a Methodist quarterly meeting," one observer noted, would present an opportunity for the candidates to "Harrangue [sic] the Sovereign people—praise and recommend themselves at the expence [sic] of their adversary's character and pretensions." A critic of this rough-and-tumble democratic style caustically noted that the candidates traveled through their districts "soliciting the favor of individuals, with whom they associate on no other occasion, and men of the first consideration condescend to collect dissolute and ignorant mobs of hundreds of individuals to whom they make long speeches in the open air."[35]

This vigorous campaigning led to a draw between Federalists and Republicans, with Adams and Jefferson each receiving five electoral votes. The overall vote in the state reflected the closeness of the race, with the Republican electors receiving 10,629 votes to 10,068 for the Federalists.[36] Adams's showing in capturing half of the electoral votes came despite the opposition of Marylander James McHenry, who had been seething with anger and resentment after having been summarily fired by Adams from his post as secretary of war. McHenry peevishly wrote a fellow Federalist that Maryland Federalists should "make little or no exertions for the federal candidate; not from any indifference to the good old cause, but from a kind of conviction that our labour would be lost" because of the "utter unfitness of one of the federal candidates to fill the office of President."[37]

North Carolina was worrisome to the Republicans. Although Adams had received only one electoral vote in 1796, the Federalists in the ensuing congressional elections had picked up almost half the seats. And North Carolina chose their electors by popular vote in districts, one of only three states that did. This meant that areas of Federalist strength would, most likely, return Federalist electors.[38]

"The state of public mind in N. Carolina appears mysterious to us," Jefferson wrote in an anxious letter to a colleague in South Carolina in August. "Doubtless you know more of it than we do." What will be the impact in the South Atlantic states, Jefferson asked, of the South Carolinian Pinckney being on the Federalist ticket? Would his being promoted by some Federalists as a substitute for Adams for president attract voters to the Federal ticket that might have gone to the Republicans?[39] Although Adams did win more electoral votes in North Carolina than he had in 1796 (when he received only one), he still ran behind Jefferson, who received eight electoral votes to Adams's four in 1800. Despite these results, it has been suggested by one historian that, based on incomplete returns, the statewide vote in North Carolina most likely favored the Federalists, 11,557 to 10,556.[40]

By late November, then, the two presidential candidates, Adams and Jefferson, were tied—at least unofficially—with sixty-five electoral votes each. So there was the presumption that the election would be decided by South Carolina—the only state whose electors had not yet been selected—the state legislators who would make the decision having only been elected in October. The political situation in that state, of course, was hard to predict, with native son Pinckney on the Federalist ticket and many anti-Adams Federalists attempting to have him elected president over the presumed head of the ticket. While there undoubtedly was substantial support in the state for Pinckney, it was unclear whether a combination of Pinckney-Jefferson, Jefferson-Burr, or Pinckney-Adams might emerge victorious.

Pinckney himself remained publicly coy about any plan for electors to support him over Adams. Nonetheless, he did, in a letter to the sacked McHenry, offer an opening. First stating that the Southern states should respect the wishes of the Federalist caucus and support Adams for president, he then went on to say that if, however, the "Eastern States" should be convinced that Adams had abandoned "federal principles" and was thus unfit to be president, these states "should consent to substitute another Candidate in his stead. This event I do not think impossible, & his [Adams's] conduct & the critical situation of our Country may require it." But such action to "preserve the Union" must originate in the "Eastward and Middle States," and "the Southern ones with propriety follow."[41]

General Charles Cotesworth Pinckney. Although the South Carolinian ran on the Federalist ticket as the presumed vice presidential nominee in 1800, Alexander Hamilton schemed to have him elected president in place of incumbent president John Adams. Worcester Art Museum, Worcester, Massachusetts. General Charles C. Pinckney by James Earl, 1796–1797, 35 × 39 inches, museum purchase.

By the time Pinckney wrote this letter to McHenry, his relationship with Adams was already strained because of a family issue. The Republican *Aurora* had dug up and published an old letter, purportedly written by Adams, charging that Thomas Pinckney, Charles Cotesworth's brother, had been appointed U.S. minister to England because of family lobbying and blatant British influence. In response, Thomas had taken offense at Adams's characterization of him and had written a letter to the *Charleston City Gazette* in September 1800 suggesting that he would investigate whether or not the letter (the original of which could not be produced by Duane of the *Aurora*) was authentic and would ask the president to explain himself. Adams responded to Pinckney's inquiry by ingratiatingly claiming that he did not remember writing the letter.[42]

The new South Carolina legislature was scheduled to meet to select the state's electors on November 24, shortly before the national deadline of December 2 for presidential electors nationwide to cast their official ballots. But, how the South Carolina legislators would vote on electors was still in question because the outcome of the voting for the legislature had been ambiguous. The Federalists had elected eleven of the fifteen members from the city of Charleston's delegation to the state's House of Representatives, but the exact makeup of the legislature was unclear because some of the newly elected legislators from elsewhere in the state seemed to be uncommitted.

A former Federalist, Charles Pinckney, second cousin to candidate Charles Cotesworth Pinckney, managed the Republican effort in the state, much to the displeasure of members of his family and the Federalists, who referred to him as "Blackguard Charlie" for what they considered to be his disloyalty. And, in a letter to Jefferson, the black-sheep cousin complained bitterly about the Federalist tactics that had affected the legislative elections in Charleston. He charged that "several Hundred more Voted than paid taxes," and the "*Lame, Crippled, diseased and blind were either led, lifted, or brought in Carriages to the Poll.*" These men, influenced by "Banks and federal officers and English Merchants," the Republican Pinckney claimed, "voted as they were directed."[43]

After their Charleston victory, the Federalists were therefore shocked when the House of Representatives elected a Republican to be speaker of the house by a large margin, thus reflecting Republican support from the more rural areas of the state. Still believing they had an opportunity to select Federalist presidential electors, the Federalists then lobbied the uncommitted legislators and also attempted to lure Republican supporters over to the Federalist side by offering a Charles Cotesworth Pinckney–Jefferson ticket. The capital at Columbia was abuzz with all kinds of rumors and intrigue, but the attempt to capitalize on the popularity of Pinckney as the state's favorite son ultimately failed when Pinckney refused to go along and publicly repudiate Adams. In the end, Jefferson and his running mate, Burr, each won all of the state's eight electoral votes, thus seemingly assuring Jefferson's election to the presidency.[44]

Subsequent to the balloting Jefferson received a jubilant letter from Charles Pinckney announcing that it had "depended upon our State entirely to secure Your Election," and that the "Election is just finished and We Have, Thanks to Heaven's Goodness, carried it." In another letter, he took credit for the victory, claiming to Jefferson that "Most of our friends believe that my Exertions and influences" have "in great measure contributed to the decision and firmly believing myself that they were indispensable to Your Success I did not suppose myself at liberty to quit Columbia until it was over." Pinckney was later rewarded for his efforts by being appointed as minister to the Spanish court.[45]

V

On election day, December 2, 1800, electors gathered in their respective state capitals to cast their votes for president and vice president. The returns were not to be officially counted until February 11, but unofficial reports filtered in from the various states throughout the month of December.[46]

Jefferson came to the capital in Washington on November 27, timing his arrival to miss Adams's address to a joint session of Congress. He wanted to avoid an embarrassing meeting between the two candidates. As every public official except the president was forced to find some kind of housing, Jefferson had obtained quarters in the boarding house of Conrad and McMunn located on the south side of Capitol Hill. It was only about "two hundred paces" from the north Senate wing, one of the few buildings in the projected Capitol complex to have been completed. As a newcomer, Jefferson was seated at the end of the residence's crowded dining table, the place furthest from the fire and therefore the coldest.

The most popular of the boarding houses, Conrad and McMunn's was where Albert Gallatin resided and shared a room with another member of Congress. The thirty boarders there each paid $15 a week for the shared rooms, meals, firewood, candles, and liquors. As to the cuisine, Gallatin praised the mutton and poultry but complained that the beef was "not very good" and that there were "hardly any vegetables."[47]

Two weeks after Jefferson's arrival, the *National Intelligencer* reported that Republican electors had been chosen by the South Carolina legislature and that "Mr. Jefferson may, therefore, be considered our future President." This report was based on the latest returns received at that point and the assumption that the distant Republican strongholds of Georgia (four votes), Tennessee (three votes), and Kentucky (four votes) would go for Jefferson.

But, with the fragmentary information coming into Washington, it was not clear whether Jefferson would poll more votes than his presumed vice president—although earlier private communications made it appear so. For example, the candidate had been assured that one of the Republican electors in South Carolina would vote for George Clinton rather than Burr. And a report from Georgia also seemed to indicate that one or two of that state's four electors might deny Burr their votes. These reports had led Jefferson happily to conclude in early December that "I believe we may consider the election as now decided."[48]

The complete returns of the Electoral College vote did not arrive in Washington until the end of December, when Jefferson, as presiding officer of the Senate, received them. The final count, which appeared in several Washington newspapers right before Christmas, showed that Jefferson had been overly optimistic about his chances of winning the election outright.[49] He and Burr led all candidates but were tied with seventy-three electoral votes apiece, followed by Adams with sixty-five, Pinckney with sixty-four, and John Jay with one, the Jay vote having come from a Rhode Island elector.

The tie in the Electoral College between Jefferson and Burr meant that the election would have to be decided by the House of Representatives in early February, with each state having one vote. This, much to the dismay of the Republicans, opened up the alarming and (to them) unacceptable possibility that Jefferson's election to the presidency might be thwarted by an unyielding bloc of votes in the Federalist-dominated House.

In addition to revealing a deadlock, the electoral votes disclosed a dangerous sectionalism. Adams had received fifty-six of his sixty-five electoral votes, or 86.2 percent, from New England and the Middle States, and only nine (or 13.8 percent) from the South and West. Of the seventy-three votes for Jefferson, fifty-three votes (or 72.6 percent) had come from the South and West, and twenty (or 27.4 percent) from the Middle States of New York and Pennsylvania. Looking at the election another way, electors from the South and West cast 85.5 percent of their ballots for Jefferson, and New England electors cast 100 percent of their ballots for Adams.

The 1800 returns also reflected a much more disciplined vote than in the previous election. In 1796 the principals, Adams and Jefferson, had run ahead of their tickets, seventy-one to sixty-eight respectively. But the votes for vice president had been scattered. While Federalist Thomas Pinckney had garnered fifty-nine votes and Republican Aaron Burr thirty, some forty-eight votes had been "wasted" by Republican and Federalist electors on other candidates, including John Jay, Samuel Adams, George Clinton, George Washington, Oliver Ellsworth, Samuel Johnston, John Henry, C. C. Pinckney, and James Iredell.[50] In 1800, the four principal candidates captured all of the electoral votes, with the exception of a single vote for John Jay.

In the 1800 elections for the U.S. Congress, which stretched throughout the year, Republicans also won an important victory. The Congress elected in 1798 had been strongly Federalist, by a margin of sixty-three to forty-three. The election of 1800, however, returned sixty-eight Republicans to thirty-eight Federalists.[51]

In New England the Federalists continued to be strong. They won all seven congressional seats in Connecticut as well as all four in New Hampshire. Massachusetts divided its congressional delegation eight to six in favor of the Federalists, and Vermont elected one congressman from each of the parties. Rhode Island elected two Republicans.

In the Middle States, the Republicans made important gains in congressional delegations. Stunned by the Republicans' capture of three of the five congressional seats in 1798, the Federalist legislature in New Jersey had changed back to an at-large congressional vote for 1800, only to find that the Republicans, with a turnout of more than seventy percent, won all five seats.[52] The presidential results were announced while that state was in the midst of its congressional campaign, thus giving considerable momentum to the Republicans in a state that had given all of its presidential electoral votes to Adams. Pennsylvania elected ten Republicans and three Federalists to Congress, while New York split six to four in favor of the Republicans. Delaware awarded its one seat to the Federalists.

In the South and West, Virginia (with nineteen seats at stake), Georgia (with two), Kentucky (with two), and Tennessee (with one) remained bastions of Republican strength. In the Old Dominion, Republicans garnered all but one of the seats, and in the other three states the Republicans made clean sweeps. Maryland (with eight), North Carolina (with ten), and South Carolina (with six) were "nearly equally divided."[53]

Although, in the end, the Federalists lost the presidency and control of Congress in 1800, they did, however, maintain considerable strength in the states. Nine states had Federalist governors, and Federalists held a majority in both houses of the legislatures in six states. And a compilation of the combined election returns from state, congressional, and presidential returns in 1800 show that the Republicans did not have a commanding majority. They polled 150,778 votes (or 52 percent) to the Federalists' 138,685 (or 48 percent).[54]

Of crucial importance to the 1800 presidential election, however, was that the new, Republican-dominated Congress would not convene until December 1801. Thus, it was the heavily Federalist Congress that would be asked to resolve the Electoral College deadlock and decide who the next president and vice president would be.

9

THE CRISIS BUILDS

February "will present us storms of a new character."
—*Jefferson to Madison, December 1800*

I

Jefferson celebrated the New Year of 1801 by taking a ferry across the Potomac from Georgetown to Alexandria, where he took lodging and then rented a horse for three dollars to ride to Mount Vernon to pay his respects to George Washington's widow, Martha, most likely unaware that she had earlier voiced such great disdain for him.[1]

But the situation he faced upon his return to Washington after this brief excursion was a daunting one. The stark reality of the seriousness of the tie in the Electoral College dominated the conversation in the raw, new capital on the Potomac. Nothing, however, could actually be done right away, since the official count of the votes could not be made until the second Wednesday in February. At that time, Jefferson, under his constitutional role as vice president, was charged with officially opening the ballots from the various states and reporting the results. So, the interval from the beginning of January through early February was a time of waiting for the residents of the isolated governmental outpost, where lawmakers were described as living "like a refectory of monks,"[2] most of them lodged in one or another of the boarding houses there.

In several letters to his wife in early 1801, Albert Gallatin vividly described the insular lifestyle at the time, reporting that "being all thrown together in a few boarding houses without hardly any other society then [*sic*] ourselves, we are not likely to be either very moderate politicians or to think of anything but politics. A few indeed drink and some gamble, but the majority drink nought but politics, and by not mixing with men of different or more moderate sentiments, they inflame one another."[3] Isolated and remote, Washington's denizens were hostage to the rumors and wild assertions that made their way to the capital in early 1801.

To say that Washington was difficult to get to was a gross understatement. Jefferson's trip to resume his role as vice president and the presiding officer of the Senate in late 1800 is a case in point. In making the arduous trip from his home just outside Charlottesville to Washington, he complained, eight rivers had to be crossed and "five have neither bridges nor boats." For those traveling from Philadelphia to the capital, it took three days just to get to Baltimore. The roads through the forests the rest of the way were so bad and poorly marked that stage drivers celebrated any trip during which their coaches didn't overturn or get mired in the mud.[4]

Aggravating the already tense and apprehensive atmosphere in the capital were two mysterious fires. The newly completed Department of War building burned on November 8, a couple of weeks before the South Carolina legislature met to choose the state's electors, and the Treasury Department building sustained damage on January 20, when the official tally was still being awaited. The Federalists rather lamely attempted to accuse the Republicans of starting the fires, while the Republicans believed the blazes to have been set by a desperate Federalist party about to lose its power. The Federalist efforts, the Republicans contended, had been motivated by a desire to destroy official documents that revealed years of corruption and lies.

One Republican editor charged that the "offices of the *War* and *Treasury Departments* were burnt down by design" (presumably by guilty Federalist officeholders), adding that innocent persons had nothing to hide and therefore would not stoop to arson.[5] Virginia governor James Monroe was told by a correspondent in Washington that "there is no doubt but that every purpose which was intended is answered" by the Treasury fire. Everyone in Washington that he had spoken to, he told the governor, agreed "that the thing was willful." He just wished that the entire Virginia legislature "were in possession of those facts."[6]

The Republicans especially targeted Samuel Dexter, the Massachusetts Federalist who served as secretary of treasury and acting secretary of war at the time of the two fires, for abuse and ridicule, the editor of the Republican *General Advertiser* pointing out that

Mr. Dexter has been rather unfortunate in *fireworks*. He had not been warm in the chair of the war department, before there was a terrible combustion: he was soon after translated to the cold calculating chair of finance, "when lo! there, cometh a *hot wind*" and the treasury office is consumed! It would not be discreet to remove this dexterous secretary to the navy office, lest our navy should follow the path of fire, and the secrets of our state department would, were he to approach them, be erased like certain *acts of the senate*, in the reign of Tiberius, even from the records of the government and of history.[7]

Accusations of arson were given additional traction by the allegations that had been published the previous summer in the *Aurora* that Federalist officials were guilty of corruption and malfeasance in office. Specifically, Federalist Speaker of the House of Representatives Jonathan Dayton, Secretary of Treasury Oliver Wolcott, and Secretary of State Timothy Pickering had been charged by the Republicans with betraying the public trust by using their official positions for private profit.[8]

Fires during normal times might have been regarded as unfortunate, but blameless, disasters. But not in late 1800 and early 1801. These were not normal times. The distrust and suspicion that separated the Republicans and Federalists transformed every difference of opinion into a fundamental and uncompromising schism; by then opposing party members' perceptions of one another had become grotesquely exaggerated.

Rumors warning of violence, or actual calls for violence, also swept through the capital in late 1800 and early 1801, further heightening the anxiety level. There was talk of militias arming and preparing to march, possible civil war, and Federalist plots to deny Jefferson the presidency either by the outright usurpation of power or by elevating Burr to the presidency instead. There were also wild reports that Jefferson would be assassinated.[9]

A Connecticut ally had reported to Jefferson in the fall that the Republicans would be threatened with "bloodshedding and civil war" if the Virginian were to win the presidency.[10] And, perhaps in response to this and other such reports, Philadelphia Republicans in December 1800 organized a citizen militia group called the "Republican Blues," "in order to defend the country against foreign and domestic enemies, and [to] support the laws." More accurately, it was an obvious effort to provide armed support to assure Jefferson's election and guard against any Federalist intrigues designed to deny him the presidency.[11]

While stories circulated about political militias and their potential role in using the force of arms to resolve the crisis, even wilder and more fantastical stories made their rounds. The Federalists were attempting nothing less than burning "the constitution at the point of a bayonet," one Republican warned. And another hysterically wailed that he had heard that "every democrat should be put to death in order to secure the government in the former hands."[12]

Wild charges were not confined to the Republicans, as the Federalists passed stories and rumors of Republican plots and intrigues. A "*Conspiracy is mentioned abroad*," a shocked and terrified *Salem Federalist* writer asserted, for it was being "whispered that when the Philosopher [Jefferson] gets into the chair, and a suitable force provided at his back, he is to declare himself permanent."[13]

This specter of despotism, frightening to both Federalists and Republicans, was no doubt closely related to the fact that in October 1799 Napoleon had overthrown the Directory that had governed the French republic since 1795. And, while maintaining the appearance of himself as the head of a republic, he had, in reality, instituted a dictatorship. The failure of republicanism in France, and the spectacle of a military hero's ascension to power there, coming within a decade of the French Revolution, was alarming to Americans, and a sober reminder that their own republic had no guarantee of success.

Viewed from the perspective of the twenty-first century, the electoral crisis might seem to have been almost comically overblown. Yet the electoral deadlock of 1801 stands as one of the two great political and constitutional crises in our nation's history. The participants believed that they were staring into an awful abyss and that all of the fruits of the American Revolution and the many accomplishments in its aftermath were in danger of being swept away in a civil war and a dismemberment of the Union.

II

The unofficial electoral vote count indicating a tie vote between Jefferson and Burr, which was to be officially certified on February 11, 1801, meant that under the Constitution the naming of the next president would become the responsibility of the House of Representatives, where each state would have one vote. Since there were sixteen states in 1801, the winning candidate would need nine votes for victory.[14]

It was not at all clear how the House of Representatives might vote. A majority of its members were Federalists. Nonetheless, the Federalists did not control the delegations in a majority of the states. Republicans controlled the delegations in New York, New Jersey, Pennsylvania, Virginia, North Carolina, Georgia, Kentucky, and Tennessee, while the Federalists had a majority of members in New Hampshire, Massachusetts, Rhode Island, Connecticut, Delaware, and South Carolina. Thus, the presumption was that Jefferson would receive the votes of eight of the sixteen states whose delegations were controlled by the Republicans, one short of a majority, while the Federalists would control the votes of six.[15] But what the Federalists would do remained a mystery. This left Maryland and Vermont, whose delegations were equally divided and most likely would not cast ballots.

The key player in this election drama was Aaron Burr. Four years earlier a number of Virginia Republicans had been suspicious about the New Yorker's loyalty to the Republican opposition when he was under consideration to be Jefferson's running mate in the 1796 election, and the suspicions had persisted even after his nomination. The Federalists had also viewed Burr as "unsettled in his politics" and someone who might "go over to the other [their] side."[16] A Federalist friend of Burr's even suggested in 1796 that the Federalists would do well to support Burr over Adams for president because it was mistakenly believed that Adams could not win. This plan was immediately scotched by another Federalist who argued that Burr would have no chance of being elected president because he did not even have the full support of the Republicans, who believed that "their views and his" were "opposite."[17]

Later, Burr had been insulted and deeply upset by the failure of the Virginians to support him as the vice presidential candidate in 1796, he having run a poor fourth in the balloting behind Adams, Jefferson, and Thomas Pinckney. Most embarrassingly, he had received only one out of a possible twenty-one Virginia Republican electoral votes. Thus, before agreeing to run on the Republican ticket again in 1800, he had insisted upon, and had been given assurances about, receiving full Republican support. But in dutifully following through on their promise to Burr and refusing to divert any votes away from him, the Republicans, including the Virginians, had contributed to the electoral crisis in 1800. In November, some Virginia Republicans had even worried that Burr might receive a *larger* number of electoral votes than Jefferson.[18]

Numerous Republican strategies for dealing with the electoral crisis of 1800–1801 were discussed in December, January, and early February. These included holding another national election, an idea that attracted little support since it would have been strictly extraconstitutional. Another proposal

Aaron Burr. Thomas Jefferson's vice presidential running mate in 1800, he earned the contempt of fellow Republicans by not publicly repudiating Federalist attempts to have him elected president in place of Jefferson. Aaron Burr by John Vanderlyn, 1809, oil on wood panel, 8 × 10 inches. Collection of the New-York Historical Society. Accession no.1859.2.

offered by Madison was for the current Federalist-dominated, lame-duck Congress to adjourn, opening the way for President Adams to summon the newly elected Seventh Congress dominated by Republicans to a special session to meet on March 4, the same day the terms of Adams and the members of the Sixth Congress were due to expire. This would give Jefferson the necessary votes in the House of Representatives to carry the election. Failing this, he recommended that on March 4, Jefferson and Burr themselves should call the Seventh Congress into special session. However, both of these suggested solutions were eventually deemed unfeasible. It was highly unlikely that the Federalist Sixth Congress would go along with the first and agree to adjourn, and both options raised serious constitutional questions.[19]

In mid-December, as it was becoming increasingly apparent that the resolution to the looming disaster would likely be in the hands of Burr, Jefferson sought to draw the New Yorker out by writing him an artfully crafted letter. Although at the time both men still thought, based on incomplete returns, that Jefferson would have at least a single electoral vote more than Burr and thus was destined to win the presidency with Burr as his vice president, Jefferson clearly was already concerned about a possible contingency—that the electoral vote between the two Republicans might be tied. And he raised that possibility in his letter. "Several of the high-flying federalists have expressed their hope that the two republican tickets may be equal," he said, and were determined "in that case to prevent a choice by the H of R, (which they are strong enough to do)."

Then, congratulating Burr on his election, Jefferson went on to cunningly and disarmingly open the possibility of Burr filling a grander and more rewarding position than the vice presidency within his administration. Burr was told that while the vice presidency was "more honorable, and doubtless more grateful to you than any station within the competence of the chief magistrate, yet for myself, and for the substantial service of the public, I feel most sensibly the loss we sustain of your aid in our new administration," for it "leaves a chasm in my arrangements which cannot be adequately filled up."[20]

It should be noted that the vice presidency in the early days of the republic—and even until the recent past—was a powerless position that seems to have been an afterthought of the Founders. In Article I of the Constitution, where the powers of Congress (importantly, not of the executive branch) are detailed, the role of the vice president is laid out: "The Vice President of the United States shall be President of the Senate, but shall have no Vote, unless they be equally divided." In Article II, in which the duties of the president are described, the Constitution specifies that upon the removal, death, resignation, or the inability of the president to perform his duties, the vice president shall become president.

And the first two vice presidents, Adams and Jefferson, had played no role whatsoever in either the Washington or Adams administrations. Not consulted on policy, nor regularly in touch with the president or his cabinet, they were neither fish nor fowl. Ostensibly members of the executive branch, they had no official or unofficial duties except a minor congressional one: presiding over and breaking tie votes in the Senate. The one attractive feature of the vice presidency was that it had been, up to 1800—at least in the case of Adams and potentially in that of Jefferson—the stepping-stone to the presidency.

Burr, writing Jefferson back the following week, was clearly interested in what alternative "service" or post Jefferson might offer him and vowed to "abandon the office of V.P. if it shall be thought that I can be more useful in any Active station." Furthermore, the New Yorker promised his Virginia running mate that any of the New Yorker's potential supporters who might be tempted to support him for the presidency were "perfectly informed of . . . [his] Wishes on the subject" and that he would "never think of diverting a single Vote" from Jefferson.[21]

This latter assertion was in line with Burr's declaration a week earlier to Maryland Republican Samuel Smith that he "would utterly disclaim all competition" with Jefferson and would have nothing to do with any possible entreaties from the Federalists.[22]

Burr's pledge of support, however, was not convincing to Jefferson and his supporters, nor for that matter was it to the Federalists, who continued to believe that Burr was "available." Burr's strategy, if he had one, is difficult to discern even in hindsight. Most Republicans and Federalists believed that he was cleverly biding his time, maintaining his support for and allegiance to Jefferson while also keeping his options open. These options, they suspected, included winning the presidency with Federalist support in the House of Representatives.

Much later James Madison even implied that an agent of Burr had *caused* the tie in the first place—Madison telling Jefferson that it had resulted from "false assurances dispatched at the critical moment to the electors of one state, that the votes of another would be different from what they proved to be." These "assurances," he alleged, could be attributed to one of Burr's "henchmen."[23]

Robert Goodloe Harper of South Carolina, a Federalist firebrand who had been a strong advocate of the Alien and Sedition Acts in 1798, wrote Burr immediately after the tie in the Electoral College had become known. The "language of the Democrats is, that you will yield your pretensions to their favorite" and support Jefferson in the upcoming House of Representatives balloting, he said. But Harper then advised Burr to look to his own benefit instead and "take no step whatever by which the choice of the House of Representatives can be impeded or embarrassed." Secrecy was essential, Harper conspiratorially asserted. Burr, he said, had to be discreet and keep "the game perfectly in . . . [his] hand" and not to answer Harper's letter "or any other that may be written . . . by a federalist; nor write to any of that party."[24]

Harper believed that the Federalists should support Burr unconditionally "without asking or expecting any assurances or Explanations respecting his future Administration." Rabidly anti-Jefferson, the Marylander was— according to the Republicans—one of those "desperadoes" willing to "go any lengths, to risqué every thing in opposition to Mr. Jefferson." To Harper, Jefferson's "Democratic Spirit" and "false Principles of Government" would severely endanger the future prospects of the country were he to become president.[25]

Burr's most recent biographer asserts that the Federalists were presumptuous in their claims to know what Burr's motives and objectives were. But they clearly did hope to be able to use Burr to fatally divide the Republicans or else to elevate the New Yorker to the presidency, and then relegate him to becoming a puppet under their control. One Federalist leader speculated that Burr would "not be able to administer the government without the aid of the federalists & this aid he cannot obtain unless his administration is federal."[26]

Many Federalists, however, made a more positive argument in support of Burr. One saw him as a "vigorous practical man" with a "strong and comprehensive mind . . . neither timid nor wavering: but firm, intrepid and energetic." The *Washington Federalist* also publicly praised Burr. Even though he has never "*penned a declaration of independence,*" it maintained, "*He has gallantly exposed his life in support of that declaration and for the protection of its* penn-man *[Jefferson]; He has been* liberal *of his* blood, *while* Mr. Jefferson *has only* hazarded *his* ink." And in another article, the same newspaper praised Burr as a man of action with a "strong and comprehensive mind" and a man not "timid nor wavering" but rather "firm, intrepid and energetic."[27]

At the end of December 1800, Republican Congressman Samuel Smith of Maryland received a letter from Burr that was shockingly different from the one Burr had written him a couple of weeks earlier. In it the New Yorker asserted that he would serve as president if elected by the House of Representatives. Reinforcing Smith's distress over this message was the rumor that a New York Federalist was in Washington lobbying Republicans to support Burr. Smith feared that if Burr's apparent declaration of his candidacy were to be made public, it might hearten his Federalist backers and tempt Middle Atlantic Republicans to change sides and support him.[28]

Attempting to soothe an angry Burr who was reacting to stories questioning his loyalty to the Republicans, Smith wrote him a letter back denying the allegation that the Virginians were "abusing" him. The Federalists "will attempt to disunite us" by floating rumors, Burr was told, and thus "we must not believe any thing that comes from them, we must be on our guards." But significantly, in an effort meant to also discourage any effort by Burr to solicit Republican support for the presidency, Smith emphatically stated that the "Democrats" of eight states were united and "*immovable*" in support of Jefferson and absolutely committed "to continue to the End of the session to vote" for him.[29] This last point was important, since Smith's vote was critical in maintaining the deadlock in the Maryland congressional delegation. Without Smith's vote, the Maryland delegation would be carried by the Federalists. In his letter Smith also signaled to Burr that he as well as other Republicans was unavailable as a supporter of a Burr presidential candidacy.

Burr defended himself in a January response to Smith by arguing that he was not a competitor with Jefferson for the presidency and denying that he had "said or written to any one a word" that contradicted his earlier pledge not to challenge the Virginian. And later in a letter to Jefferson intended to reassure his running mate of his loyalty, Burr indignantly condemned "the most malignant Spirit of slander and intrigue" that was "calculated to disturb our harmony."[30]

Despite Burr's denials, however, in late December and early January many Federalists and Republicans believed that the New Yorker's candidacy for the presidency was in play.

So, in hindsight, what is to be made of Burr's intentions? The chronology perhaps offers a partial explanation. When Burr wrote Jefferson in mid-December assuring him of his support, the final electoral vote totals were unknown, and indeed some reports indicated that Jefferson had won, thanks to a Vermont elector who supposedly had cast his second vote for him. By the end of the year, however, after it had become clear that both men were unofficially tied with seventy-three Electoral College votes apiece, Burr might have become more amenable to considering his own candidacy for the top position.[31]

Furthermore, while Burr privately disclaimed and renounced his interest in the presidency, he never did so publicly. And this suggests that despite the assurances he made to Jefferson and the Republicans to the contrary, he did not want to jeopardize any chance he had to become president. Certainly, rumor upon rumor about Burr's possible apostasy circulated throughout the insular Washington community. And based upon the assumption that if Burr were to be elected president he would serve, the Federalists lobbied certain Republicans who, they believed, could be induced to become possible defectors. These included Smith of Maryland, Edward Livingston of New York, and James Linn of New Jersey. Jefferson himself understood that Burr had "agents" at work in Washington who were hoping to entice Republicans to support him.

Hamilton, who was unalterably opposed to Burr's candidacy, stated that the Republicans "as a body prefer Jefferson, but among them are many who will be better suited by the *dashing projecting* spirit of *Burr.*" These Republicans, after initially supporting Jefferson, he predicted, "will go over to Mr. Burr," especially Livingston, who "has declared among his friends that his first ballot will be for Jefferson, his second for Burr."[32]

III

The strategy involving elevating Burr to the presidency was only one of a number of possible schemes the Federalists discussed in the weeks before the House of Representatives began to ballot in February. Whereas the election of Burr to the presidency in place of Jefferson was clearly contrary to the public will, another plan that bypassed both Republican frontrunners was overtly usurpatious. As early as December 1, Gouverneur Morris, a prominent New York Federalist, wrote Hamilton that some Federalists planned "to prevent any Election and thereby throw the Government into the Hands of a President [pro tempore] of the Senate."[33]

This Federalist proposal, while provocative and perilous, was not that farfetched. Under the provisions of a 1792 statute, it was provided that "in case of removal, death, resignation or inability both of the President and Vice President of the United States, the President of the Senate pro Tempore, and in case there shall be no President of the Senate, then the Speaker of the House of Representatives, for the time being shall act as President of the United States until the disability be removed or a President shall be elected."[34]

In order to implement this plan, the Federalists would need to forestall any presidential election by the House of Representatives. And with Adams's and Congress's term of office expiring on March 4, the ensuing vacancy in the office of the president would be filled by the Federalists under the provisions of the 1792 statute. This would guarantee that a Federalist would be named president, since the Federalists controlled both houses of Congress.[35]

Jefferson was aware of this idea as early as December 19, when he wrote Madison reporting that the anticipated nondecision in the Electoral College was producing "great dismay & gloom on the republican gentlemen here" and "equal exultation on the federalists, who openly declare they will prevent an election" and name a president pro tem of the Senate to be president. It was a plan that Jefferson claimed the Federalists saw as "only . . . a *stretch* of the constitution." February, he ruefully concluded, "will present us storms of a new character."[36]

Apparently, the proposal to elevate the president pro tem of the Senate to the presidency was further discussed in January by the Federalist caucus convened for the "express object of organizing measures for defeating the election of Mr. Jefferson" or "of the Election of a President." Unable to reach an accord on a strategy, however, the caucus "broke up without concluding upon any decisive measures."[37]

The inability of the caucus to agree upon a course of action indicated a split among the Federalists about how to proceed. Hamilton, although aghast by the prospect of either a Jefferson or a Burr administration, opposed the plan to block an election in the House of Representatives. He warned that while "the Federalists may be disposed to play the game of preventing an election and leaving Executive power in the hands of a future President of the Senate," this, "if it could succeed, would be . . . a most dangerous and unbecoming policy."[38] Perhaps smarting over his disappointing loss, President Adams somewhat surprisingly disagreed, declaring that there was "no more danger of a political convulsion, if a President, *pro tempore*, of the Senate, or a Secretary of State, or Speaker of the House, should be made President by Congress, than if Mr. Jefferson or Mr. Burr is declared such."[39]

For their part, Jefferson and the Republicans vowed to resist, by force if necessary, any Federalist ploy whereby the election would be set aside and the Federalists would seize power by elevating a president pro tem of the Senate to the presidency. Jefferson later reflected on this possible usurpation of power by the Federalists in a diary entry, contending that such radical action would have been "a very dangerous experiment" that would have produced "resistance by force." Such irresponsible and extreme Federalist action, he said, would have brought "a suspension of the federal government, for want of a head" and would have opened "upon us an abyss, at which every sincere patriot must shudder."[40]

As the February date for balloting drew near, a kind of hysteria increasingly pervaded Washington. At least some Republicans feared that extreme and violent action would be taken by the Federalists. The Republican *General Advertiser*, for instance, charged that the Federalists were plotting to renew the expiring Sedition Act and to mobilize and assemble in the capital a "considerable . . . portion of the Marines" to support by arms their efforts to contravene the will of the people and supplant Jefferson with a Federalist minion.[41] An even more incredible scenario was put forth by Henry Brackenridge of Pennsylvania in a letter to Jefferson. He visualized Hamilton, Cromwell-like, at the head of an army, capturing military arsenals and forts in a desperate Federalist effort to retain power.[42]

IV

But while all sorts of plots and subplots, rumors and counter-rumors, were hatched, discussed, and circulated through the Washington incubator, most Federalists by early 1801 seem to have concluded that the best course of action was to launch an immediate effort to support Burr's election. For the Federalists, supporting Burr would be the least dangerous alternative, and one that would still leave open other options. Burr's election, they reasoned, might be achieved by intimidating wavering Republicans desperately hoping to prevent a constitutional crisis. Or, failing this, support for Burr might at least lead to an impasse and no election, and this might well open up an opportunity for a Federalist to be appointed by Congress.

The question Federalist supporters of Burr had to answer for their colleagues and potential renegade Middle State Republicans was this: why should Burr be supported? One argument made by Theodore Sedgwick was that Jefferson was far more dangerous than Burr because Jefferson had been "hostile to all those great systems of Administration" that had been the foundation for "our national prosperity." Furthermore, Jefferson's support for the principle of states' rights was decried by the Speaker of the House of Representatives. It would undermine the national government, he said, and render it as ineffective as the government under the Articles of Confederation had been.

In contrast to Jefferson, Sedgwick explained, Burr was "a mere matter-of-fact man" who held "no pernicious theories" and whose "very selfishness prevents his entertaining any mischievous predilections for foreign nations" (an obvious jab at Jefferson for his support of France). In a less than ringing endorsement, the speaker lamely concluded that Burr's "unworthiness is neither so extensively known, nor so conclusive as that of . . . [Jefferson]." Thus, he saw the Federalists as reduced to embracing either a bad choice or a worse one and trying to at least avoid being "disgraced . . . by assenting to the election of Jefferson."[43]

Another Federalist argument for Burr was that his elevation to the presidency would destroy the Republicans by "sow[ing] among them . . . seeds of a mortal division." Federalist support of Burr "against the hearty opposition of the Jacobins," it was argued, would so wound and split the Republicans that it would create an "incurable" breach.

In addition, a Burr presidency founded on Federalist backing was envisioned as resulting in the New Yorker becoming the Federalists' creature, for he "must depend on good men for his support and that support he cannot receive but by a conformity to their views."[44]

The most compelling and powerful motive behind the Federalists' support for Burr, however, was their deeply felt fear of the Virginians' political power—a fear underlain by a profound sectional antagonism. To the Federalists, Virginia, the wealthiest and most populous state in the Union, was striving for political dominance.[45]

Federalist James Bayard from Delaware, who would later play a reluctant but key role in the election, reflected this concern about what he called the "State ambition of Virginia." The "Faction who govern . . . [Virginia] aim to govern the UStates," he was convinced, and "Virginia will never be satisfied, but when this state of things exists."[46] Bayard was outraged by what he deemed the hypocrisy of the Virginians. They were, he pointed out, "Men who can count in their train a hundred slaves, whose large domains, like feudal barons, are people[d] with the humblest vassals." These self-styled "democrats" and "high priests of liberty are zealously proclaiming freedom on one hand while on the other they are rivetting the chains of slavery."[47]

V

As the momentum to support Burr increased within Federalist ranks, Hamilton became more frantic in his opposition to the New Yorker, claiming that there was no one in his home state who did not believe that Burr was the "most unfit man in the U.S. for the office of President."[48] "For heaven's sake let not the Federalist party be responsible for the elevation of this Man," he pleaded.[49]

Burr's "private character is not defended by his most partial friends," Hamilton insisted. He "is bankrupt beyond redemption except by the plunder of his country," and "he will certainly disturb our institutions to secure to himself *permanent power* and with it *wealth*."[50] Burr, Hamilton charged, was a "profligate; a voluptuary in the extreme, with uncommon habits of expense;" a debtor with all "his visible property . . . deeply mortgaged;" and someone who had "*constantly* sided with the party hostile to federal measures before and since the present constitution."[51]

Federalists who imagined that Burr would be a passive sycophant beholden to them for their support were misguided, Hamilton said, for Burr would attract the "young and profligate" and the "worst men of all parties." Hamilton even questioned Burr's patriotism and discounted his military record, avowing that Burr had resigned from the army "at a critical period" of the Revolutionary War by faking poor health.[52]

Hamilton said he recognized that Jefferson was only marginally superior to Burr. The Virginian was "crafty and persevering," not "very mindful of the truth," and "a contemptible hypocrite." Yet he was preferable because "a true estimate of Mr. J's character warrants the expectation of a temporizing rather than a violent system." Burr, however, was much more dangerous, for he was a man "of *extreme and irregular* ambition," a man "far more *cunning* than *wise*, far more *dexterous* than *able*," and "inferior in real ability to Jefferson." Hamilton envisioned Burr as a person who might even blunder into a war with England that would be a "death warrant" for the country. [53]

The trump card of Hamilton's anti-Burr tirade was his claim that by supporting Burr the Federalists would disgrace themselves and would become a "disorganized and contemptible party." On the other hand, if they maintained a principled opposition to a Jefferson administration, they would gain stature and become formidable and cohesive.[54]

However, Jefferson should not get a free pass to the presidency, Hamilton advised his Federalist colleagues. In return for the Federalists' withdrawal of their support for Burr, Jefferson should be forced to give certain assurances. He would have to agree to support the Federalist fiscal system, sustain American neutrality, implement the plan to increase the navy, and continue in office all Federalists, with only a few limited exceptions.

For the most part, Hamilton's condemnation of Burr fell on deaf ears. Having played a powerful leadership role in shaping Federalist policy both in and out of office during the 1790s, Hamilton was puzzled and distressed by his seeming inability to convince his colleagues of Burr's unfitness for the presidency. No doubt the loss of Washington as his powerful patron as well as his intemperate outburst against Adams in the fall of 1800 were important factors contributing to the diminution of his influence.

One of Hamilton's colleagues bemoaned that an "opinion has grown . . . which at present obtains almost universally, that [Hamilton's] character *is radically deficient in discretion,* and therefore the federalists ask, what avail the most preeminent talents—the most distinguished patriotism—without the important quality of discretion?" Sorrowfully, it was concluded, Hamilton was "considered as an unfit head of the party," and because of that the Federalists were "without a rallying point."[55]

What animated Hamilton's almost frenzied fear of Burr's election? One clue, perhaps, lies in Hamilton's *Federalist 68* discussion of the qualifications and characteristics that would be required of a president. Granted that his objective at the time he was writing the essay—in 1787–1788, prior to the adoption of the Constitution—was to convince Americans that they had little to fear from the increased power of the chief executive in the new Constitution, the discussion nevertheless reflects Hamilton's very positive view of strong leadership.

The Electoral College system, he said in describing the careful way a president would be chosen, was a way of filtering and screening candidates that would afford "a moral certainty that the office of the President will seldom fall to the lot of any man who is not in an eminent degree endowed with the requisite qualifications."

Popularity in an individual state might result from "talents for low intrigue, and little arts of popularity may alone suffice to elevate a man to the first honors." But on the national level, "it will require other talents, and a different kind of merit, to establish him in the esteem and confidence of the whole Union." This would ensure that the presidency would be "filled by characters pre-eminent for ability and virtue."[56] Or, in one historian's words, Hamilton saw the president as being "a patriotic leader . . . above party . . . [and able] to furnish leadership that was fundamentally moral and in accord with a higher law."[57]

To Hamilton, then, it was painfully and frighteningly clear that Burr, as one of those individuals with "talents for low intrigue, and little arts of popularity," failed to measure up.[58] And Burr had other Federalist detractors as well.

VI

Thus, on the eve of the announcement of the official vote count, after which the House of Representatives would be given the responsibility for solving the electoral crisis, Republicans were discussing a number of strategies to deal with the various possible scenarios. The likely outcomes, as they saw them, were: Jefferson being elected and serving as president; Burr being elected (and then either serving or resigning in favor of Jefferson); the deadlock being extended beyond the end of the presidential term on March 4 (possibly allowing the Federalists to appoint the president pro tem of the Senate to the office of chief executive); the calling of a new election; or the issuance of a joint request by Jefferson and Burr for an early meeting of the next, Republican-dominated Congress to solve the stalemate.[59]

Initially upon arriving in the capital in early January 1801, Albert Gallatin had been cautiously optimistic, feeling hopeful that the more moderate Federalists in Maryland, Delaware, and Vermont might "acquies[ce] in Mr. Jefferson's election."[60] But he soon changed his mind.

As he came up against the hardening of the Federalist opposition to Jefferson, he began to despair of the possibility of a harmonious settlement to the deadlock, particularly fearing the possibility that "violent Federals" would "attempt to defeat the election [of Jefferson] under pretence of voting for Burr." This anticipated Federalist stonewalling in order to prevent a resolution of the crisis was seen by him as a blatant tactic designed to bring about a usurpation of power and one that would "most certainly . . . [be] resisted."[61]

Gallatin was accurate in his analysis of the motives of the more radical Federalists, as stories persisted that some of them did indeed want to prolong the impasse and force the "appoint[ment of] a [Federalist] president pro tem [of the Senate] who will act as the president of the U.S."[62]

In a draft memorandum sent to Jefferson as well as other Republican leaders, Gallatin outlined the possible scenarios and suggested appropriate Republican responses. Nevertheless, certain that Jefferson's eight votes in the House of Representatives were secure and that Burr supporters could not mobilize enough support to get the New Yorker elected, Gallatin argued that in the end the Federalists would either be forced to yield to Jefferson's election or else to pursue a more dangerous action by assuming power and ignoring the will of the people as expressed through the election.

If the Federalists chose to pursue this latter tactic and attempted to seize executive power, that action, Gallatin contended, had to be "resisted by freemen whenever they have the power of resisting"—for to "admit a contrary doctrine would justify submission in every case, and encourage usurpation for ever hereafter."

It was necessary for Republicans to decide, however, how they could resist most effectively, Gallatin maintained. In those states where the state government supported the usurpation, "the minority must submit for a while, because they are under actual coercion," he said.

On the other hand, in Republican-controlled states, his words echoing the strong states' rights sentiments of the Kentucky and Virginia resolutions,

Gallatin recommended that any measure or policy initiated by a usurper president should be ignored. Where the Republicans control a state government, "we shall run no risk of civil war by refusing to obey only those acts which may flow from the usurper as President." Thus, while certain federal laws, such as the "collection of duties, payment of debt, etc.," should be strictly adhered to, all proposals coming from a usurper president, especially the calling up of the militia, should be disobeyed.

Still, all of this, he advised, would have to be carried out deliberately and with great discretion and caution in order to avoid and thwart "every partial insurrection, or even individual act of resistance, except when supported by the laws of the particular state."

Gallatin also brought up again the option of having a new election if efforts to break the impasse in the House of Representatives failed. But he pointed out that such a tactic had political dangers, since the Federalists controlled at least one house of the state legislatures in New York, Pennsylvania, Maryland, and South Carolina. These Federalist-controlled houses might be able to block these states, which had given thirty-three electoral votes to the Republicans in 1800, from participating in any new election. The math, Gallatin pointed out, was against the Republicans here because the forty-nine votes the Federalists would be guaranteed in New England, New Jersey, and Delaware would defeat the forty-four assured votes the Republicans could count on from Virginia, North Carolina, Georgia, Kentucky, and Tennessee.

But Gallatin saw an even greater potential danger in a new election. It might cause a "reanimation of the hopes and exertions of the Federal party in some States, and despair of success on the part of the Republicans." And this further inflaming of the political and sectional antagonisms might lead to a possible "dissolution of the Union."[63]

Although Gallatin strenuously objected to the idea of a new election, apparently a few other Republicans believed, at least for a while, that it might be an suitable option. The Pennsylvanian told his wife that despite his opposition to the idea, he might "be overruled by our friends."[64] However, in the end most Republicans evidently did agree with Gallatin, and the new election alternative was not seriously entertained.

VII

Thus, with the tie in the Electoral College between Jefferson and Burr, the new republic, with only twelve years of history under its new Constitution, now had come face-to-face with a severe political crisis; and a group of isolated and bitterly divided members of a lame-duck House of Representatives would soon be called upon to deal with it. There was no clear path to a solution. Rumors abounded, and both sides seem to have been resolved to pursue a course of action that counted on the other side to blink first.

Despite their serious doubts and fears, most Republicans believed that, if they were resolute in their support of Jefferson, the Federalists would flinch before precipitating a constitutional crisis. Moderate Federalists from Vermont, Delaware, and Maryland, it was reasoned, would feel vulnerable and be susceptible to pressure.[65] In the end, the Republicans concluded their opponents would come to their senses, abandon Burr, and bring an end to the stalemate.

The Federalists, although desperate to retain power, also did not seem ready to pursue any of the more radical schemes that were being proposed. They appear to have been in general agreement that supporting Burr was the alternative most likely to be successful in dealing with the crisis that was heading toward destroying the Union. In order to elevate Burr to the presidency, they needed to convince some Middle State Republicans to switch their allegiances to the New Yorker, and they had received some encouraging reports that Federalist James Bayard of Delaware was offering government positions in a Burr administration to Republicans Samuel Smith of Maryland and Edward Livingston of New York in exchange for their betrayal of Jefferson.

10 THE CRISIS RESOLVED

The Federalists "meant to go without a constitution and take the risk of a Civil War."
—*James Bayard, February 1801*

I

A severe snowstorm hit the new capital on Wednesday, February 11, making travel from the various boarding houses to the capitol building difficult. Nonetheless, at noon, members of both houses of Congress met in the Senate chamber to witness the president of the Senate Thomas Jefferson fulfill his constitutional duty to, "in the presence of the Senate and House of Representatives, open all of the certificates, and," according to Article II, "the Votes shall then be counted." As expected, Jefferson's report of the official, certified election results mirrored the unofficial returns that had been circulating in Washington for weeks. It showed Jefferson and Burr to have seventy-three votes each, Adams sixty-five, Pinckney sixty-four, and John Jay one.

Unbeknownst to most, if not all, the assembled members of Congress, however, was a potential complication that could have shaken the new government and fundamentally altered the dynamic of the election. There were irregularities in regard to the official report of the balloting in Georgia. That state's four votes for Jefferson and four votes for Burr had not been properly certified.

Interestingly, Jefferson did not raise questions about or make public the improper reporting by Georgia officials. And subsequent reports did confirm that, while the state had improperly reported its electoral vote, it was an *accurate* tally.

One historian who has studied this situation has observed that "it was bad lawyering, not fraud, that accounted for . . . [Georgia's] defective ballots."[1]

Nonetheless, however, had the Georgia votes been invalidated, it would have reduced each of Jefferson's and Burr's vote totals to sixty-nine, one vote shy of the seventy votes needed for each to have a majority of the possible one hundred and thirty-eight electoral votes. Thus, as specified in the Constitution, this would have meant that, in addition to Jefferson and Burr, the three Federalist vote getters would have become eligible to be candidates for the presidency on an equal footing with Jefferson and Burr. And, having all five candidates, instead of just the two Republican front runners, competing for votes would have completely changed the nature of the election. With Adams, Pinckney, and John Jay back in contention, the possible outcomes would have increased dramatically. Given the unpopularity of Adams with a number of members of his own party, for instance, the South Carolinian might have had great appeal to southern Republicans if a Federalist-led impasse in the House had blocked Jefferson's election.

However, since House members were not made aware of this potentially history altering situation with the problematic Georgia ballots, after hearing the official announcement of the electoral results they returned to their own chamber to begin to resolve the tie vote in the Electoral College between Jefferson and Burr. The representatives that made up each state delegation sat together so that they could caucus and then report their votes. Nobody knew how long they would be there. What *was* known was that the House had resolved that it would continue in session until the deadlock was broken. It had been agreed that no other business would come before the chamber until a decision had been reached.

So, closeted in the only partially completed capitol building in the isolated new capital of Washington, D.C., the congressmen began their deliberations. And, as they did, Americans around the country waited, their attention focused on what these bitterly divided men would decide—and also on the rumors circulating in their midst about possible civil unrest and even armed conflict.

The first ballot, taken at 1 P.M., went as expected. Jefferson received support from the eight states whose delegations were controlled by the Republicans: New York, New Jersey, Pennsylvania, Virginia, North Carolina, Kentucky, Georgia, and Tennessee. Burr received support from the six states whose delegations were controlled by the Federalists: New Hampshire, Massachusetts, Rhode Island, Connecticut, Delaware, and South Carolina. The delegations of two states, Vermont and Maryland, were evenly split, so they

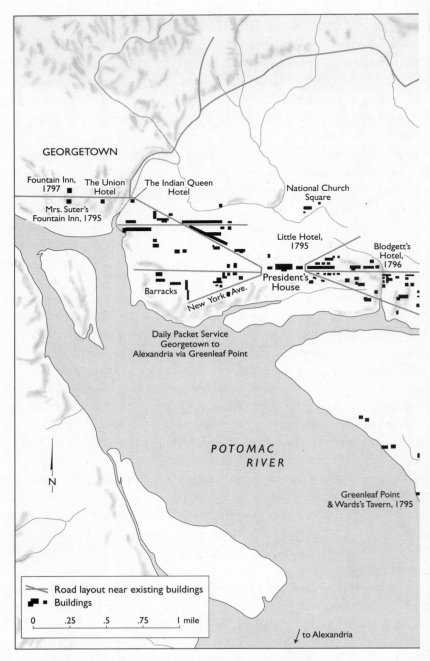

GEORGETOWN

Fountain Inn, 1797   The Union Hotel

The Indian Queen Hotel

National Church Square

Mrs. Suter's Fountain Inn, 1795

Little Hotel, 1795

Blodgett's Hotel, 1796

President's House

Barracks

New York Ave.

Daily Packet Service
Georgetown to
Alexandria via Greenleaf Point

POTOMAC
RIVER

N

Greenleaf Point
& Wards's Tavern, 1795

Road layout near existing buildings
Buildings

0   .25   .5   .75   1 mile

to Alexandria

*Map of Washington, D.C., in 1800. (Map by historian Judd Olshan
and cartographer Bill Nelson)*

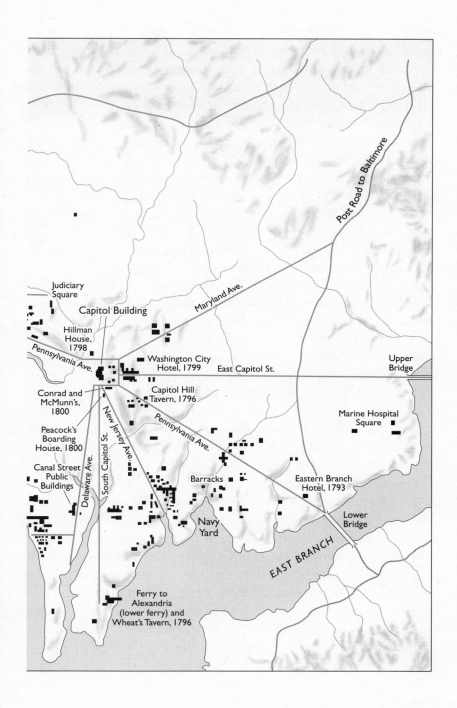

Judiciary
Square

Capitol Building

Hillman
House,
1798

Pennsylvania Ave.

Washington City
Hotel, 1799

East Capitol St.

Maryland Ave.

Post Road to Baltimore

Upper
Bridge

Conrad and
McMunn's,
1800

Capitol Hill
Tavern, 1796

Peacock's
Boarding
House, 1800

New Jersey Ave.

Pennsylvania Ave.

Marine Hospital
Square

Canal Street
Public
Buildings

Delaware Ave.

South Capitol St.

Barracks

Eastern Branch
Hotel, 1793

Navy
Yard

Lower
Bridge

EAST BRANCH

Ferry to
Alexandria
(lower ferry) and
Wheat's Tavern, 1796

could not vote.[3] Since nine votes were required for a decision, the House continued to ballot during the rest of the day and hourly through the night until 8 A.M. the next morning, Thursday the 12th. In all, twenty-seven votes were taken, with an eight-to-six result each time. At that point, Gallatin reported to his wife, the House agreed "to suspend the further balloting till twelve o'clock, and during that time I went to sleep."

The nineteen-hour marathon of conversations, caucuses, and day-and-night voting that had continued until Thursday morning had been mentally and physically exhausting. One House member described his colleagues as having looked "banged badly" as a result of the ordeal. And a newspaper reported that it was "ludicrous to see some . . . [representatives] running with anxiety from the committee rooms, with their nightcaps on."[4]

Republican Joseph Nicholson of Maryland had been quite ill at the beginning of the session but had made the heroic decision to risk his health and participate anyway. Knowing that if he failed to cast a vote, the Maryland vote would no longer be tied and would go to Burr, Nicholson's friends had carried him the two miles from his lodgings to the capitol through the snowstorm. Gallatin wrote his wife, "A bed was fixed for him [Nicholson] in the committee room, and he lay there and voted all night the 11th to 12th," with his wife carrying his vote on every ballot onto the floor of the House to give to the clerk. One admiring Federalist feared that the Marylander's actions might kill him, asserting, "I would not thus expose myself for any President on Earth." Apparently, however, the bitter weather and the makeshift bed in a cold and drafty room had no ill effects, as Gallatin reported later that Nicholson "recovered amazingly, notwithstanding the risk he ran in exposing himself to cold."[5]

When the twenty-eighth vote at the Thursday session continued the deadlock, it was agreed that the next ballot would not be until the following day, Friday the thirteenth. Nonetheless, stories continued to circulate that the Federalists were trying to entice potentially unsettled and apprehensive Republicans to switch their votes, believing that the "Jeffersonians can acquiesce in Burr with less reproach than the federalists can agree to Jefferson." Jefferson was told, for example, that Federalist James Bayard of Delaware had offered the post of secretary of the navy to Republican Samuel Smith if Smith would change his vote to Burr. And Bayard had said that he had been "authorized to make the offer."[6]

The next day, in the midst of continued widespread gossiping, fearmongering, and contingency planning, the House of Representatives once again tried to resolve the crisis. However, the standoff persisted with the twenty-ninth vote. Neither side seemed willing to concede or compromise. Another balloting was not called for until the next day, Saturday the fourteenth, during which the thirtieth, thirty-first, thirty-second, and thirty-third canvasses were taken. They yielded the same result.

II

Jefferson had clearly had enough. On Saturday the fourteenth, the day the House completed four inconclusive ballots, he paid a call on President Adams at the president's home, only later to be called the White House. During that visit, the alarmed vice president recounted years later, he warned Adams against any Federalist attempt at a coup d'etat and put him on notice that any congressional usurpation would be opposed by force. He then asked Adams to try to prevent "this desperate measure."

In response, Jefferson went on, Adams became angrier than Jefferson had ever seen him, testily answering that the Virginian's election was within his "own power." All Jefferson had to do, he said, was to vow he would "do justice to the public creditors, maintain the navy, and not disturb those holding office, and the government . . . [would] instantly be put into . . . [his] hands." These were similar conditions to the ones Hamilton had outlined a month earlier as the price Federalists should insist on before agreeing to a Jefferson presidency.

Jefferson replied saying that he had never done anything in his public or private life that would lead anyone to doubt his "fidelity to the public engagements." On the other hand, he told Adams, he would "not come into the government by capitulation," nor enter it, "but in perfect freedom to follow the dictates of my own judgment." Jefferson then changed the subject of the conversation and soon left, commenting later that it was "the first time in our lives we had ever parted with anything like dissatisfaction."[7]

The next day Jefferson reported to Governor James Monroe of Virginia that the Federalists had been told that he would not make deals with them and "would not receive the government on capitulation." The Federalists had been further warned "openly and firmly," he said, that if they attempted to usurp power by blocking an election in the House and putting a Federalist president pro tem of the Senate in the presidency on March 4, this would be opposed by force. The "day such an act passed, the middle States would arm, and . . . no such usurpation, even for a single day, should be submitted to." Finally, the Federalists had been told that the Republicans were thinking about requesting "a convention to re-organize the government, and to amend it." The "very word convention gives them the horrors," Jefferson observed, "as in the present democratical spirit of America, they fear they should lose some of the favorite morsels of the constitution."[8]

Jefferson's admonition that force would be used to combat a "congressional usurpation" was not just an empty threat. Two key Republican governors, both with distinguished records of serving their country—James Monroe of Virginia and Thomas McKean of Pennsylvania—clearly thought that the situation could lead to a violent confrontation.

McKean had been a delegate to the Stamp Act Congress as well as to the Continental and the Articles of Confederation congresses. Initially a resident and officeholder in Delaware, he held office for a time in both Delaware and Pennsylvania before settling permanently in the latter state. Opposed to the radical 1776 Pennsylvania constitution, he nonetheless served as chief justice under that frame of government before his years as governor of the state from 1799 to 1808.

In the summer of 1800, Virginia governor James Monroe had sent a congratulatory letter to McKean after his election to the governorship, suggesting a political alliance between the two most populous states in the country. McKean's election, Monroe contended, marked the beginning "of a change in our political system, which promised to restore our country to the state it formerly enjoyed" and to safeguard "those liberties we acquired by our revolution, and which ought never to have been put in danger." Therefore McKean and the Keystone State, Monroe stressed, were essential in promoting "the sacred cause of our country."[9]

As the balloting in the House of Representatives progressed, then, both governors followed the events in Washington intently, maintaining daily contact with agents in the capital. Monroe even believed that the "state of things" was so "critical and alarming" that he created a "chain of expresses" between Richmond and Washington that involved messengers riding on the road "day and night with the dispatches entrusted to their care."[10]

Both governors were also in close contact with the legislatures of their respective states in the event that a crisis in Washington might necessitate some kind of legislative action. The Pennsylvania legislature was kept in session by McKean, while Monroe stood ready to call the Virginia legislature into session "without delay" if "any plan of usurpation [were to] be attempted at the federal town."[11]

McKean had made preparations, if necessary, to take some drastic steps— including the use of force—to prevent a "usurper" from ascending to the presidency. In a letter written to Jefferson about a month after the crisis was resolved, the Pennsylvania governor outlined the plans he had made and arrangements he had undertaken at the time. The militia, he said, "would have been warned to be ready, arms for upward of twenty thousand were secured, brass field pieces etc. etc. and an order would have been issued for the arresting and bringing to justice every Member of Congress and other persons found in Pennsylvania who should have been concerned in the treason." In addition, a proclamation would have been delivered "enjoining obedience on all officers civilian and military and the citizens of this State to you as President and Mr. Burr as Vice President."[12]

Governor Monroe was also preparing for a possible armed clash with the Federalist central government. Because he was fearful that a large stock of weapons captured from the British at the end of the Revolution and later stored in a federal arsenal at New London, Virginia, might be used against the state by federal forces, he sent a Republican militia officer to spy on the arsenal. From this reconnaissance mission the governor learned that the facility contained "4000 excellent muskets and bayonets with about 3000 cartridge boxes" as well as "two good brass field pieces with their carriages and a very large quantity of musket cartridges, powder and ball." Worried that federal authorities might remove these arms from Virginia, Monroe instructed his informant to recruit local militia men who were loyal Republicans to intercept any attempted transfer of these arms from the state.[13]

And the newspapers, especially those sympathetic to the Republicans, clearly saw the nation's future as in jeopardy, taking seriously the threats of violence, civil war, and disunion.

The Republican *General Advertiser* reported that the "Anglofederalists," as the Federalists were styled in an effort to cast them as stooges of England, were prepared to initiate an armed conflict that would destroy the Union unless Pinckney should be chosen president. Already, the paper continued, the Federalists were using intimidating and aggressive language with their threats to burn "the constitution . . . at the point of a bayonet," to assassinate Jefferson, or to "support a usurper" with "70,000 Massachusetts militia."[14] Another Republican newspaper warned that if the Federalists refused to allow the rightful election of Jefferson, the federal government would be disbanded as of March 4, when the present government's term expired.[15]

The *Washington Federalist* also saw the country as facing a "momentous" disaster but did not agree on the cause. It charged that it was the excesses of liberty that were threatening public order, and it ridiculed Republican warnings of a possible civil war, predicting that any disorder would be easily put down by the force of the authorities.

The "tumultuous meetings of a set of factious foreigners in Pennsylvania, or a few *fighting* bacchanals of Virginia" were not representative of the American people, the paper scornfully asserted, describing threats like those coming from Pennsylvania and Virginia as preposterous and absurd. The militias in those two states, it went on, were inept and would quickly be overwhelmed by government forces aided by "the militia of Massachusetts consisting of 70,000 (*regulars let us call them*) in arms" united with militias from "New Hampshire and Connecticut . . . [along] with half the number of at least the citizens of eleven other states ranged under the federal banner in support of the Constitution." This mighty force would easily crush the Virginia and Pennsylvania militias, who were "untrained and farcically perform . . . the manual exercise with cornstalks instead of muskets."[16]

III

With all the passions aroused by the talk about possible conflict, the Republican leadership believed it was absolutely essential that the public peace be maintained outside Washington during the voting, worrying that over-zealous followers, frustrated by the events in the capital, might take matters into their own hands and initiate some form of violent action. After hearing a rumor that "the people had seized the public arms" in Philadelphia, which later turned out to be false, Gallatin wrote a 3 A.M. note to A. J. Dallas in Philadelphia condemning any precipitous action and pleading with his colleague to by "all means preserve the city quiet." Dallas was further instructed that "anything which could be construed into a commotion would be fatal to us."[17] Any provocative action that might arouse negative public opinion against the Republicans, Gallatin feared, would give the Federalists a legitimate excuse to react harshly against what they would surely consider to be an insurrection against the government.

Gallatin, however, was assured by John Beckley, the longtime Republican loyalist and political strategist from Philadelphia, that while the city's Republicans were on high alert, and steadfast in their dedication to meet and defeat any Federalist provocation, they were "solemn, calm and deliberate" and had not engaged in any confrontational actions.

Nonetheless, Beckley went on, the city's Republicans were sending letters to every Pennsylvania member of Congress vowing that, if an act of usurpation passed Congress, that would be "the first day of revolution and civil War." Furthermore, Beckley informed Gallatin that if such an act were to be passed, Republican congressmen had the responsibility "to solemnly protest against the Act, appeal to their constituents and the World and [to] withdraw from Congress." Beckley also relayed the disturbing news that local Federalists had confiscated "several hundred stands of arms and 18 pieces of cannon, heretofore in the hands of the [Pennsylvania] Militia . . . [and moved them] into the public arsenals of the U.S."[18]

Greatly intensifying the widespread apprehension about a possible outbreak of violence and civil unrest were the armed militias in the various states that could be used, it was feared, for political purposes. The organization of these state militias had been a response, at least in part, to the 1792 law passed by Congress requiring universal militia service for able-bodied males. However, since the federal government provided little regulation and oversight, much of the organization and responsibility for enforcement of this law was left to the states.

And while information about militias and their political role is sketchy, they were important institutions that state and federal authorities could call upon not only to defend the country against an external foe but also to restore and maintain public order in the event of an internal rebellion or insurrection. Indeed, militias had been instrumental in putting down the Whiskey and Fries rebellions in Pennsylvania.

The militias' role was further complicated in Pennsylvania, and most likely in other states as well, by the two-tiered militia system that had evolved. There were public militia organizations, often made up of the less affluent and workingmen who had little or no social standing, but there were also private or volunteer militia companies, usually composed of the wealthier elites. Membership in either fulfilled the universal militia service requirement.

Resplendent in their colorful uniforms and bearing fancy arms, the private companies marched and played a very visible role in public celebrations, such as those on Washington's birthday and the Fourth of July. In addition, some of these private companies doubled as social clubs that "kept close ties with elite fraternities such as the Society of the Cincinnati."[19]

The danger of the private militia companies was that they could be used to intimidate local populations or to defend or promote the fortunes of a political party. In Virginia, for example, the Federalists organized private militia companies in Richmond and Petersburg, which, it was explained, was for the explicit purpose of frightening the "sans culottes,"[20] or lower classes. And one historian of Philadelphia has concluded that there is "good evidence" that in that city the officers in the private militias were associated with "political party activity."[21]

William Duane, the intrepid Republican editor of the *Aurora* in Philadelphia, had organized a Republican "militia Legion," a force made up of artisans, laborers, and immigrants from working-class neighborhoods, to counterbalance the more elite Federalist militias in the city. In addition to its role in making appearances at public festivals and celebrations, the Legion also operated as a political organization that protected prominent Republicans from Federalist mobs and provided them with help during political campaigns.

Duane certainly needed protection on one occasion, when he was targeted and severely beaten by a gang of Federalist militia members who dragged him from his office, encircled him, and then took turns punching him. Duane's son, who attempted to break through the ring of soldiers to protect his father, was also beaten. Not to be silenced, Duane ran several long stories in his newspaper in the days after the beating, giving full details of his treatment at the hands of the Federalist bullies, who were members of the city's volunteer cavalry.[22]

Duane's militia Legion, however, was unusual in that most private militias in Philadelphia were not made up by working-class members but by elites like those who presumably made up the group of tormentors who administered Duane's beating.

So in 1800–1801, both parties were threatening to mobilize the public and volunteer militias under their control. Militias sympathetic to the Republicans were envisioned as being called into action to assure Jefferson's rightful election, while the Federalist militias were seen as possibly necessary to respond to any provocation by the Republicans or else to maintain civil order.

IV

After a Sunday break, the House on Monday, February 16, made its thirty-fourth and thirty-fifth unsuccessful attempts to break the impasse.[23] However, over the weekend, a crack had appeared in the Federalist solidarity. James Bayard, in a caucus of the Federalist members in the House of Representatives, had stunned his colleagues by declaring that since the chief Federalist strategy of electing Burr over Jefferson had failed, he was "determined to end the contest by voting for Mr. Jefferson." The other alternative, of preventing an election by the House of Representatives, would endanger the Union and the Constitution, he said.

The shocking declaration by the Delaware congressman was greeted by "clamour prodigious" and "reproaches vehement," the Delaware Federalist reported. And afterward, the meeting had broken up in confusion. Nonetheless, at a subsequent caucus, despite much recrimination and frustration, the Federalists did finally agree to concede to the election of Jefferson.[24]

Thus, on Tuesday, February 17, Federalist congressmen in the two tied delegations, Vermont and Maryland, "retired" from the House chamber. This allowed their Republican colleagues to cast their states' votes for Jefferson. Bayard, as the single congressman from Delaware, as well as the South Carolina Federalists cast blank ballots. The result was that Jefferson was elected with ten states supporting him, four die-hard New England states supporting Burr, and two states (Delaware and South Carolina) voting neither for nor against Jefferson or Burr.[25]

Why did Bayard and other Federalists decide to withdraw their support from Burr and allow Jefferson's victory?

For one thing, Bayard had earlier shown himself to be somewhat of a maverick. Despite his grave suspicions about Jefferson and the power of Virginia, he had not immediately seen merit in the tactic of supporting Burr. In a stormy meeting in January, despite the wish of the Federalist caucus to throw its support to Burr, Bayard had insisted that he was undecided and that his colleagues' decision would "not bind me," even though "it might cost me a painful struggle to disappoint the views and wishes of many gentlemen . . . [with] whom I have been accustomed to act."[26] Bayard's subsequent backing of Burr on the first ballots had been critical since he was the *only* representative from Delaware, and, as such, had total control over his state's vote in the House of Representatives.

Secondly, in the late afternoon on Monday, the Federalists had apparently received word from Burr that he was "explicitly" resigning "his pretentions" to the presidency, causing the Federalist speaker of the house, Theodore Sedgwick, ruefully to declare that the "gigg is up." Evidently, Burr refused to agree "to shackle himself with federal principles" or to accept Federalist conditions in order to gain Federalist support.[27]

This news undoubtedly increased the pressure on Bayard and other moderate Federalists to acquiesce in Jefferson's election. For with the Burr "option" no longer available, the Federalists' only other alternative was to prolong the stalemate beyond March 4, when Adams's term of office was scheduled to expire. Thus, after thirty-five ballots without resolution, Bayard and a few other fellow Federalists were unwilling to stand firm, push the contest to the brink, and risk the dissolution of the Union and perhaps civil

James Bayard. This Delaware Federalist initiated the Federalists' reluctant acquiescence to Jefferson's election during the tense negotiations in 1801 to break the electoral deadlock between Aaron Burr and Thomas Jefferson. James A. Bayard, nineteenth century (1803–1805), attributed to Gilbert Stuart, American, 1755–1828, oil on canvas, 26⅝ × 23 inches (67.6 × 58.4 cm). The Baltimore Museum of Art: Bequest of Ellen Howard Bayard. BMA 1939.178.

war. For his part Bayard was absolutely convinced that the New Englanders had been determined to do just that, claiming that "they meant to go without a constitution and take the risk of a Civil War."[28]

Thirdly, Bayard later revealed that he believed that he had brokered a deal with Jefferson in return for securing the Virginian's election. The arrangement had been worked out, he insisted, between himself and Republican Samuel Smith of Maryland, after an attempt to negotiate with Republican John Nicholas of Virginia had failed.[29] The supposed deal with Smith, who was a fellow inhabitant with Jefferson at Conrad and McMunn's boarding house and regarded as a spokesman for the Virginian, called for Jefferson's support "of the public credit," his maintenance of the "naval system," and his pledge not to remove "subordinate public officers [from their posts] . . . on the ground of their political character."[30] These Federalist "conditions" had earlier been proposed by Hamilton and then mentioned by Adams in his conversation with Jefferson on Saturday, February 14.

Lending credibility to Bayard's claim is a letter he wrote shortly after Jefferson's victory to a fellow Federalist and federal officeholder, Allan McLane, assuring McLane that the Republicans would not purge Federalists from office. "I have taken good care of you, and think if prudent, you are safe," Bayard promised.[31]

Six years later, however, Jefferson vigorously denied as "absolutely false" that he had given any assurances to the Federalists, claiming that neither Smith "nor any other republican ever uttered the most distant hint to me about submitting to any conditions, or giving any assurances to anybody."[32]

And in 1848, the year before he died, Gallatin supported Jefferson's claim by arguing that Smith, "who was very erroneously and improperly afraid of a defection" of some Republicans, took it upon himself to make certain promises that he had not been authorized to make.[33] Gallatin's defense of Jefferson, coming many years after the election, is somewhat suspect given that several Republican leaders attempted much later to rewrite history, to make some of their earlier actions appear more idealistic and national rather than politically self-interested and sectional.

Also tending to support Jefferson's denial of a deal, however, were his communications with Adams and Monroe on the weekend before the final vote. At the stormy meeting on Saturday with Adams, the vice president had declared that he would "not come into the government by capitulation," nor enter it "but in perfect freedom to follow the dictates of my own judgment."[34] The following day, on Sunday, Jefferson had written Monroe that the Federalists had been told that he would not make deals with them and "would not receive the government on capitulation."[35]

So, in the final analysis, the question remains: did Jefferson or his representatives make a deal with Bayard? Jefferson's record as president did seem to bear out, at least partially, Bayard's allegations. As president he did preserve "the public credit," maintain Hamilton's Bank of the United States, and retain the Federalist "naval system." What is not so obvious is Jefferson's record on Federalist officeholders. While Jefferson did, in fact, retain McLane in his post as collector of the port of Wilmington, Delaware, the president fired another Federalist that Bayard sought to protect and also let other Federalists go.[36]

Certainly, Bayard *believed* that he had secured an agreement with Jefferson to abide by those Federalist "conditions." And Smith himself supported Bayard's account in sworn testimony five years later.[37] Nonetheless, while it cannot be said for certain that Jefferson did not make some sort of a deal in order to get elected, the evidence seems to indicate that he himself probably did not. His supporters, eager to hold the pro-Jefferson coalition in the House together, could very well have made assurances they were not authorized to make. Furthermore, it is not impossible that, at a time of great tension and anxiety, Bayard heard what he wanted to hear and that Smith, eager, like Bayard, to bring the crisis to a close, couched his language in such an ambiguous way that it was misconstrued by the Delaware representative.

V

But what of Burr? Was he the political innocent who, through no fault of his own, became so entangled in a web of political intrigue and conspiracy that he was hopelessly ensnared and unable to extricate himself?

In a new Burr biography, Nancy Isenberg argues that the New Yorker acted appropriately by properly keeping his distance from turmoil in Washington. The confusion, she says, comes from the Federalists "arrogantly" and mistakenly assuming "that they knew Burr's motives better than he did." And thus, despite Burr's sincere disavowal of any competition with Jefferson, she explains, many Federalists as well as Republicans refused to believe him, regarding his demurral as a subterfuge to mask his goal of capturing the presidency.

And this, according to Isenberg, has led to a misunderstanding of Burr's role in the electoral crisis. Instead, she maintains Burr properly kept his distance from Washington during the crisis, annoyed that Republican colleagues continually questioned his loyalty.[38] Furthermore, she asserts that

Hamilton, Burr's archenemy, was the source of many of the rumors about Burr's double-dealing and skullduggery. And finally, she downplays the idea that Burr would have been willing to sacrifice his political reputation and future by getting involved in risky behavior that would certainly have ruined any chance he might have had to be in line for the presidency after Jefferson's two terms.

Isenberg's argument still does not fully explain Burr's refusal to *publicly* pledge to resign—a refusal that was seen by all as a strong signal that he intended to keep his options open. In bolstering her argument, Isenberg points to several Republican endorsements of Burr's honorable intentions, including a letter by Jefferson. These documents, however, seem to have been circulated in early to mid-January 1801, and may well have reflected the Republicans' eagerness to convince themselves and others of Burr's trustworthiness.

Burr's actions or inaction are perplexing at best. Clearly the prize of the presidency enticed him. The alliance between Burr and the Virginia Republicans had been an uneasy one, with Burr still smarting from their betrayal in 1796 and many Virginians remaining deeply suspicious of a man whom they regarded as opportunistic and "unsettled in his politics."[39] And no doubt these wounds were reopened in early 1801, as numerous hostile accusations had come from the New Yorker's erstwhile allies reminding him of his earlier humiliation. Indeed, it is likely that Burr believed he could keep open a possible election by the Federalists by staying above the fray in Albany, far from the center of the contest, by neither courting Federalist support nor burning his bridges with the Republicans.

In any case, the New Yorker's high-wire performance proved disastrous. Ultimately, his political instincts failed him, and he emerged from the crisis with his reputation ruined—a man condemned and reviled by both sides.

Bayard, for one, condemned Burr for having played "a miserable paltry part" in the election and for failing to act when the "election was in his power." Burr would "never have another chance of being President of the U. states," Bayard predicted, because he had "made little use . . . of the one which has occurred," thus giving "me but a humble opinion of the talents of an unprincipled man."[40]

The consideration of Burr as a candidate for the presidency in 1801, however, also raises another question. How had a man with such a limited résumé compared to many of his peers risen to such high standing? Burr, forty-five at the time of the crisis, was twenty-four years younger than Washington, twenty-one younger than Adams, and thirteen younger than

Jefferson. In addition to his abbreviated, though loyal and brave service in the Continental Army, he had held the offices of state attorney general, state assemblyman, and U.S. senator for a total of about ten years of public service. All told, however, his background paled when compared to those of his more distinguished contemporaries.

Jefferson wrote a harsh assessment of Burr in his autobiography. Remembering a visit with the New Yorker early in 1804, Jefferson said he was put off by Burr's obsequious flattery and did not respond to Burr's request for some presidential "mark of favor" to put an end to the attacks on him by his enemies. Jefferson also recalled in his diary that he had never met Burr until the latter served in the Senate during the Washington administration. At that time, the New Yorker's "conduct very soon inspired me with distrust," Jefferson said, and because of that he "habitually cautioned Mr. Madison against trusting him too much." Jefferson had only chosen Burr as his running mate in 1800, he said, out of "respect" for his "extraordinary exertions and successes in the N.Y. election in 1800."[41]

Considering Burr's role in the electoral deadlock in 1801, it is hardly surprising that Jefferson's opinion in 1804 was so negative. In fact, within a month of Jefferson's meeting with his vice president that year, the Republican caucus chose George Clinton of New York to replace Burr as the candidate for vice president in that year's election. Burr did not receive even a single vote for the nomination.[42]

John Adams must surely have been reflecting the sentiments of many when he wrote a Massachusetts friend in the midst of the 1800 crisis, regretting that all "the old Patriots, all the Splendid Talents, the long experience, both of Feds and Antifeds, must be subjected to the humiliation of seeing this dexterous Gentleman [Burr] rise like a balloon, filled with inflatable air, over their heads." The result would be a "discouragement to all virtuous exertion" and "an encouragement to Party intrigue and corruption," he mourned.[43] Even while discounting to some extent the elder Adams's remarks as reflecting his bruised ego from his own defeat, his criticisms are important ones. Adams was right in his belief that Burr was not among that top tier of political leaders in the early republic.

One of the major questions about Burr that remains, therefore, is: how did a man clearly not of the stature of Adams, Jefferson, Hamilton, Madison, as well as numerous others, rise to the position of contending for the presidency in 1800–1801? It is certainly true that Burr played a key role in the critical New York election of 1800, one that ultimately made the difference in giving Jefferson and Burr the margin of victory in the Electoral College.

Yet Burr's ascent to a position of political prominence in 1800–1801 also reflected the acute polarization of the country and the desperation of both Federalists and Republicans. After the tie in the Electoral College, both parties viewed the New Yorker, despite his limitations, as the instrument through which they might be able to retain or gain power. This in and of itself is a testament to how despairing they both were.

VI

Jefferson's election prompted celebrations, but there were laments of doom and gloom as well. The Republicans, of course, were euphoric. Parishioners in one Philadelphia church sang a song written for the occasion of his inauguration that thanked the "God of Life and Liberty" for assisting in saving the nation from "ruin." An elaborate parade, featuring a float formed in the shape of a schooner called the *Thomas Jefferson*, was also part of that city's festivities. In addition, pageants were presented in several communities that included a young woman portraying Liberty being assailed by kings, soldiers, and clergy only to be rescued by a character representing Thomas Jefferson. In New York City the celebration included a parade, fireworks, and colored lamps that curiously illuminated two hearts representing the friendship between Jefferson and Burr.[44]

A Connecticut Federalist offered a much different take on Jefferson's election, hysterically predicting that there was "scarcely a possibility that we shall escape a Civil War. . . . Murder, robbery, rape, adultery and incest will be openly taught and practiced, the air will be rent with the cries of distress, the soil will be soaked with blood and the nation black with crimes."[45]

Another New England Federalist told his supporters after Jefferson's victory that an "active spirit must be roused in every town to check the incessant proselytizing arts of the Jacobins," and the Federalists "must speak in the name and with the voice of the good and the wise, the lovers of liberty and the owners of property."[46]

VII

Before dawn on inauguration day—March 4, 1801—a disappointed and embittered John Adams boarded a stage to leave the capital for his home in Massachusetts. Yet this was not a spontaneous act of petulance, but a trip that had been planned in advance—the 4 A.M. departure necessary in order to arrive in Baltimore in one day of traveling. Thus, there is little evidence of an enraged and ill-tempered Adams skulking out of Washington at the last moment to avoid public humiliation.

His political enemies, however, showed him no mercy. He should be thrown like "polluted water out the back door," the *Aurora* asserted. And "May he return in safety to Braintree, that Mrs. Adams may wash his befuddled brains clear."

Adams's friends, however, regretted that he had left before the inauguration, observing that "Sensible, moderate men of both parties would have been pleased had he tarried until after the installation of his successor. It certainly would have had good effect."[47]

Abigail had left Washington earlier and received the news of Jefferson's election by the House of Representatives as she traveled through Philadelphia. "I have heard some of the Democratic rejoicing such as ringing bells and firing cannon," she reported to her husband. And true to her satirical nature, she related a comment made to her: "What an inconsistency, said a lady to me today, the bells of Christ Church ringing peals of rejoicing for an infidel president."[48]

As he rode away from the capital in the coach, Adams himself must have regretfully reflected on his presidency, remembering the defeats and mortifications: his battles with Hamilton, his having been betrayed by members of his cabinet, and his repudiation by former political friends. However, the more optimistic side of his personality may also have allowed him to dwell more on the triumphs: his building of a strong naval force of fifty ships in a very short time, his successful coping with a divided country and a divided Federalist party at a time of national crisis, and his determination and courage to make the extremely difficult and politically costly decision to negotiate an end to the quasi-war with France.

It is a great irony that Adams's greatest success, the peace treaty with France signed in September 1800, came within a month of Hamilton's public denunciation of him. Later Adams himself wrote that peace with France was his most rewarding achievement and that he desired "no other inscription over my gravestone than: 'Here lies John Adams, who took upon himself the responsibility of peace with France in the year 1800.'"[49]

VIII

In Washington, however, March 4 was Jefferson's day.

His inaugural address was notable for its substance rather than its oratory. Not a comfortable or accomplished public speaker, he, like Washington before him, spoke in such a soft, tremulous voice that the crowd in the Senate chamber must have had trouble hearing him.

The speech was a mostly conciliatory one, reaching out to those who had bitterly opposed the Virginian's bid for the presidency by assuring the audience that a broad consensus existed among all Americans on certain shared inalienable and fundamental rights. Thus, Jefferson urged that his "fellow citizens unite with one heart and one mind" to "restore to social intercourse that harmony and affection without which liberty and even life itself are but dreary things."

However, while not naming the Federalists, the incoming president did condemn them for their bigotry and fanaticism in passing the Alien and Sedition Acts. The Revolution, he asserted, had "banished from our land that religious intolerance under which mankind so long bled and suffered," but "we have yet gained little if we countenance a political intolerance as despotic, as wicked, and capable of as bitter and bloody persecutions."

Jefferson also outlined the basic principles of his administration. In foreign policy, like Washington, he promised "honest friendship, with all nations—entangling alliances with none." Domestic policies articulated by Jefferson echoed Republican beliefs that had been embraced since the development of the party's early opposition during Washington's administration: the importance of states' rights (as the states were "the surest bulwarks against anti-republican tendencies"); the "absolute acquiescence in decisions of the majority"; the "honest payment of our debts and sacred preservation of the public faith"; and the importance of a frugal government. Jefferson also gave a ringing endorsement to the protection of the citizenry under the Bill of Rights: "Freedom of religion; freedom of the press; freedom of person under the protection of the habeas corpus."

And in some of the most well-remembered and often-quoted lines from his speech, Jefferson urged unity, maintaining that "every difference of opinion is not a difference of principle. We have called by different names brethren of the same principle. We are all republicans—we are federalists." And if "there be any among us who would wish to dissolve this Union or to change its republican form, let them stand undisturbed as monuments of the safety with which error of opinion may be tolerated where reason is left free to combat it."[50]

IX

On March 4, 1801, as Jefferson and the Republicans were poised to assume power, there must have been a huge collective sigh of relief (at least on the part of the Republicans) that the bitter division over the deadlock in the Electoral College and the House of Representatives had been solved peacefully. The nation had met its first electoral crisis and survived.

Today the frenzied rhetoric of democratic politics is often viewed as an exercise of exaggeration and hyperbole in which politicians demonize their opponents and extol their own virtues. Claims and counterclaims are made and refuted, with the public largely responding by regarding the words as "just politics."

To read this cynical perspective back into the late eighteenth and early nineteenth centuries, however, would be a mistake. The seemingly, almost hysterical, language of fear and foreboding had a far greater grounding in the reality of the time. Few in 1800 would have predicted that the Constitution would have survived for over 200 years. Then, given the experimental nature of the young republic, the newness of its political institutions, and the lack of precedents for guidance, the new nation was struggling to survive in a world of European monarchies. And the threat of being drawn into the epic battle between England and France further intensified and magnified political differences, with each side viewing the other in hideously distorted terms. Doubts about the future had to be taken seriously.

So, the fact that the dangerous stalemate was resolved peacefully does not suggest that there was not the potential for violence and the destruction of the Union in 1801. With frightening rumors swirling around them, the participants themselves did not know that the electoral deadlock would be resolved without armed conflict. Looking back much later in his life, Adams himself wrote that during that time of crisis in 1801 he had thought that the Federalists and Republicans were looking into a disastrous abyss and that "a civil war was expected."[51]

11 THE REVOLUTION OF 1800

"The revolution of 1800 . . . was as real a revolution in the principles of our government as that of 1776 was in its form."
—Thomas Jefferson, 1819

I

The presidential election of 1800 was one of the two most critical elections in American history. But unlike the election of Lincoln in 1860, which was followed by the Civil War, the deeply divisive 1800 election was settled off the battlefield. Nonetheless, it did lead to a crisis that had the potential for destroying the Union.

Why was the 1800 contest so wrenching and potentially devastating? It was because in a world of despotic governments in which republican government was seen as an experiment, it marked the first time that political power was transferred from one party to the other in an era in which political opposition was not accepted as legitimate. And since both Federalists and Republicans fervently believed that their conception of the public good was the authentic and faithful one for the collective best interests of the country and that their opponents' conception jeopardized the country's continued existence, the election became a polarized do-or-die political struggle. The nation was fortunate indeed to escape without some type of civil disorder or armed conflict.

Jefferson himself believed that the election of 1800 was one of those profoundly defining or transformative moments in history. Referring to it as "the revolution of 1800" in a letter he wrote ten years after leaving office, he claimed that his presidential victory was "as real a revolution in the principles of our government as that of 1776 was in its form."[1]

The distinction between "form" and "principles" that Jefferson makes in the letter is critical. While he saw the American Revolution as having established republicanism as the "form" of government, he believed that his election over the Federalists in 1800 had preserved the legacy of that revolution in that it had saved the "principles" of republicanism.

The future of the young republic, he argued, had been imperiled by the Federalists, who had sought to concentrate power at the federal level, to move the country into a dangerously dependent relationship with Great Britain, and to curb basic individual liberties by the passage of the Alien and Sedition Acts.

One Federalist leader, the maliciously eloquent and frequently venomous Fisher Ames of Massachusetts, reluctantly agreed with the Republican assessment of what the election meant. Jefferson's accession to the presidency, he said, was "no little cabinet scene, where one minister comes into power and another goes out, but a great moral revolution proceeding from the vices and passions of men, shifting officers today, [in order] that measures, and principles, and systems, may be shifted tomorrow."[2]

There is little doubt that the Republicans believed, fervently believed, that the election in 1800 had saved the republic and the fruits of the American Revolution.

In their minds, the election was a great, epoch-changing moment in the history of the country. And it was this conviction and the narrative created to explain it that were powerful influences in shaping political events after 1801.

Party labels had been used in the past to confuse and distract Americans. But Jefferson maintained that with his victory in 1801 they eventually would become meaningless, and the victorious Republicans would become the political embodiment of a broad-based republican consensus that would, in time, establish political hegemony.

In the future, he wrote to a correspondent during the standoff in the House of Representatives, political divisions in the United States, if there were to be any, would be between "republican and monarchist." The "body of the nation, even that part which French excesses forced over to the federal side," would "rejoin the republicans, leaving only those who were pure monarchists, and who will be too few to form a sect."[3] Thus, only the most fanatical, intransigent, diehard Federalists would remain outside a broad republican—and Republican—consensus.

In a letter to Elbridge Gerry less than a month after his inauguration, Jefferson made a similar point, perceiving Gerry's New England as lagging behind the other sections. The United States, he told his friend, "from N.Y. southwardly, are as unanimous in the principles of '76, as they were in '76," but your "part of the Union tho' as absolutely republican as ours, had drunk deeper of the delusion, & is therefore slower in recovering from it." "The aegis of government & the temples of religion & of justice, have all been prostituted there [in New England] to toll us back to the times when we burnt witches. But your people will rise again."[4]

The future safety of the country and the preservation of the Union and the Constitution, Jefferson believed, depended on the continuation of the Republicans in power. A couple of days before he was finally elected president by the House, Jefferson had written his daughter that if he were to be elected he would bring the government "back to its republican principles," so that when he left office it would be "so established . . . [that] it may be under full security that we are to continue free and happy."[5]

This meant that once in power the Republicans were resolute in their determination to make certain that the Federalists should never again be entrusted with the control of the national government. The truth, as the Republicans saw it, was that the Federalists were perfidious and untrustworthy opponents who had betrayed the public trust and threatened the future of republican government. They could never again be allowed to endanger Republican hegemony and the well-being of the nation that accompanied it. As a result, as time went by the Republicans were sometimes willing to adopt extreme measures to accomplish this, measures that were contradictory to their own stated beliefs, especially those beliefs celebrating the limited role of the federal government.

Jefferson himself, looking back after he had left office, attempted to explain what Republican dominance of the federal government meant, declaring that the Republicans were not a political party, which to him even in 1810 was a debasing and unbecoming term. Reflecting a prominent civic humanist theme, he proclaimed instead that the "Republicans are the *nation*."[6]

Jefferson's statements obviously must be viewed within the context of the United States in the early nineteenth century. The country's first attempt at governing itself under the Articles of Confederation had lasted less than a decade, and its second attempt under the Constitution was only a dozen years old in 1800. Few Americans then would have predicted that the Constitution would endure more than two hundred years.

Americans in 1800 believed that they were living in a treacherous world governed by hostile autocratic governments. Republicanism in France, after having been euphorically hailed in the United States in the aftermath of the French Revolution, had failed to flourish, and the French were again under authoritarian rule, that of Napoleon, who would soon become emperor. The future existence of republicanism in the United States thus seemed to be precarious and vulnerable as well.

II

Bolstering Jefferson's perception of his election as a revolution is the fact that in the years after 1800 the Federalists did virtually disappear as a national political force. While they maintained strength in New England and a few other areas, in most of the country the name "Federalist" became an epithet (like "Tory" earlier) that was often invoked to blacken the reputation of an opponent. The name "Republican," on the other hand, became synonymous with the "*nation*."

And it is true that the Republicans were not a political party in any modern sense. Instead, they constituted a broad-based coalition led by Virginians that symbolized and embodied a nationwide political consensus embracing republicanism, the Union, and the Constitution. As such they dominated the American political scene for the next twenty-four years.[7]

The powerful and influential role that Virginia played in this coalition as well as the nation during that quarter century is illustrated by the fact that Jefferson's presidency began a succession of Virginia Republican presidencies. His two terms in office, covering the years 1801 to 1809, were followed by the two terms of James Madison, 1809 to 1817, and the two terms of James Monroe, 1817 to 1825. In fact, the Republicans became so dominant that there was no more than token opposition to Monroe in his two elections.

In hindsight it can also be seen that the Republican victory in 1800 began a sixty-year period of Southern dominance of national political power, first by the Republican Party and later by its successor, the Democratic Party. And, if the three presidential terms of Virginian George Washington and New Englander John Adams are included, Southerners held the presidency forty-nine years, provided twenty-three of the thirty-six speakers of the House, and twenty of the thirty-five Supreme Court justices in the seventy-two-year period from 1789 to 1861.

A major contributor to this Southern dominance, and one that also played a crucial role in Jefferson's election, was the "three-fifths clause" in the Constitution that counted each slave as three-fifths of a person for allotting representation in Congress as well as for levying taxes. According to one historian, Jefferson would have lost twelve votes in the election of 1800, but Adams only two, without the three-fifths clause. This would have given the election to Adams, sixty-three to sixty-one.[8] This three-fifths arrangement, as might be expected, was resented by the Federalists in the Northeast, who saw it as unfairly advantaging Southern Republicans. The Boston *Columbian Centinel*, for example, complained in early January 1801 that the Republican victory was due to the "suffrages of a minority of the free citizens [and] the weight of about half a million black cattle thrown into their scale."[9]

III

What were the underlying factors, issues, and public images of the two parties that influenced and shaped the election of 1800?

First, the nature of the election system itself had a major impact on the outcome. The three-fifths compromise, as noted, was an important piece of the puzzle, as were the indirect voting method involving the Electoral College, the use of local notables as electors, and the varied methods of choosing the electors.

Second, the two most important issues in determining the result of the election were the Federalists' enthusiasm for the quasi-war with France (along with their support for the defense buildup and the accompanying taxes), and their passage of the repressive Alien and Sedition Acts. All this proved to be unpopular. Also, the bitter division between Adams and Hamilton, which led the Federalists almost to self-destruct, was another major determinant. For the rest of his life, Adams himself believed that Hamilton's intriguing had been responsible for the Federalists' defeat in New York and that this intriguing had cost him the election. They "killed themselves and ... indicted me for the murder," the embittered Adams said of Hamilton and his followers.[10]

Third, by 1800 the Federalists had come to be viewed by many Americans as undemocratic and elitist, while the Republicans had come to be seen as more democratic and as reflecting the increasingly democratic ethos of the country. The Federalists struggled throughout the 1790s under a barrage of epithets—monarchists, aristocrats, Anglo-men, Tories, members of a British faction—while the Republicans labored against charges of being Jacobins, atheists, levelers, and naïve or sycophantic supporters of France. While these charges were exaggerations and caricatures, they did influence how citizens came to perceive the two parties.

And, despite the hyperbole and distortion, there was an element of truth in each depiction. The Federalists did support England against France, did fear the excesses of the French Revolution more than the Republicans, and did favor a stronger and more vigorous federal government. The Republicans, on the other hand, did favor France over England, did embrace the French Revolution (although during the quasi-war with France, this lost much of its appeal), did fear a stronger federal government, and did support strengthening the states. Furthermore, the charges made by the parties against one another were important not so much because they were true, but because many *thought* they were true. These charges, therefore, seemed to confirm the rough perceptions that Republicans and Federalists had of one another.

And by 1800 the Republican critique of the Federalists and its leaders, as well as the Republicans' own positive image of themselves as a party dedicated to saving the republic, the Constitution, the Union, and the democratic heritage of the American Revolution, resonated with voters and contributed to Jefferson's electoral victory.

IV

In addition to controlling the presidency in the quarter century after 1800, the Republicans also held strong majorities in the House of Representatives. After the Federalists had earlier won an important victory in 1798–1799 that secured them a sixty-to-forty-six majority, the Republican superiority was never again seriously challenged, beginning with the party's win in 1800, when the Republicans gained a sixty-eight-to-thirty-eight or 64.2 to 35.8 percent margin. The Federalists did eke out 37.4 percent of the seats in 1812, but that was because of a bitter political conflict over the diplomatic crisis leading to the war with England that year. From that point afterward, their national political strength dramatically declined, with their membership in the House eventually falling to 14 percent after the election of 1818.[11]

Despite the fading away of the Federalists at the national level, however, there was for a time some evidence of increased competitiveness between Federalists and Republicans at the state level. In 1808, for example, the Federalists contested "virtually every legislative seat in the five Middle States, [and] captured the New York assembly and the Maryland House of Delegates for the first time since 1799." They also gained seats in the New Jersey legislature, retained control of Delaware, and swept New England, winning all five governorships and four of the five legislatures.[12] But as the years wore on, the Federalists disappeared as a viable political opposition to the Republicans on the state level as well.

Eventually, however, the stresses and strains of being *too successful* took their toll on the Republicans. Ideological factions increasingly arose within the party around questions about what the role and scope of the federal government should be, with a states' rights wing becoming more and more frustrated with those who were more nationalistic. And in the election of 1824, these fractures within the party led to five Republican candidates contending against one another to become Monroe's successor.

V

In addition to ushering in an era of Republican rule on the national level, the 1800 election was a pivotal milestone in the process of transforming national politics from deferential, elitist, and narrowly based to what would eventually become a more democratic, mass-based, two-party system. This is *not* to say, however, that it marked a major step toward democratizing national politics. Neither the Federalists nor the Republicans accepted the notion of a loyal opposition. This acceptance and a modern national two-party system evolved haltingly and incrementally over time. The anti-party, civic humanistic view of politics was slow to die.

It does seem clear, however, that a more democratic, more vigorous politics, organized around national issues, began to emerge in certain areas in the 1790s. The example of John Beckley is illustrative. Although framing his work in civic humanist ideology, he became an activist grassroots organizer in the presidential campaigns of 1796 and 1800 in Pennsylvania, canvassing the state and distributing pamphlets and printed tickets with the names of Republican electors.[13] In New York it was Burr's masterful job in organizing the state for the Republicans that provided the key to their stunning victory in 1800. In Virginia as well, the Republicans did not leave anything to chance in 1800. A general committee was established in Richmond to oversee and coordinate county committees, whose activities included circulating printed and handwritten tickets listing the names of the twenty-one Republican electors. This was essential because voters in the state were long used to voting orally, and in 1800 they had to contend with a ballot listing twenty-one individual candidates, since all electors were selected on a general, statewide ticket. And one historian has concluded that in 1800 in "no other state were the methods of campaigning so advanced" as in Maryland, where there was extensive canvassing and statewide electioneering in the presidential campaign.[14]

In the election of 1800 and during the years after, newspaper editors also were at the forefront of an increasingly democratic style of politics even though their lower economic and social standing was of special concern to the elites. The conventional wisdom of classical republicanism, accepted by both Republicans and Federalists, held that public virtue was essential for sustaining republican government. Only established gentlemen, theoretically independent and therefore not tempted by self-interest or man's baser instincts, were deemed autonomous enough to objectively legislate for the public good. Thus, it did not seem suitable for artisans and craftsmen who worked as editors to have the power to threaten the established order through their ability to influence public opinion, as they increasingly were able to do.

One Federalist, for instance, complained about the plentiful availability of newspapers and ridiculed those non-elite Americans he saw as influenced by them. Too many Americans, he scoffed, "are able to lay out their earnings in buying Newspapers, books, etc., and having leisure to read, they of course become mighty politicians, acquainted beforehand with all that ought to be done by government & with all that ought not to be done, are ready to pronounce what is done right & what wrong, & so will condemn public measures which happen not to comport exactly with their great knowledge, or what might cross their present interests."[15]

But despite the fears and suspicions of the leadership elite, editors did publicize and critique the actions of the government and provide important grassroots oversight of public officials in 1800. And while the Sedition Act had been expected by the Federalists to curtail popular press criticism of the Adams administration, it ended up having the opposite effect, with the number of Republican presses increasing dramatically after its passage.[16]

VI

The older deferential politics associated with the anti-party, civic humanistic system seems to have retained its hold on national elections long after it had faded at the state level, as most of the democratic advances after 1800 had to do with state issues and state elections. This is undoubtedly because state politics were less intimidating and more familiar, accessible, and relevant than national politics, with each state having its own significant and singular history of political divisions, most going back to pre-Revolutionary days. There was a comfort level with a state's political culture—made up by loosely formed factions often focused around a single leader or family contending for power. In comparison, the national government seemed far removed.

Even though the Constitution had invested the federal government with considerably more power than the state governments, the voters were only directly involved on the national level when they cast their ballots for members of the House of Representatives. Their votes for president, of course, were once or twice removed, depending on the state in which they lived. In addition, one historian has pointed to the national hegemony of the Republicans that made the election results a foregone conclusion and produced "presidential elections [that] did not arouse voter interest as much as did those for governor, state legislators, or even members of Congress."[17]

In any case, state politics were characterized by robust, competitive contests that generally had significantly higher voter turnouts than national ones, at least until the 1820s and 1830s. The average voter participation of adult white males in all states in the election of Andrew Jackson in 1828 was 56.3 percent. In state elections, however, fifteen of the twenty-two states had exceeded that percentage before 1824. And in some state gubernatorial elections, the percentages exceeded 70 percent, including Delaware (81.9 percent, 1804), New Hampshire (80.8 percent, 1814), Tennessee (80 percent, 1817), and Vermont (79.9 percent, 1812).[18]

In addition, in a number of states, an increased number of appointive offices were made elective. And, while it was not uncommon in 1800 for congressmen to be elected in a statewide at-large poll or from multiple member districts, by 1842 single-member districts, which made congressmen more accountable, had early on become mandatory. Whereas only Maryland of the original states had embraced universal white manhood suffrage, by 1824 suffrage reforms in most states—Rhode Island, Virginia, and Louisiana were exceptions—gave most adult white males the right to vote in presidential elections. Furthermore, the six new states to join the Union from 1816 to 1822 all provided for universal white manhood suffrage. *Viva voce* voting with its lack of privacy was also gradually replaced by the ballot.

And finally, the selection of presidential electors also became more democratic. Whereas in the presidential election of 1800 the legislatures chose the electors in ten out of sixteen states, by 1832 every state except South Carolina selected its electors by popular vote.[19]

VII

What ultimately was the significance of the election of 1800? It marked the beginning of the end of the Federalist party and began a twenty-four-year period of national political domination by Virginia Republicans. And it stimulated the development of a more democratic politics, especially in the states. It was not, however, as has been suggested, "a mandate from the People for sweeping transformation." And it did not signal "the invention of recognizably democratic political parties," nor did the 1790s mark "the two-party system" becoming "rooted in American politics."[20]

A recognizable, modern two-party system did not develop until after Andrew Jackson's election in 1828. And it was not until 1844 that a political party, the Democratic Party, was able to regain the presidency after it had lost it. Prior to this, there was an expectation that a victorious party had received an almost permanent mandate.

President Jackson asserted as much in 1835 when he declared that "it was only by preserving the identity of the Republican party as embodied and characterized by the principles introduced by Mr. Jefferson that the original rights of the states and the people could be maintained." Therefore, Jackson claimed that he had "labored to reconstruct this great Party" in order to preserve "its *permanent ascendancy*."[21] Despite the obvious strong partisanship exhibited by the Old Hero's declaration, his words also revealed the continued strength of certain eighteenth-century assumptions about the nature of political conflict—namely the permanency of victory and the absolutist character of political struggle.

Thus, when Jefferson talked about the "Revolution of 1800," he was not referring to his election to the presidency as a victory for the Republicans in any modern sense. Neither he and the Republicans nor the Federalists would have been comfortable with the two-party system that eventually developed. Instead, they believed that these who opposed them could not be trusted with exercising the power of the federal government. Members of both parties continued to embrace a classical republican view of politics that idealized a virtuous leadership elite, exercising their superior judgment, discerning the general good of society, and legislating to achieve that goal. Leaders of both parties passionately and stubbornly believed that they, and they alone, were the ones who could divine the true or authentic vision of the general good.

EPILOGUE

"Thomas Jefferson survives."
—*John Adams, July 4, 1826*

I

Many American leaders played major roles in the impassioned drama surrounding the election of 1800, but none were more intimately involved than Alexander Hamilton, Aaron Burr, John Adams, and Thomas Jefferson. Three of the four—Adams, Jefferson, and Burr—lived for more than two decades after that critical election, while Hamilton died tragically only a few years later. Nonetheless, only Jefferson continued for some time to be active in politics, remaining in the presidency until 1809.

II

Hamilton's reputation never recovered from his public denunciation of John Adams during the 1800 election campaign. His gift for political acumen and his concern for his country, however, did at least keep him active on the margin of politics as a commentator. Within months of Jefferson taking office, he founded the *New York Post*. And the next year he fiercely took the Jefferson administration to task for repealing the Federalist Judiciary Act of 1801 that had expanded the federal judiciary and allowed Adams, in the waning days of his administration, to make a number of midnight appointments. Hamilton denounced the Republican action as one that would destroy the independent judiciary and the Constitution.[1]

At about the same time, Hamilton suffered personal family tragedies that devastated him. His son Philip, "the eldest and *brightest* hope of my family," was killed in a duel, ironically not far from the place Hamilton himself would die in a duel a few years later. Compounding the heartbreaking death of his son, Hamilton's seventeen-year-old daughter, Angelica, suffered an emotional and mental breakdown. In a futile effort to comfort her, South Carolinian Charles Cotesworth Pinckney sent her, at Hamilton's request, watermelons and four parakeets. But despite efforts like this and the loving attention of Hamilton and his family, Angelica only occasionally recognized members of the family and referred to her dead brother as if he were still living. For the rest of her seventy-three years she lived in a childlike, semi-lucid state.[2]

In early 1802, Hamilton poured his heart out in a letter to a friend. "Mine is an odd destiny," he lamented. "Perhaps no man in the UStates has sacrificed or done more for the present Constitution than myself—and contrary to all my anticipations of its fate . . . I am still laboring to prop the frail and worthless fabric. Yet I have the murmurs of its friends no less than the curses of its foes for my rewards. What can I do better than withdraw from the Scene? Every day proves to me more and more that this American world was not made for me."[3]

Hamilton's political and personal adversities did not, however, actually cause him to withdraw from the scene or deter him from continuing to make harsh criticisms of the Jefferson administration. Yet, unlike most Federalists, he did endorse Jefferson's purchase of the Louisiana Territory from France in 1803. The New Yorker must have felt vindicated in the irony of Jefferson's action. Not only had the Virginian and his supporters always styled themselves as strict constructionists in respect to the Constitution, they had earlier denounced Hamilton's financial plan during the Washington administration as a dangerous effort to increase the power of the executive and the federal government. But in order to justify the purchase, Jefferson—to the horror of some Republicans—used the doctrine of implied powers, which was first articulated by Hamilton himself to support the creation of a national bank. John Adams's son, John Quincy, astutely pointed out the contradiction when he observed that the Louisiana Purchase was "an assumption of implied powers greater in itself, and more comprehensive in its consequences, than all the assumptions of implied powers in the years of the Washington and Adams administrations."[4]

Although Hamilton supported the addition of Louisiana to the American empire, the acquisition alarmed the New England Federalists, and the issue became a factor in shaping the last and fatal conflict between Hamilton and Burr. Fearing that the immense increase in territory associated with the purchase would dramatically diminish the political strength of New England and the Northeast and correspondingly increase the power of the slaveholding South, a number of New England Federalists, including Timothy Pickering, began to talk about secession from the Union and forming a Northeastern confederacy.[5] They hoped that New York might also join the plot, and Vice President Aaron Burr, who seemed to be near the center of a number of conspiracies and intrigues in the early republic, was seen as the key player in any such alliance. Abandoned by the Virginia Republican leadership as Jefferson's second-term vice presidential running mate, Burr was at this time being supported in his 1804 run for governor of New York by the Federalists even though he was being coyly noncommittal (as he had been during the election crisis in 1801) about the planned secession.

Hamilton publicly condemned the secessionist talk and deplored Burr's role in it. Federalists should think twice about their support of Burr for governor, he argued, for, if elected, he said, Burr would use the position to lead New York out of the Union and become the chief contender for leadership in any new Northern confederacy.

A report in early March 1804 in the malevolent *American Citizen* attempted to goad the two men into a confrontation by its explanation of Hamilton's position. "General Hamilton did not oppose Mr. Burr because he was a *democrat* . . . but because HE HAD NO PRINCIPLE, either in morals or in politics," it was asserted. "The sum and substance of his [Hamilton's] language was that no *party* could trust him [Burr]." Whether or not Hamilton's opposition to Burr was critical, Burr did lose the election the next month. Enraged by Hamilton's repeated attacks on his public and private character, which he saw as responsible for the ruination of his career, Burr challenged his protagonist to a duel.[6]

While duels or affairs of honor were not uncommon among gentlemen at the time, there was a great discrepancy between the number of duels fought by the two protagonists. At the time he made the challenge, Burr had fought one duel in 1799, while Hamilton had been a principal in eleven affairs of honor from 1779 to 1804, both as a challenger and as someone who had been challenged.[7]

Thus, on July 11, after making out his will and writing farewell notes to his wife, Hamilton, along with his physician and his second, met Burr and his entourage at Weehawken, New Jersey, near the spot where his son had been killed a few years earlier. There, the Federalist stalwart was mortally wounded by Burr's first shot. The next day, after suffering agonizing pain for thirty-six hours, Hamilton died at the age of forty-nine.[8]

III

Aaron Burr surely is one of the most enigmatic leaders in American history. Hailed as a master politician after engineering the Republican electoral victory in New York in 1800, he nonetheless alienated both Republicans and Federalists by his evasiveness during the deadlock between himself and Jefferson in 1801. Was his inaction a terrible miscalculation or a failure of nerve?

Extremely ambitious, Burr was an adventurer, intrigant, and conspirator whose name was associated with almost every plot to break up the Union in the early nineteenth century. A man obviously attracted to large and often fanciful schemes, he also seems to have had an unerring capacity to make bad decisions.

His personal life was characterized by contradictions. He was a loving father who adored his daughter, whom he raised after the death of his wife; yet he also cruelly seduced, used, and discarded other women like yesterday's newspapers. And he displayed a shocking insensitivity in the aftermath of his slaying of Hamilton, showing little or no remorse. A debtor consistently in financial difficulties, as well as a voluptuary and sexual reprobate, Burr scandalized polite society, whose members were appalled and outraged by his actions.

And yet this was a man, who, despite his paucity of experience and his disturbing reputation, was elected and served a term as vice president and came close to being elected president. With Burr, it is often exceedingly difficult to distinguish between fact and fiction, but in the final analysis his story presents a dramatically flawed figure who, even so, was larger than life.

Burr was not immediately forsaken by Jefferson after the 1801 election, but he did find himself increasingly isolated and ignored during his first year as vice president. And by early 1804, the message of disapproval was clear when the Republican congressional caucus met in February to nominate candidates for president and vice president for the upcoming presidential election and Burr did not receive a single vote. After nominating Jefferson for a second term, the Republicans chose another New Yorker, Governor George Clinton, as their vice presidential nominee.

But that did not end Burr's political ambitions. Irrepressible, he ran in 1804—with Federalist backing—to become governor of New York state. After his defeat and his subsequent killing of Hamilton, Burr, however, did become a pariah, forced to flee south from New York to escape being arrested on murder charges in both his home state and New Jersey. Occasionally traveling incognito, he ended up spending time in both Georgia and Florida, wryly wondering in a letter to his daughter which state "shall have the honour of hanging the vice president."[9] Burr's macabre wit about his legal predicament showed itself again a little later when he quipped, "In New York, I am to be disfranchised and in New Jersey hanged. Having substantial objections to both, I shall not, for the present, hazard either but shall seek another country."[10]

When Congress met in November 1804, the sight of the disgraced Burr presiding over the Senate while facing murder charges seemed to some a terrible and cruel travesty, causing one Federalist to declare, "The man whom the grand jury in the county of Bergen, New Jersey, have recently indicted for the murder of the incomparable Hamilton appeared yesterday and today at the head of the Senate . . . ! It certainly is the first time—and God grant that it may be the last—that ever a man, so justly charged with such an infamous crime, presided in the American senate."[11]

After Burr's tainted vice presidential term was up, he traveled to the trans-Appalachian West, in part to escape the murder charges still pending in the East but also to pursue grand plans to found a new empire. While in the West, Burr considered various intrigues, including one with England that would have split Louisiana and other western territories off from the United States in order to create a new and independent western nation. There were also discussions about annexing Mexico after liberating it from Spanish rule. This scheming, in the end, led the Jefferson administration in 1807 to charge and try Burr with treason for attempting to incite war with Spain; but Burr was eventually acquitted for lack of evidence.

Thoroughly discredited, hounded by his creditors, and often using an assumed name, Burr fled the country the following June and lived for four years in Europe, where he continued to be involved in attempting to organize filibustering expeditions against Spanish territories in America. Returning to the United States in 1812, he struggled to rebuild his legal practice in New York, but without much success.

It was at the end of this year that a tragedy—perhaps the greatest of his life—struck. His beloved daughter Theodosia and her son, on a voyage coming north from their home in South Carolina to see him, were lost at sea.

Even in his advancing years, however, Burr was still a rake and courted controversy. At the age of seventy-seven, he married a wealthy widow, almost twenty years his junior. Within the year, however, she filed for divorce, accusing her husband of both adultery and squandering her money. On the day of Burr's death at the age of 81, September 14, 1836, the divorce decree was awarded.[12]

IV

The contrast between Aaron Burr and John Adams could not have been greater. Adams was a celebrated founder of the country as one of the authors of the Declaration of Independence and a leader of the American Revolution. He was also a devoted husband and man of high moral character.

After leaving Washington in the early morning hours of March 4 (Jefferson's inauguration day), he did not arrive home until the evening of March

18. Little did he know at the time that, as a sixty-five-year-old man living in a society in which the life expectancy was fifty-five, he still had almost a third of his life to live. And although he was someone who had traveled extensively abroad prior to becoming president, Adams's retirement years were spent almost exclusively within a fifteen-mile radius of home. Only occasionally did he travel as far as Boston or Cambridge for a Harvard commencement or meeting of the American Academy of Sciences.

The practical necessity of earning a living was foremost on his mind. He did not have the luxury or comfort of being a gentleman farmer, for his modest farms had to sustain not only Abigail and himself, but the family of his deceased son Charles, as well as other family members who were occasional guests. All told, the farms, which included three houses and 600 acres of fields and woods, were large enough that the summer harvest required hiring help. Nonetheless, while Adams busied himself with farm chores, daily walks, and reading the classics, old political wounds continued to fester. In fact, Abigail once noted overhearing him swear to himself at various political enemies in the summer of 1801 as he worked outside alongside his farmhands in the fields.[13]

Thus, retirement for Adams was not the sedentary life of a cloistered scholar, but an active one of work and exercise. "I walk every fair day . . . ," he said, "sometimes three and four miles. Ride now and then, but very rarely more than ten or fifteen miles."

As Adams aged, he suffered the heartache of losing loved ones and dear friends. In the spring of 1813 he heard that his longtime and very close friend, Benjamin Rush, had died in Philadelphia. And within a few months, his daughter Nabby, who was suffering from incurable cancer, returned home with her two children. Adams wrote, "My dear, my only daughter lies, in the next chamber, consumed with cancer . . . my daughter-in-law, Charles's widow [Sally], lies in the next chamber extremely weak and low. . . . My wife, a valetudinarian through a whole life of 69 years, is worn down by care." And after suffering from agonizing and excruciating pain and a horrifying mastectomy surgery while conscious and numbed only by opium, Nabby died.[14]

But despite his grief at the death of children, grandchildren, and friends, Adams remained an optimist. "I assure you in the sincerity of a father," he wrote his son John Quincy Adams in 1815, "the last fourteen years have been the happiest of my life."[15]

However, a major preoccupation of Adams in that lengthy retirement period was his work to justify and correct the historical record about his own public career. This was especially true in regard to an 1806 history of the American Revolution that was highly critical of Adams for betraying the Revolution, saying he was corrupted by his admiration of English monarchy. Incensed, Adams wrote to the author, Mercy Otis Warren: "Madame! . . . Corruption is a charge that I cannot and will not bear. I challenge the whole human race, and angels and devils, too, to produce an instance of it from my cradle to this hour!" Even more outrageous, Adams charged, was the accusation that he had a "partiality for monarchy."[16]

Adams also nursed a continuing resentment toward his successor in the presidency. Jefferson, he believed, had "not a clear head, and never pursues any question through. His ambition and his cunning are the only steady qualities in him. His imagination and ambition are too strong for his reason."[17] And upon Jefferson's retirement from office, Adams questioned how the Virginian "will get rid of his remorse in retirement," for he "must know that he leaves the government infinitely worse than he found it, and that from his own error or ignorance." Adams claimed that he had "no resentment" against Jefferson, although this is unlikely, because he was convinced that Jefferson had "honored and salaried almost every villain he could find who had been an enemy to me."[18] This last was in connection with Adams's deep suspicion that Jefferson had actively supported Callender's attacks on him, which, in fact, he had. These extremely offensive assaults had included such slanders as calling Adams a "repulsive pedant," a "gross hypocrite," and "one of the most egregious fools on the continent."[19]

Jefferson's growing reputation as the author of the Declaration of Independence and symbol of the Revolution was also galling to Adams, who saw his own star as being eclipsed. Adams's recollection was that Jefferson had been a secondary figure, so passive that "during the whole Time I sat with him in Congress [Continental Congress], . . . I never heard him utter three sentences together."[20]

V

Jefferson's two terms in office were mirror opposites. His first term was one of unqualified success, especially since the country paid off its national debt and doubled its size as a result of the purchase of Louisiana from France.

His second term, when the country became embroiled once again in the great war between France and England and the neutrality of American ships was violated by both powers, was a disaster. Finally, in an act of desperation intended to pressure the warring belligerents to recognize American neutrality, the Jefferson administration imposed an embargo that closed all of the country's ports to foreign trade. But not only did the embargo fail to achieve its stated objectives, its restriction on trade caused great hardships in the commercial areas of the country and aroused a widespread condemnation of the Jefferson administration. Furthermore, repressive and authoritarian in its use of state power, the embargo was a direct contradiction to Jefferson's philosophical dedication to minimum government and individual freedom.

Years earlier Jefferson had observed that no public official would ever leave office with as good a reputation as the one he had when he entered it. And in the final days of his presidency, by which time he had become deeply unpopular, Jefferson was experiencing the truth of those words and longing to return to private life. "Never did a prisoner, released from his chains," he wrote, "feel such relief as I shall on shaking off the shackles of power." "Nature intended me," he lamented, "for the tranquil pursuits of science. . . . But the enormities of the time in which I have lived, have forced me . . . to commit myself to the boisterous ocean of political passions." And perhaps with a bit of self-delusion, he concluded, "I thank God for the opportunity of retiring from . . . [public office] without censure, and carrying with me the most consoling proofs of public approbation."[21]

Once retired, Jefferson described his daily routine: "From breakfast to dinner, I am at my shops, my garden, or on horseback among my farms; from dinner to dark, I give to society and recreation with my neighbors and friends; and candle light to early bed-time, I read." "My mornings are devoted to correspondence," he observed. And keeping up with his correspondence must have been a great burden. In one year alone he received more than 1,200 letters.[22]

Upon returning to Monticello, Jefferson found that, despite the paper value of owning 10,000 acres of land and 200 slaves, he was deeply and irretrievably in debt. And this debt, which continued to mount, dogged him throughout the rest of his life. Contributing to the problem were Jefferson's generosity and the large numbers of people who came to visit the former president at his home. As many as fifty guests a night would sometimes have to be put up and fed, since there were no inns or taverns close by. His farm manager recounted that often when "I have killed a fine beef . . . it would all be eaten in a day or two."[23]

Jefferson's munificence and hospitality in retirement followed a lifelong habit of spending beyond his means. In line with this, the Virginian once confessed to Adams's son, John Quincy, that the "*Epicurean* philosophy came nearest to the truth, in his opinion, of any ancient system of philosophy." And this was shown, John Quincy somewhat disapprovingly noted, in Jefferson's love of discoursing on fine wines. This refined appreciation of superior vintages was further reflected in the Virginian's wine bill. While Jefferson was president, it exceeded $2,500 a year.[24]

A nationwide financial crisis in 1819, which drove down the price of land and commodities, deepened Jefferson's financial woes. Failing banks, in an effort to save themselves, called in debts, and this restricted Jefferson's credit, which in turn forced him to borrow more money to cover his debts and to pay interest on old loans. All of this increased his bank debt alone to more than $10,000. The predatory actions of banks, the former president said at the time, was all the result of Hamilton's establishment of the Bank of the United States. It was Hamilton, he charged, who had "let in this torrent of swindling institutions which have spread ruin and wretchedness over the face of our country."[25]

The public activity that consumed much of Jefferson's time and called upon his political and persuasive skills during his retirement was the founding of the University of Virginia. The effort was not an easy one, but finally, after long and arduous battles with legislators and clergymen, the university was chartered in 1819. Indeed, Jefferson considered the creation of this institution as one of the three greatest achievements of his long and distinguished career. In line with this was his request that the inscription on his tombstone read: "Author of the Declaration of Independence, of the Statute of Virginia for Religious Freedom, and Father of the University of Virginia." Remarkably, Jefferson did not mention his presidency among those accomplishments for which he wished "most to be remembered."[26]

In time Jefferson's retirement brought with it a healing of the estrangement between himself and Adams. In 1812, their mutual friend Benjamin Rush played the mediator and brought the former Revolutionary comrades back together. It was at this point that the two former presidents began an extraordinary correspondence that lasted until their deaths more than a decade later. The 158 letters that resulted from this reconciliation, written at the end of their lives, represent, according to one historian, "the intellectual capstone to the achievements of the revolutionary generation and the most impressive correspondence between prominent statesmen in all of American history."[27]

The letters ran the gamut from reminiscing about the American Revolution, examining political differences (albeit without pushing any argument

beyond polite limits), exchanging news of family and friends, and philoso-
phizing about the nature of religion. The institution of slavery was one topic
that Adams opened only gingerly, in line with the custom of silence or avoidance that was practiced throughout most of the antebellum period—a time
when what became known as "the peculiar institution" was off limits, un-
mentionable for most political leaders.

Initially, in 1812, the resumed relationship between Jefferson and Adams
was rather awkward. But after a time both men began to feel more comfortable and less wary of the other. So, ultimately, a genuine friendship developed
between the aging heroes of the Revolutionary generation. Each wanted to
explain his historical role, not only to his correspondent, but also to posterity. As Adams remarked in an early letter to Jefferson, "You and I ought not
to die" before we have the chance to explain "ourselves to each other."[28]

In October 1818, Adams's dearest Abigail died of typhoid fever. Right
before her death, an anguished Adams poured out his heart to Jefferson.
"The dear partner of my life for fifty-four years as a wife, and for many more
years as a lover, now lies in extremis, forbidden to speak or be spoken to."[29]
Her death eight days later ended one of the most remarkable marriages
in American history. She and her devoted husband seem to have been the
perfect match, complementing and strengthening each other. Abigail was a
fierce defender of her husband and family, a woman not afraid to publicly
voice her opinions—ones that were often full of both insight and naughty,
ironic wit.

Abigail and Jefferson had had an exchange of frosty letters in 1804, when
Abigail had written the Virginian expressing sympathy to him upon the
death of his daughter, Mary Jefferson Eppes. Jefferson mistook the letter
as an effort to rekindle the comradeship that the families had shared years
earlier. And in his response he talked about his long friendship with the Adamses. However, he also suggested that Adams's "midnight judges" appointments were "personally unkind." This was too much for Abigail. She angrily
replied that the appointments were for Adams to make and reminded Jefferson about the hurtful way he had "cherished and warmed" Callender, the
"serpent" who had been Adams's nemesis.[30] There was no further exchange
of letters between Jefferson and the Adamses until the correspondence between Adams and Jefferson was resumed in 1812.

Among the many different subjects Adams and Jefferson discussed, the
disagreement between the two over the concept of "aristocracy" is one of the
most revealing. Adams agreed with Jefferson that the differences between
the "few and the many" had characterized social and political divisions since

the time of Aristotle. But Adams maintained that this was the result of an almost immutable law—that aristocracies inevitably held the power, and the few were deferred to by the many. Jefferson's claim of human equality, Adams asserted, was simply disproven by human nature and the natural order of inequality.

Jefferson agreed that there was "a natural aristocracy among men" rooted in the "virtue and talents" of individuals. But there was also, he said, a "pseudo-aristocracy founded on wealth and birth, without either virtue or talents." And, he professed, it had been a major objective of American republicanism to provide an institutional mechanism that would make it possible for the people, in free elections, to select those of the natural aristocracy to serve as their rulers instead of the pseudo-aristocrats.

It was the passage of the Missouri Compromise in 1820 that prompted a discussion of the hitherto avoided subject of slavery. Jefferson had evaded the topic most of his public life, arguing that the abolition of slavery was an unavoidable problem for the next generation to solve. The Missouri Compromise, however, had raised profound fears that a race war might be inevitable sooner than that.

"The real question, as seen in the states afflicted with this unfortunate population is," Jefferson argued, "Are our slaves to be presented with freedom and a dagger?" If "Congress has a power to regulate the conditions of the inhabitants of states," he apprehensively acknowledged, it logically followed that Congress also had the power to free the slaves. The consequences of that were unthinkable, Jefferson stressed. "Are we then to . . . wage another Peloponnesian War to settle the ascendancy between them. The question remains to be seen; but not I hope by you or me. Surely, they will parlay awhile, and give us time to get out of the way." It was an issue, Jefferson confessed, that brought a fear and foreboding that rivaled "the gloomiest moments of the Revolutionary War."

Adams, in correspondence with others, strongly condemned slavery. "Negro Slavery is an evil of Colossal magnitude" that should never be allowed in the Missouri Territory, he forcefully declared. In letters to Jefferson, however, Adams was uncharacteristically evasive, presumably out of a sensitivity to Jefferson's strong feelings. "Slavery in this Country I have seen hanging over it like a black cloud for half a Century," Adams wrote to Jefferson— but he then promised to defer to Jefferson's view and support "no measure against your judgments."[31]

One of the most remarkable exchanges between the two concerned the French Revolution, Jefferson acknowledging that Adams had been more accurate in his predictions about it. "Your prophecies," he wrote, "proved truer than mine; and yet fell short of the fact, for instead of a million, the destruction of eight or ten millions of human beings has probably been the effect of those convulsions." At the beginning of the French Revolution in 1789, Jefferson confessed, "I did not . . . believe . . . [that it] would have lasted so long, nor have cost so much blood." On a more optimistic note, however, Jefferson said he hoped that the "idea of representative government" had "taken root" and ultimately would be demanded by the people of France.[32]

Adams, delighted with Jefferson's letter, absolved the Virginian from ever having used the issue of the French Revolution in an opportunistic and political manner for partisan advantage. Jefferson, he allowed charitably, had been sincere in his support of the idealism of the French Revolution, honestly believing that it had represented a repudiation of the past with its aristocratic and absolutist governments and a hope for the future with its embracement of republicanism.[33]

The last years of Jefferson's life were spent struggling with an ever-increasing debt load that forced him to sell land and slaves at the same time that he was coping with his own physical decline. Nonetheless, despite his infirmities, which included crippling arthritis and urinary problems, he remained optimistic.

Asked to attend the Fourth of July celebration in Washington in 1826, he wrote to decline the invitation by proclaiming in an outpouring of idealistic enthusiasm that the nation's birth had been the "signal" that had aroused men "to burst the chains under which monkish ignorance and superstition had persuaded them to bind themselves, and to assume the blessings and security of self-government. . . . All eyes are opened, or opening, to the rights of man. The general spread of the light of science has already laid open to every view the palpable truth, that the mass of mankind has not been born with saddles on their backs, nor a favored few booted and spurred, ready to ride them."[34]

As fate would have it, the date Jefferson was invited to come to Washington to celebrate the Fourth of July holiday in 1826 was the date of death for both Jefferson and Adams. Among ninety-one-year-old John Adams's last words as he lay dying were, "Thomas Jefferson survives." Little did he know, or would he ever know, that Jefferson, his junior by eight years, had preceded him in death by about five hours. The two Revolutionary War patriot leaders, authors of the Declaration of Independence, and former presidents had died hours from each other on that fiftieth anniversary of Independence Day.

METHODS OF SELECTING PRESIDENTIAL ELECTORS, 1796 AND 1800

	1796	1800
New Hampshire	GT and L*	L
Massachusetts	D and L†	L
Rhode Island	L	GT
Connecticut	L	L
New York	L	L
New Jersey	L	L
Pennsylvania	GT	L
Delaware	L	L
Maryland	D	D
Virginia	D	GT
North Carolina	D	D
South Carolina	L	L
Georgia	GT	L
Vermont	L	L
Kentucky	D	D
Tennessee	‡	‡

Source: U.S. Department of Commerce, Bureau of the Census, *A Statistical Abstract Supplement: Historical Statistics of the United States, Colonial Times to 1957* (Washington, D.C.: U.S. Government Printing Office, 1961), 681.

Note: L = Legislature; GT = By people on general ticket; D = By people in district.

*A majority vote was necessary for a choice. When this failed, the legislature made the choice.

†In 1796, the legislature chose nine electors, the people seven.

‡In 1796 and 1800, Tennessee chose electors by a confusing mix of district voting and legislative appointment.

ELECTORAL VOTE, 1796

	TJ	AB	JA	TP	SA	OE	GC	JJ
New Hampshire			6			6		
Massachusetts			16	13		1		
Rhode Island			4			4		
Connecticut			9	4				5
New York			12	12				
New Jersey			7	7				
Pennsylvania	14	13	1	2				
Delaware			3	3				
Maryland	4	3	7	4				
Virginia	20	1	1	1	15		3	
North Carolina	11	6	1	1				
South Carolina	8			8				
Georgia	4						4	
Vermont			4	4				
Kentucky	4	4						
Tennessee	3	3						
Totals	68	30	71	59	15	11	7	5

Source: Edward Stanwood, *A History of the Presidency: From 1788 to 1897* (Clifton, N.J.: Augustus M. Kelley, 1975), 1:51.

Note: TJ = Thomas Jefferson; AB = Aaron Burr; JA = John Adams; TP = Thomas Pinckney; SA = Sam Adams; OE = Oliver Ellsworth; GC = George Clinton; JJ = John Jay. There were ten other votes, scattered among James Iredell of North Carolina (three votes from North Carolina); George Washington (one vote from Virginia and one vote from North Carolina); Samuel Johnson of North Carolina (two votes from Massachusetts); John Henry of Maryland (two votes from Maryland); and Charles C. Pinckney of South Carolina (one vote from North Carolina).

ELECTORAL VOTE, 1800

	TJ	AB	JA	CCP	JJ
New Hampshire			6	6	
Massachusetts			16	16	
Rhode Island			4	3	1
Connecticut			9	9	
New York	12	12			
New Jersey			7	7	
Pennsylvania	8	8	7	7	
Delaware			3	3	
Maryland	5	5	5	5	
Virginia	21	21			
North Carolina	8	8	4	4	
South Carolina	8	8			
Georgia	4	4			
Vermont			4	4	
Kentucky	4	4			
Tennessee	3	3			
Totals	73	73	65	64	1

Source: Edward Stanwood, *A History of the Presidency: From 1788 to 1897* (Clifton, N.J.: Augustus M. Kelley, 1975), 1:63.

Note: TJ = Thomas Jefferson; AB = Aaron Burr; JA = John Adams; CCP = C. C. Pinckney; JJ = John Jay.

PARTY DIVISIONS IN THE 5TH, 6TH, AND 7TH CONGRESSES

5th Congress (1797–1799): 106 members
  57 Federalists
  49 Republicans

6th Congress (1799–1801): 106 members
  60 Federalists
  46 Republicans

7th Congress (1801–1803): 106 members
  38 Federalists
  68 Republicans

Source: Office of the Clerk of the U.S. House of Representatives, http://clerk.house.gov/art_history/house_history/index.html.

Note: Party affiliation was sometimes worn very lightly in the early republic; to categorize someone as a Federalist or Republican is sometimes a leap of faith, so these figures should be used as approximations and not as absolute. Also, members of the House sometimes served only partial terms, and special elections were held to choose their replacements, thus complicating any final count. See Michael J. Dubin's marvelous *United States Congressional Elections, 1788–1997: The Official Results of the Elections of the 1st through 105th Congresses* (Jefferson, N.C.: McFarland, 1998) for a discussion of the complexities of the electoral process with different dates and special and runoff elections. Dubin provides a breakdown by state of each election, each candidate, and the margin of victory—a truly monumental achievement.

NOTES

AUTHOR'S PREFACE

1 Robert A. Dahl, ed., *Political Opposition in Western Democracies* (New Haven, Conn.: Yale University Press, 1966), xiii.

2 D. E. Apter, "Some Reflections on the Role of a Political Opposition in New Nations," *Comparative Studies in Society and History* 4 (1961–1962): 154, 165.

3 Washington to the secretary of war, November 17, 1799, in *The Writings of George Washington*, ed. John C. Fitzpatrick (Washington, D.C.: U.S. Government Printing Office, 1931–1944), 37:428.

4 Gordon S. Wood, "Ideology and the Origins of Liberal America," *William and Mary Quarterly* 44 (July 1987): 633.

5 See Gordon Wood's new book, *The Empire of Liberty: A History of the Early Republic, 1789–1815* (New York: Oxford University Press, 2009), for a comprehensive and masterful account of this critical and transformative period.

CHAPTER 1 INAUGURATION DAY, MARCH 4, 1801

1 Henry Adams, *History of the United States of America during the First Administration of Thomas Jefferson* (New York: Antiquarian Press, 1962), 1:198–199; and Merrill D. Peterson, *Thomas Jefferson and the New Nation: A Biography* (New York: Oxford University Press, 1970), 654–655.

2 Joseph J. Ellis, *His Excellency: George Washington* (New York: Vintage Press, 2005), 184–185.

3 Edward J. Larson, *Magnificent Catastrophe: The Tumultuous Election of 1800, America's First Presidential Campaign* (New York: Free Press, 2007), 271–272; Jerry W. Knudson, *Jefferson and the Press: Crucible of Liberty* (Columbia: University of South Carolina Press, 2006), 58; and "Marine Band and the Presidents," *"The President's Own": United States Marine Band*, http://www.marineband .usmc.mil/learning_tools/our_history/marine_band_and_presidents.htm.

4 From our modern understanding of the role and practice of political parties, these early political organizations were, in reality, embryo parties. It was not until the 1830s that "political parties" in any modern sense or definition were established. However, to avoid confusion I will use the term "party," with the caveat that these early "parties" were quite different from what they eventually became.

5 While the Federalists had a majority in the House, they did not control the majority of the sixteen state delegations. This was critical, since each state had only one vote in the balloting in the House to break the deadlock.

6 As quoted in John E. Ferling, *Adams vs. Jefferson: The Tumultuous Election of 1800* (New York: Oxford University Press, 2004), 189.

7 Woody Holton, *Unruly Americans and the Origins of the Constitution* (New York: Hill & Wang, 2007), 5. See also Richard R. Beeman's excellent *The Varieties of Political Experience in Eighteenth-century America* (Philadelphia: University of Pennsylvania Press, 2004).

8 Cecelia M. Kenyon, ed., *The Antifederalists* (Indianapolis, Ind.: Bobbs-Merrill, 1966), 132–134.

9 Richard Norton Smith, *Patriarch: George Washington and the New American Nation* (Boston: Houghton Mifflin, 1993), xix.

10 Ibid.

11 Jefferson to Dr. Walter Jones, January 2, 1814, in *The Life and Selected Writings of Thomas Jefferson*, ed. Adrienne Koch and William Peden (New York: Modern Library, 1944), 173–176.

12 Ellis, *His Excellency: George Washington*, xiv.

13 As quoted in Marcus Cunliffe, *George Washington: Man and Monument* (New York: New American Library, 1960), 20.

14 As quoted in Ron Chernow, *Alexander Hamilton* (New York: Penguin Press, 2004), 3.

15 Ibid.

16 As quoted in Joseph Ellis, *American Sphinx: The Character of Thomas Jefferson* (New York: Alfred A. Knopf, 1997), 66.

17 William Maclay, *The Journal of William Maclay: United States Senator from Pennsylvania, 1789–1791*, introduced by Charles A. Beard (New York: F. Ungar Publishing, 1965), 265–266.

18 Madison to Jefferson, June 30, 1789, in *The Papers of Thomas Jefferson, 1743–1826*, ed. Julian P. Boyd (Princeton, N.J.: Princeton University Press, 1950), 15:224.

19 Paul Goodman, "First Party System," in *The American Party System: Stages of Political Development*, ed. William Nisbet Chambers and Walter Dean Burnham (New York: Oxford University Press, 1967), 64.

20 As quoted in Harry Ammon, *James Monroe: The Quest for National Identity* (New York: McGraw Hill, 1971), 86.

21 Henry Lee to James Madison, April 3, 1790, Madison Papers, Library of Congress. See also Edmund Randolph to Madison, May 20, 1790.

22 Rhys Isaac, *Transformation of Virginia, 1740–1790* (Chapel Hill: University of North Carolina Press, 1982), 319–320.

23 Jefferson to William Short, January 3, 1793, in *The Works of Thomas Jefferson*, ed. Paul L. Ford (New York: G. P. Putnam's Sons, 1904), 6:153–157.

24 As quoted in Claude Milton Newlin, *The Life and Writings of Hugh Henry Brackenridge* (Mamaroneck, N.J.: P. P. Appel, 1971), 132–133. See also *National Gazette*, May 8, 1793, and the *General Advertiser*, December 14, 1793, for similar sentiments.

CHAPTER 2 THE ORIGINS OF NATIONAL POLITICS IN THE EARLY REPUBLIC

1 James Roger Sharp, *American Politics in the Early Republic* (New Haven, Conn.: Yale University Press, 1995), 139.

2 James Madison, *Federalist 10*, in *The Federalist Papers*, ed. Clinton Rossiter (New York: New American Library, 1961), 82.

3 *General Advertiser*, February 28, 1795.

4 Philip S. Foner, ed., *The Democratic-Republican Societies, 1790–1800: A Documentary Sourcebook of Constitutions, Declarations, Addresses, Resolutions, and Toasts* (Westport, Conn.: Greenwood Press, 1976), 22.

5   Eugene Perry Link, *Democratic Republican Societies, 1790–1800* (New York: Octagon Books, 1942), 13–15. In her excellent 2010 Ph.D. dissertation at Syracuse University, Michelle Orihel shows the number of societies to have been more than thirty-five. See her "Political Fever: The Democratic Societies and the Crisis of Republican Governance in 1790s America."

6   See Lloyd S. Kramer, "French Revolution and the Creation of American Political Culture," in *The Global Ramifications of the French Revolution*, ed. Joseph Klaits and Michael H. Haltzel (Cambridge: Cambridge University Press, 1994), 33, for a discussion of the usefulness of Jürgen Habermas's *Structural Transformation of the Public Sphere: An Inquiry into a Category of Bourgeois Society* (Cambridge, Mass.: MIT Press, 1989) in analyzing the development of a new democratic political culture.

7   See Thomas R. Slaughter's *Whiskey Rebellion: Frontier Epilogue to the American Revolution* (New York: Oxford University Press, 1986) for the best account of the insurrection.

8   As quoted in Kramer, "French Revolution," 37.

9   U.S. Congress, *Annals of the Congress of the United States, 1793–1795*, 3rd Cong., 2d sess., 921–922.

10 Edmund Morgan, *Inventing the People* (New York: Norton, 1988). Quotations are from 286, 256; see also 235–306. Albrecht Koschnik offers an account of the development of a political public sphere in Philadelphia that includes a discussion of Democratic societies. See his *"Let a Common Interest Bind Us Together": Associations, Partisanship, and Culture in Philadelphia, 1775–1840* (Charlottesville: University of Virginia Press, 2007), especially 11–40.

11 Rossiter, *Federalist Papers*, 314–315. See also Sharp, *American Politics*, 124, 125.

12 As quoted in Gordon Wood, *The Creation of the American Republic, 1776–1787* (Chapel Hill: University of North Carolina Press, 1969), 373–374. Jeremy Belknap of New Hampshire expressed the same sentiments: "Let it be stated as a principle that government originates from the people: but let the people be taught . . . that they are not able to govern themselves." See Barbara Karsky, "Agrarian Radicalism in the Late Revolutionary Period (1780–1795)" in *New Wine in Old Skins: A Contemporary View of Socio-Political Structures and Values Affecting the American Revolution*, ed. Erich Angermann et al. (Stuttgart: Klett, 1976), 87.

13 Sharp, *American Politics*, 42.

14 Jefferson to Francis Hopkinson, March 13, 1789, in *Papers of Thomas Jefferson*, ed. Julian P. Boyd (Princeton, N.J.: Princeton University Press, 1958), 14:649–650.

15 See R. R. Palmer, *Age of the Democratic Revolution: A Political History of Europe and America, 1776–1800* (Princeton, N.J.: Princeton University Press, 1964), 2:518–546, for a discussion of politics in the United States after the "revolutionizing" of the French Revolution in 1792. See especially 525 for a discussion of Federalist and Republican perceptions of their own positions in relationship to France. See also Lawrence S. Kaplan, *Jefferson and France: An Essay on Politics and Political Ideas* (New Haven, Conn.: Yale University Press, 1967), chapter 3; and Alexander DeConde, *Entangling Alliance: Politics and Diplomacy under George Washington* (Durham, N.C.: Duke University Press, 1958), 86–87, for an analysis of the impact of the French Revolution after 1793. Howard Mumford Jones, in his *American and French Culture, 1750–1848* (Chapel Hill: University of

North Carolina Press, 1965), discusses the American reception of various aspects of French culture. See also James Roger Sharp, "France and the United States at the End of the Eighteenth Century," in *Rethinking the Atlantic World: Europe and America in the Age of Democratic Revolutions*, ed. Manuela Albertone and Antonio DeFrancesco (London: Palgrave MacMillan, 2009).

16 Chauncey Goodrich to Oliver Wolcott, February 17, 1793, in *Memoirs of the Administrations of Washington and John Adams*, ed. George Gibbs (New York: W. Van Norton, 1846), 1:88.

17 Robert A. Dahl, ed., *Political Opposition in Western Democracies* (New Haven, Conn.: Yale University Press, 1966), xiii.

18 Henry Steele Commager, ed., *Documents of American History* (New York: Appleton-Century-Crofts, 1958), 172–173.

19 Jeffrey L. Pasley, *"The Tyranny of the Printers": Newspaper Politics in the Early American Republic* (Charlottesville: University of Virginia Press, 2001), 181–182.

20 See Sharp, *American Politics*, 9–10.

21 Jeffrey L. Pasley, "'A Journeyman, Either in Law or Politics': John Beckley and the Social Origins of Political Campaigning," *Journal of the Early Republic* 16 (Winter 1996): 531–569; Noble E. Cunningham, Jr., "John Beckley: An Early American Party Manager," *William and Mary Quarterly*, 3rd ser., 13 (January 1956): 40–52; Edmund Berkeley and Dorothy Smith Berkeley, *John Beckley: Zealous Partisan in a Nation Divided* (Philadelphia: American Philosophical Society, 1973).

22 J. G. A. Pocock, "Civic Humanism and Its Role in Anglo-American Thought," in *Politics, Language and Time: Essays on Political Thought and History* (New York: Atheneum, 1971), 87.

23 As quoted in Noble Cunningham, Jr., *The Jeffersonian Republicans: The Formation of Party Organization, 1789–1801* (Chapel Hill: University of North Carolina Press, 1957), 100–101.

24 As quoted in Pasley, "A Journeyman," 534.

25 Sharp, *American Politics*, 123.

26 As quoted in David Waldstreicher, *In the Midst of Perpetual Fetes: The Making of American Nationalism, 1776–1820* (Chapel Hill: University of North Carolina Press, 1997), 128, 129.

27 As quoted in Simon P. Newman, *Parades and the Politics of the Street: Festive Culture in the Early American Republic* (Philadelphia: University of Pennsylvania Press, 1997), 90–92, 83–119.

28 Ibid., 1, 5, 11, 99, and 148.

29 As quoted in Susan Branson, *These Fiery Frenchified Dames: Women and Political Culture in Early National Philadelphia* (Philadelphia: University of Pennsylvania Press, 2001), 55.

CHAPTER 3 THE FAILURE OF NATIONAL UNITY

1 David McCullough, *John Adams* (New York: Simon & Schuster, 2001), 464.

2 Jefferson to Madison, December 28, 1794, in *The Works of Thomas Jefferson*, ed. Paul L. Ford (New York, G. P. Putnam's Sons, 1904), 6:516–519; Jefferson to Madison, April 27, 1795, Madison Papers, Library of Congress. For an analysis of the second letter and how historians have been misled by an error in the

transcribing of it, see my "Unraveling the Mystery of Jefferson's Letter of April 27, 1795," *Journal of the Early Republic* 6 (Winter 1986): 411–418.

3 As quoted in James Roger Sharp, *American Politics in the Early Republic* (New Haven, Conn.: Yale University Press, 1995), 145; see also 144.

4 As quoted in Edward Stanwood, *A History of the Presidency*, ed. Charles Knowles Bolton (Clifton, N.J.: A. M. Kelley, 1975), 1:43.

5 As late as December 1796, Madison was not sure that Jefferson would be willing to serve as vice president. See Madison to Jefferson, December 19, 1796, in *The Writings of James Madison*, ed. Gaillard Hunt (New York: Russell & Russell, 1908), 6:296–302.

6 Stanwood, *History of the Presidency*, 1:51.

7 As quoted in John Ferling, *John Adams: A Life* (Newtown, Conn.: American Political Biography Press, 2009), 316.

8 As quoted in Walter Isaacson, *Benjamin Franklin: An American Life* (New York: Simon & Schuster, 2004), 428.

9 As quoted in McCullough, *John Adams*, 318.

10 Ibid., 448.

11 As quoted in Zoltan Haraszti, *John Adams and the Prophets of Progress* (Cambridge, Mass.: Harvard University Press, 1952), 4.

12 One is reminded here of Socrates' admonishment that "an unexamined life is not worth living," which is obviously not true of Jefferson. However, the degree of Jefferson's self-awareness is, I believe, remarkably less than Adams's.

13 McCullough, *Adams*.

14 Oliver Wolcott, Sr., to Oliver Wolcott, Jr., March 20, 1797, in *Memoirs of the Administrations of Washington and John Adams*, ed. George Gibbs (New York: W. Van Norton, 1846), 1:475–477.

15 As quoted in Sharp, *American Politics*, 159.

16 See especially *Federalist 10*.

17 Stephen Higginson to Hamilton, January 12, 1797, in *The Papers of Alexander Hamilton*, ed. Harold C. Syrett (New York: Columbia University Press, 1974), 20:465–466.

18 Gerry to Adams, January 30, 1797, Gerry Papers, Library of Congress.

19 Earlier Adams had been offended by Jefferson's public remark in 1791 about "political heresies," which Adams took to be aimed at him. See Jefferson to Adams, July 17, July 29, and August 30, 1791, in *The Adams-Jefferson Letters: The Complete Correspondence between Thomas Jefferson and Abigail and John Adams*, ed. Lester J. Cappon (Chapel Hill: University of North Carolina Press, 1959), 1:245–246, 247–250, and 250–252.

20 Adams to Tristram Dalton, January 19, 1797; and Adams to Gerry, February 20, 1797, Adams Papers, Massachusetts Historical Society.

21 *General Advertiser*, March 11, 13, and 14, 1797.

22 Chauncey Goodrich to Oliver Wolcott, Sr., January 9, 1797, in Gibbs, *Memoirs of Administrations*, 1:417–418; and Hamilton to Rufus King, February 15, 1797, in Syrett, *Hamilton*, 20:515–516.

23 Jefferson's note, March 2, 1797, in *The Anas of Thomas Jefferson*, ed. Franklin Sawvel (New York: Da Capo Press, 1903), 184–185.

24 Sharp, *American Politics*, 164–165; Ferling, *Adams*, 341–342.

25 As quoted in Ferling, *Adams*, 333.

26 Gordon Wood, "Conspiracy and the Paranoid Style: Causality and Deceit in the Eighteenth Century," *William and Mary Quarterly*, 3rd ser., 39 (July 1982): 432, 434, and passim.

27 Jefferson to Edward Rutledge, June 24, 1797, in Ford, *Works of Jefferson*, 7:152–155.

28 Jefferson to Aaron Burr, June 17, 1797, in ibid., 145–149.

29 Sedgwick to unknown, March 7, 1798, as quoted in James Morton Smith, *Freedom's Fetters: The Alien and Sedition Laws and American Civil Liberties* (1956; reprint, Ithaca, N.Y.: Cornell University Press, 1966), 21; "Stand No. 1," March 30, 1798, in Syrett, *Hamilton*, 21:384.

30 Gallatin to his wife, January 19, 1798, Gallatin Papers, New York Historical Society Collection.

31 Jefferson to Monroe and to Madison, March 21, 1798, in Ford, *Works of Jefferson*, 7:218–222.

32 Jefferson to John Wise, February 12, 1798, as quoted in Dumas Malone, *Jefferson and the Ordeal of Liberty* (Boston: Little, Brown, 1962), 364–365.

33 As quoted in Simon P. Newman, *Parades and the Politics of the Street* (Philadelphia: University of Pennsylvania Press, 1997), 154, 162–163.

34 Jefferson to Madison, May 10 and 17, 1798, in Ford, *Works of Jefferson*, 7:251–254.

35 Hamilton to Rufus King, June 6, 1798, in Syrett, *Hamilton*, 21:490–491.

36 Quoted in McCullough, *John Adams*, 500. See also Ferling, *Adams*, 355–356. Benjamin Franklin Bache was the grandson of Benjamin Franklin; he was a bitter critic of the Federalists and edited the Philadelphia *General Advertiser* and later the *Aurora*. Under the Sedition Act, he was arrested and paroled. He died shortly thereafter of yellow fever.

37 David Waldstreicher, *In the Midst of Perpetual Fetes: The Making of American Nationalism, 1776–1820* (Chapel Hill: University of North Carolina Press, 1997), 161–163; Ferling, *Adams*, 357.

38 McCullough, *John Adams*, 504.

39 Jefferson to Madison, June 21, 1798, in Ford, *Works of Jefferson*, 7:272–275.

40 Ibid.

41 Boston *Centinel*, August 19, 1797, as quoted in Manning J. Dauer, *The Adams Federalists* (Baltimore: Johns Hopkins University Press, 1968), 160–161.

42 As quoted in McCullough, *John Adams*, 505.

43 Susan Branson, *These Fiery Frenchified Dames: Women and Political Culture in Early National Philadelphia* (Philadelphia: University of Pennsylvania Press, 2001), 57. Branson says there were 5,000 French in Philadelphia by the late 1790s.

44 Jefferson to Edmund Randolph, May 9, 1798, Jefferson Papers, Library of Congress; and Jefferson to Madison, May 3, 1798, in Ford, *Works of Jefferson*, 7:246–249.

45 John Ferling, *Adams vs. Jefferson: The Tumultuous Election of 1800* (New York: Oxford University Press, 2004), 122.

46 For texts of the laws, see Smith, *Freedom's Fetters*, 435–442.

47 Dauer, *Adams Federalists*, 157–158; *Annals of the Congress of the United States, 1797–1799*, 5th Cong., 2d sess., 2004.

48 As quoted in Jeffrey L. Pasley, *"The Tyranny of the Printers": Newspaper Politics in*

the *Early American Republic* (Charlottesville: University of Virginia Press, 2001), 119, 122.

49 Nancy Isenberg, *Fallen Founder: The Life of Aaron Burr* (New York: Viking Press, 2007), 174; and McCullough, *John Adams*, 505.

50 Speech in Congress, *Annals of Congress, 1797–1799*, 5th Cong., 2d sess., 2110.

51 Ibid., 2093–2094.

CHAPTER 4 THE REPUBLICANS' RESPONSE: THE KENTUCKY AND VIRGINIA RESOLUTIONS

1 As quoted in Stanley Elkins and Eric McKitrick, *The Age of Federalism: The Early American Republic, 1788–1800* (New York: Oxford University Press, 1993), 597.

2 Ibid., 583–584.

3 Ibid., 623–631.

4 Ibid., 596.

5 As quoted in Manning J. Dauer, *The Adams Federalists* (Baltimore: Johns Hopkins University Press, 1968), 169; see also 170–171.

6 The terminology is confusing surrounding the various "Armies" discussed in 1798. For simplicity's sake I will use the term "army." For a good discussion of the differences between the Regular Army, Additional Army, Provisional Army, and the Eventual Army, see editor's note in *The Papers of Alexander Hamilton*, ed. Harold C. Syrett (New York: Columbia University Press, 1975), 22:383–390; and Richard H. Kohn, *Eagle and Sword: The Federalists and the Creation of the Military Establishment in America, 1789–1802* (New York: Free Press, 1975), 229.

7 David McCullough, *John Adams* (New York: Simon & Schuster, 2001), 510–511.

8 Hamilton to Harrison Gray Otis, December 27, 1798; Hamilton to Theodore Sedgwick, February 2, 1799; Hamilton to McHenry, February 6, 1799, in Syrett, *Hamilton*, 22:393–394, 452–454, 466–467. Washington to McHenry, September 30, 1798, as quoted in Kohn, *Eagle and Sword*, 243–244. See Syrett, *Hamilton*, 22:87–146, 270–313, 316–339, for elaborate lists of candidates' names and comments about them. See also Robert Gough, "Officering the American Army, 1798," in *William and Mary Quarterly*, 3rd ser., 43 (July 1986): 460–471.

9 "Petition," August 1797, in *The Works of Thomas Jefferson*, ed. Paul L. Ford (New York: G. P. Putnam's Sons, 1904), 7:171–174. See also Dumas Malone, *Jefferson and the Ordeal of Liberty* (Boston: Little, Brown, 1962), 334–337; and Adrienne Koch and Harry Ammon, "The Virginia and Kentucky Resolutions: An Episode in Jefferson's and Madison's Defense of Civil Liberties," *William and Mary Quarterly*, 3rd ser., 5 (April 1948): 152–153.

10 *Aurora*, May 31, 1797, as quoted in Dauer, *Adams Federalists*, 154.

11 Jefferson to Monroe, September 7, 1797, in Ford, *Works of Jefferson*, 8:339. See also 7:171–174.

12 Koch and Ammon, "Virginia and Kentucky Resolutions," 153–154. "Petition," August 1797, in Ford, *Works of Jefferson*, 7:158–164.

13 *Boston Gazette*, December 12, 1798, as quoted in Dauer, *Adams Federalists*, 156.

14 *Gazette of the United States*, October 10, 1798, as quoted in ibid., 165.

15 Jeffrey L. Pasley, *"The Tyranny of the Printers": Newspaper Politics in the Early American Republic* (Charlottesville: University of Virginia Press, 2001), 105–106 and passim.

16 Ibid., 153, 125–126.
17 Ibid., 110–111; McCullough, *John Adams*, 494, 536, 537.
18 Pasley, *Tyranny of Printers*, 109–111; and John C. Miller, *The Federalist Era: 1789–1801* (New York: Harper & Row, 1963), 236.
19 Pasley, *Tyranny of Printers*, 111.
20 Madison to Jefferson, May 20, 1798, in *The Writings of James Madison: Comprising His Public Papers and His Private Correspondence*, ed. Gaillard Hunt (New York: G. P. Putnam's Sons, 1900–1910), 6:320–322. Monroe to Jefferson, to Madison, and to Jefferson, April 8, June 24, and June [no date], 1798, in *The Writings of James Monroe*, ed. Stanislaus M. Hamilton (New York: G. P. Putnam's Sons, 1900), 3:116–118, 129–139.
21 Jefferson to Madison and to Monroe, April 19, 1798, in Ford, *Works of Jefferson*, 7:240–244; Robert Troup to Rufus King, June 10, 1798, in *The Life and Correspondence of Rufus King*, ed. Charles R. King (New York: G. P. Putnam's Sons, 1894–1900), 2:344–346.
22 John Taylor added "of Caroline," meaning the Virginia county he was from, to distinguish himself from another John Taylor.
23 Jefferson to Taylor, June 1, 1798, in Ford, *Works of Jefferson*, 7:263–266. The quoted words are Jefferson's paraphrase of Taylor's letter, which has presumably been lost.
24 Ibid.
25 Taylor to Jefferson, June 25, 1798, in "John Taylor Correspondence," ed. William E. Dodd, *John P. Branch Historical Papers of Randolph Macon College* 2 (June 1908): 271–276.
26 John Dawson to Monroe, July 29, 1798, Monroe Papers, Library of Congress.
27 Jefferson to Archibald Hamilton Rowan, September 26, 1798, in Ford, *Works of Jefferson*, 7:280–281.
28 Jefferson to John Cabel Breckinridge, December 11, 1821, in ibid., 7:290–291n. Koch and Ammon, in their "Virginia and Kentucky Resolutions," 149–150, call into question the reliability of Jefferson's memory on some specific points in this letter. For a question of general strategy, however, I see no reason to doubt Jefferson's recollection.
29 "Drafts of the Kentucky Resolutions of 1798," in ibid., 289–309.
30 Ibid.
31 Jefferson to Madison, November 17, 1798, and Jefferson to Taylor, November 26, 1798, in ibid., 288, 309–312.
32 Joan Wells Coward, *Kentucky in the New Republic: The Process of Constitution Making* (Lexington: University of Kentucky Press, 1979), 113.
33 Jefferson to Wilson Cary Nicholas, November 29, 1798, in Ford, *Works of Jefferson*, 7:312–313.
34 As quoted in Richard Beeman, *The Old Dominion and the New Nation* (Lexington: University of Kentucky Press, 1972), 191–193.
35 As quoted in ibid., 192–193.
36 Ibid., 191.
37 Madison to Jefferson, December 29, 1798, in Hunt, *Madison*, 6:327–329n.
38 Beeman, *Old Dominion*, 194.

39 Taylor to Jefferson, December 11, 1798, Jefferson Papers, Library of Congress.
40 John Page to Jefferson, June 21, 1798, in ibid.
41 Ibid.

CHAPTER 5 THE FEDERALIST COUNTERATTACK:
THE ELECTION OF 1798

1 Noble Cunningham, Jr., *The Jeffersonian Republicans: The Formation of Party Organization, 1789–1801* (Chapel Hill: University of North Carolina Press, 1957), 135.
2 Frank Maloy Anderson, "Contemporary Opinion of the Virginia and Kentucky Resolutions," *American Historical Review* 5 (January 1900): 228.
3 Ibid., 233.
4 Frank Maloy Anderson, "Contemporary Opinion of the Virginia and Kentucky Resolutions," *American Historical Review* 5 (October 1899): 57.
5 Ibid., 46–47; 58–59.
6 Frank Maloy Anderson, "Contemporary Opinion of the Virginia and Kentucky Resolutions," *American Historical Review* 5 (January 1900): 237–238.
7 Jefferson to Madison, January 30, 1799, in *The Works of Thomas Jefferson*, ed. Paul L. Ford (New York: G. P. Putnam's Sons, 1904), 7:338–339.
8 Taylor to Harry Innes, April 25, 1799, Innes Papers, Library of Congress.
9 As quoted in Cunningham, *The Jeffersonian Republicans*, 135.
10 Taylor to Jefferson, May 6, 1799, and Taylor to Jefferson, February 15, 1799, in "John Taylor Correspondence," ed. William E. Dodd, *John P. Branch Historical Papers of Randolph-Macon College* 2 (June 1908): 278–281, 281–282.
11 Sedgwick to King, January 20 and March 20, 1799, in *The Life and Correspondence of Rufus King*, ed. Charles R. King (New York: G. P. Putnam's Sons, 1895), 2:514–518, 579–583.
12 Pickering to King, May 4, 1799, in ibid., 3:12–13.
13 William Heath to Hamilton, January 14 and 18, 1799, in *The Papers of Alexander Hamilton*, ed. Harold C. Syrett (New York: Columbia University Press, 1961–1987), 22:413–416 and 422–424.
14 Adrienne Koch and Harry Ammon, "The Virginia and Kentucky Resolutions: An Episode in Jefferson's and Madison's Defense of Civil Liberties," *William and Mary Quarterly* 5 (April 1948): 163, 163n. See also Richard Beeman, *The Old Dominion and the New Nation* (Lexington: University of Kentucky Press, 1972), 202.
15 As quoted in Koch and Ammon, "Virginia and Kentucky Resolutions," 164–165; William Heath to Hamilton, January 14 and January 18, 1799, in Syrett, *Hamilton*, 22:413–416, 422–424; and Sedgwick to King, November 15, 1799, in King, *Life of Rufus King*, 3:145–148.
16 As quoted in Robins Dice Anderson, *William Branch Giles* (Gloucester, Mass.: Peter Smith, 1965), 69–70.
17 James Roger Sharp, *American Politics in the Early Republic* (New Haven, Conn.: Yale University Press, 1995), 206.
18 Hamilton to Otis, December 27, 1798, and Hamilton to Sedgwick, February 2, 1799, in Syrett, *Hamilton*, 22:393–394, 452–454.
19 Hamilton to Jonathan Dayton, [October–November 1799], in ibid., 23:599–604.
20 See Paul Douglas Newman's *Fries Rebellion: The Enduring Struggle for the*

American Revolution (Philadelphia: University of Pennsylvania Press, 2004), ix. He argues, "[Fries] was a rebellion in a figurative sense, as a popular, localized resistance movement against perceived injustices by aggrieved citizens who employed logical but illegal methods and Revolutionary ideals, but not in a literal way as an attempt to make war against the government."

21 Jefferson to Edmund Pendleton, February 14, 1799, in Ford, *Works of Jefferson*, 9:45–50.

22 Newman, *Fries Rebellion*; Peter Levine, "The Fries Rebellion: Social Violence and the Politics of the New Nation," *Pennsylvania History* 40 (July 1973): 241–259; and W. H. Davis, *The Fries Rebellion, 1798–1799* (1899; reprint, New York: Arno Press, 1969).

23 Davis, *Fries Rebellion*, 33.

24 See Newman, *Fries Rebellion*, 112–141, for a very detailed account of the rescue.

25 As quoted in ibid., 142.

26 "Report, Fall 1799," in *Memoirs of the Administrations of Washington and John Adams*, ed. George Gibbs (New York: W. Van Norton, 1846), 2:298–306.

27 As quoted in Newman, *Fries Rebellion*, 152.

28 Hamilton to McHenry, March 18, 1799, in Syrett, *Hamilton*, 22:552–553.

29 As quoted in Lisle Rose, *Prologue to Democracy: The Federalists in the South, 1789–1800* (Lexington: University of Kentucky Press, 1968), 219.

30 Hamilton to Washington, May 19, 1798, in Syrett, *Hamilton*, 21:466–468.

31 As quoted in Beeman, *Old Dominion*, 158.

32 Ibid., 157–158.

33 As quoted in Dumas Malone, *Jefferson and the Ordeal of Liberty* (Boston: Little, Brown, 1962), 417.

34 Sedgwick to King, July 26 and December 29, 1799, in King, *Life of Rufus King*, 3:69–71, 162–163.

35 As quoted in Beeman, *Old Dominion*, 207.

36 Ibid., 205–206.

37 As quoted in Manning J. Dauer, *The Adams Federalists* (Baltimore: Johns Hopkins University Press, 1968), 236.

38 Taylor was responding to Jefferson's suggestion that Monroe be put up to replace the recently deceased Henry Tazewell in the United States Senate. Taylor to Jefferson, February 15, 1799, Jefferson Papers, Library of Congress; Jefferson to Taylor, January 24, 1799, in Ford, *Works of Jefferson*, 7:322–323; and John Guerrant to Monroe, October 14, 1799, Monroe Papers, Library of Congress.

39 Taylor to Madison, March 4, 1799, as quoted in Koch and Ammon, "Kentucky and Virginia Resolutions," 163–164.

40 Walter Jones and others to Madison, February 7, 1799, Madison Papers, Library of Congress.

41 These figures are from Rudolph M. Bell, *Party and Faction in American Politics: The House of Representatives, 1789–1801* (Westport, Conn.: Greenwood Press, 1973), 256–259. One difficulty in giving precise figures is that in some states, representation was rather fluid, with incoming midterm replacements. See Michael J. Dubin, *United States Congressional Elections, 1788–1997* (Jefferson, N.C.: McFarland, 1998), 18–21. Noble Cunningham has somewhat different figures in *Jeffersonian Republicans*, 133–135. He writes that in "the last session of the

Fifth Congress the party division was fifty-six Federalists and fifty Republicans. But at the beginning of the next Congress, the Federalists'majority of six was estimated to have grown to about twenty, although the majority was diminished somewhat during the course of the session." And the official data from the Clerk of the House indicates a smaller Federalist increase from an eight- to a fourteen-vote advantage over the Republicans. See Office of the Clerk, House of Representatives, http://clerk.house.gov/art__ history/house__history/index .htm/.

42 Lampi's data from the First Democracy Project at the American Antiquarian Society, Worcester, Mass. (http://www.americanantiquarian.org/fdp.htm), indicates from incomplete information that Marshall won 771 to 705. All electoral data, unless it is otherwise noted, comes from this marvelous collection.

43 Jefferson to Tench Coxe, May 21, 1799, Jefferson Papers, Library of Congress; as quoted in Rose, *Prologue to Democracy*, 222.

44 Lampi, First Democracy Project. These votes like most in the early republic are incomplete but do give a sense of how closely the state was divided.

45 Norman Risjord and Gordon DenBoer, "The Evolution of Political Parties in Virginia, 1782–1800," *Journal of American History* 60 (March 1974): 982–983.

46 Lampi, First Democracy Project.

47 Norman Risjord, *Chesapeake Politics, 1781–1800* (New York: Columbia University Press, 1978), 536–538.

48 As quoted in Rose, *Prologue to Democracy*, 181–182.

49 Ibid., 187; and Lampi, First Democracy Project.

50 As quoted in Cunningham, *Jeffersonian Republicans*, 134; and Lampi, First Democracy Project.

51 Dubin, *Congressional Elections*, 14–19; and Lampi, First Democracy Project.

52 Washington to Marshall, May 5, 1799, in *The Writings of George Washington*, ed. John Fitzpatrick (Washington, D.C.: U.S. Government Printing Office, 1940), 37:199.

CHAPTER 6 EARLY CRACKS IN THE FEDERALIST
HEGEMONY, 1799–1800

1 David McCullough, *John Adams* (New York: Simon & Schuster, 2001), 523. See John Ferling, *John Adams: A Life* (Newtown, Conn.: American Political Biography Press, 2009), 372–380, for a discussion of Adams's thinking in making this decision.

2 As quoted in McCullough, *John Adams*, 513.

3 Sedgwick and Pickering to Hamilton, February 19 and 25, 1799, in *The Papers of Alexander Hamilton*, ed. Harold C. Syrett (New York: Columbia University Press, 1961–1987), 22:487–490, 500–503, and as quoted in ibid., 22:523–524.

4 Sedgwick to Hamilton, February 7, 1799, in Syrett, *Hamilton*, 22:469–472.

5 As quoted in Manning J. Dauer, *The Adams Federalists* (Baltimore: Johns Hopkins University Press, 1968), 238–241.

6 Hamilton to King and to Miranda, August 22, 1798, in Syrett, *Hamilton*, 22:154–156.

7 King to Hamilton, January 21, 1799, in *The Life and Correspondence of Rufus King*, ed. Charles R. King (New York: G. P. Putnam's Sons, 1894–1900), 2:519.

8   Hamilton to Otis, January 26, 1799, in Syrett, *Hamilton*, 22:440–441.

9   See Darren Staloff, *Hamilton, Adams, Jefferson: The Politics of Enlightenment and the American Founding* (New York: Hill & Wang, 2005), 44–131.

10 As quoted in ibid., 44.

11 Sedgwick to Hamilton, February 7, 1799, in Syrett, *Hamilton*, 22:469–472.

12 As quoted in McCullough, *John Adams*, 518 and 522; and Ferling, *Adams*, 360.

13 Peter Shaw, *The Character of John Adams* (Chapel Hill: University of North Carolina, 1976), 260–261.

14 McCullough, *John Adams*, 513; Ferling, *Adams*, 384; and Jeffrey L. Pasley, "The Tyranny of the Printers": Newspaper Politics in the Early American Republic (Charlottesville: University of Virginia Press, 2001), 183.

15 Robert Troup to King, June 5, 1799, and George Cabot to King, October 6, 1799, in King, *Life of Rufus King*, 3:33–35 and 113–114.

16 Alexander DeConde, *The Quasi-War: The Politics and Diplomacy of the Undeclared War with France, 1797–1801* (New York: Scribner & Sons, 1966), 215–216; Stephen G. Kurtz, *The Presidency of John Adams: The Collapse of Federalism, 1795–1800* (New York: A. S. Barnes, 1961), 387–388; and John C. Miller, *Alexander Hamilton: Portrait in Paradox* (New York: Harper & Brothers, 1959), 501–502.

17 McCullough, *John Adams*, 526; and Ferling, *Adams*, 384–385.

18 McCullough, *John Adams*, 528; and Ferling, *Adams*, 384.

19 As quoted in McCullough, *John Adams*, 528; and Ferling, *Adams*, 384–386.

20 Adams's letter as quoted in *Memoirs of the Administrations of Washington and John Adams*, ed. George Gibbs (New York: W. Van Norton, 1846), 2:271; Adams to Pickering, October 16, 1799, in *The Works of John Adams, 2nd President of the United States*, ed. Charles Francis Adams (Boston: Little, Brown, 1854), 9:39; DeConde, *Quasi-War*, 215–222; Miller, *Alexander Hamilton*, 501–502; Shaw, *Character of Adams*, 260–265; John Ferling, *Adams vs. Jefferson: The Tumultuous Election of 1800* (New York: Oxford University Press, 2004), 124.

21 Morse to Olcott, November 8, 1799, in Gibbs, *Memoirs of Administrations*, 2: 287.

22 Jefferson to Madison, August 23, 1799, Madison Papers, Library of Congress.

23 Ibid.

24 Jefferson to Wilson C. Nicholas, September 5, 1799, in *The Works of Thomas Jefferson*, ed. Paul L. Ford (New York: G. P. Putnam's Sons, 1904), 7:389–392. See also Adrienne Koch and Harry Ammon, "The Virginia and Kentucky Resolutions: An Episode in Jefferson's and Madison's Defense of Civil Liberties," *William and Mary Quarterly* 5 (April 1948): 115–118, for a discussion of Jefferson's change of position.

25 Breckinridge to Jefferson, December 13, 1799, Jefferson Papers, Library of Congress; and Koch and Ammon, "Virginia and Kentucky Resolutions," 169.

26 Koch and Ammon, "Virginia and Kentucky Resolutions," 171–173.

27 Dumas Malone, *Thomas Jefferson and the Ordeal of Liberty* (Boston: Little, Brown, 1962), 422–423.

28 Kurtz, *Presidency of Adams*, 412–413.

29 The figures are from Philip J. Lampi, "Election of 1800 Re-visited," unpublished paper presented to the American Historical Association Meeting in Chicago, January 9, 2000, 11.

30 Malone, *Jefferson and the Ordeal*, 462–463.

31 Ferling, *Adams vs. Jefferson*, 127.

32 See Nancy Isenberg, *Fallen Founder: The Life of Aaron Burr* (New York: Viking Press, 2007), for an attempt to restore Burr's reputation. For a discussion of his legal work, see 87–98.

33 Ibid., 135–136 and 162–164.

34 William Smith to Ralph Izard, May 18 and November 8, 1796, in U. B. Phillips, ed., "South Carolina Federalist Correspondence, 1789–1797," *American Historical Review* 14 (July 1909): 784–785; Oliver Wolcott to Wolcott Senior, October 17, 1796, and to Jonathan Dayton, September 15, 1796, in Gibbs, *Memoirs of Administrations*, 1:386–388, 383–384. See also Noble Cunningham, Jr., *The Jeffersonian Republicans: The Formation of Party Organization, 1789–1801* (Chapel Hill: University of North Carolina Press, 1957), 91–92; Malone, *Jefferson and the Ordeal*, 277–278; Kurtz, *Presidency of Adams*, 93–94. Oliver Wolcott, the secretary of treasury, was making inquiries as late as September 1796 among his colleagues about who would run with Jefferson. See Jonathan Dayton to Wolcott, September 15, 1796, in Gibbs, *Memoirs of Administrations*, 1:383–384.

35 Isenberg, *Fallen Founder*, 162.

36 As quoted in ibid., 178–179 and 180.

37 Cunningham, *Jeffersonian Republicans*, 177.

38 As quoted in Isenberg, *Fallen Founder*, 197.

39 As quoted in Elkins and McKitrick, *The Age of Federalism: The Early American Republic, 1788–1800* (New York: Oxford University Press), 733.

40 As quoted in Milton Lomask, *Aaron Burr* (New York: Farrar, Straus & Giroux, 1979), 1:244.

41 As quoted in Cunningham, *Jeffersonian Republicans*, 182–183.

42 Matthew L. David to Gallatin, March 29, 1800, and George J. Warner to Gallatin, May 2, 1800, Gallatin Papers, New York Historical Society; and Lomask, *Burr*, 1:236–246.

43 Ferling, *Adams vs. Jefferson*, 131; and Isenberg, *Fallen Founder*, 197.

44 As quoted in Ferling, *Adams vs. Jefferson*, 127.

45 Hamilton to Jay, May 7, 1800, and Hamilton to Sedgwick, May 4, 1800, in Syrett, *Hamilton*, 24:464–467, 444–453. Also, Pickering and C. Gore to King, May 7 and May 5, 1800, in King, *Life of Rufus King*, 3:232–333.

46 John Chester Miller, *Federalist Era: 1789–1801* (New York: Harper & Bros., 1960), 258–259.

47 James M. Smith, *Freedom's Fetters: The Alien and Sedition Laws and American Civil Liberties* (Ithaca, N.Y.: Cornell University Press, 1956), 288–289, 300 and 300n.

48 Sharp, *American Politics*, 218–220; Malone, *Jefferson and the Ordeal*, 464–467; and Dauer, *Adams Federalists*, 244.

CHAPTER 7 ADAMS VERSUS HAMILTON: THE SPLIT BECOMES UNBRIDGEABLE

1 Hamilton to King, January 5, 1800, in *The Life and Correspondence of Rufus King*, ed. Charles R. King (New York: G. P. Putnam's Sons, 1900), 3:173–174.

2 Sedgwick to King, May 11, 1800, in ibid., 3:236–239; and Hamilton to Sedgwick a week earlier, May 4, 1800, in *The Papers of Alexander Hamilton*, ed. Harold C. Syrett (New York: Columbia University Press, 1976), 24:452–453.

3 John Dawson to Madison, December 12, 1799, Madison Papers, Library of Congress.

4 As quoted in Nancy Isenberg, *Fallen Founder: The Life of Aaron Burr* (New York: Viking Press, 2007), 134–135.

5 As quoted in ibid., 201.

6 Ibid., 201–202.

7 Letter of John Nicholson, December 26, 1803, *American Historical Review* 8 (1902–1903): 511–513; James Nicholson to Gallatin, May 7, 1800, Mrs. Albert Gallatin to her husband, May 7, 1800, and Albert Gallatin to his wife, May 12, 1800, in Henry Adams, *The Life of Albert Gallatin* (New York: Peter Smith, 1943), 242, 243. Milton Lomask, in his *Aaron Burr: The Years from Princeton to Vice President, 1756–1805* (New York: Farrar, Straus, & Giroux, 1979), argues that Clinton had wanted the nomination, but that Burr had "tricked him out of it," 1:247–255.

8 James McHenry to Adams, May 31, 1800, enclosed with McHenry to Hamilton, June 2, 1800, in Syrett, *Hamilton*, 24:550–565.

9 As quoted in David McCullough, *John Adams* (New York: Simon & Schuster, 2001), 538.

10 As quoted in Gerard H. Clarfield, *Timothy Pickering and American Diplomacy, 1795–1800* (Columbia: University of Missouri Press, 1969), 212. See also Adams to Pickering, May 10, 1800, Pickering to Adams, May 12, 1800, and Adams to Pickering, May 12, 1800, in *The Works of John Adams, 2nd President of the United States*, ed. Charles Francis Adams (Boston: Little, Brown, 1854), 9:53–55.

11 See Paul Douglas Newman, *Fries Rebellion: The Enduring Struggle for the American Revolution* (Philadelphia: University of Pennsylvania Press, 2004), 183–188.

12 As quoted in ibid., 184–185.

13 As quoted in ibid., 185.

14 *The Trenton Federalist; or New-Jersey Gazette*, June 2, 1800, as quoted in Syrett, *Hamilton*, 24: 482–486n.

15 Hamilton to McHenry, June 6, 1800, in ibid., 573.

16 Campbell Gibson, "Population of the 100 Largest Cities and Other Urban Places in the United States: 1790–1990," Population Division, U.S. Bureau of the Census (Washington, D.C.: U.S. Government Printing Office, 1998).

17 Elaine C. Everly and Howard H. Wehmann, "'Then Let Us to the Woods Repair,'" in *Establishing Congress: The Removal to Washington, D.C., and the Election of 1800*, ed. Kenneth R. Bowling and Donald R. Kennon (Athens: Ohio University Press, 2005), 56–59.

18 Nathan Schachner, *Thomas Jefferson: A Biography* (New York: Thomas Yoseloff, 1960), 646.

19 As quoted in James Sterling Young, *The Washington Community, 1800–1828* (New York: Harcourt, Brace & World, 1966), 49.

20 As quoted in ibid., 45.

21 As quoted in ibid., 47; and Henry Adams, *History of the United States during the First Administration of Thomas Jefferson* (New York: Antiquarian Press, 1962), 1:188.

22 As quoted in Young, *Washington Community*, 41.

23 Everly and Wehmann, "Let Us to the Woods," 56, 66–67.

24 It was not called the "White House" until named so by President Theodore Roosevelt in 1901.
25 As quoted in Young, *Washington Community*, 44, 75.
26 As quoted in ibid., 75.
27 Ibid., 51.
28 As quoted in Edward J. Larson, *A Magnificent Catastrophe: The Tumultuous Election of 1800; America's First Presidential Campaign* (New York: Free Press, 2007), 259.
29 As quoted in Young, *Washington Community*, 47; and Adams, *History of the United States*, 1:188.
30 Hamilton to Sedgwick, May 4, 1800, Syrett, *Hamilton*, 24:452–453.
31 Hamilton to Pickering, May 14, 1800, in *The Works of Alexander Hamilton*, ed. Henry Cabot Lodge (New York: G. P. Putnam's Sons, 1904), 10.
32 John Ferling, *Adams vs. Jefferson: The Tumultuous Election of 1800* (New York: Oxford University Press, 2004), 142–143.
33 As quoted in Stephen G. Kurtz, *The Presidency of John Adams: The Collapse of Federalism, 1795–1800* (New York: A. S. Barnes, 1961), 401–402.
34 Abigail Adams to Thomas Boylston Adams, July 12, 1800, as quoted in Syrett, *Hamilton*, 24:574–577n.
35 As quoted in Noble E. Cunningham, Jr., *The Jeffersonian Republicans: The Formation of Party Organization, 1789–1801* (Chapel Hill: University of North Carolina Press, 1957), 186.
36 Fisher Ames to Chauncey Goodrich, June 12, 1800, in *Memoirs of the Administrations of Washington and John Adams*, ed. George Gibbs (New York: W. Van Norton, 1846), 2:366–367.
37 Cabot to King, August 9, 1800, in King, *Life of Rufus King*, 3:291–292.
38 Ames to Wolcott, June 12, 1800, in Gibbs, *Memoirs of Administrations*, 2:367–370.
39 Wolcott to Ames, August 10, 1800, ibid., 400–405.
40 Ibid.
41 Letter 17 to the *Boston Patriot*, in Adams, *Works of Adams*, 9:300–301.
42 I am grateful to my colleague, Professor Margaret Susan Thompson, for information about presidential campaigning.
43 Kurtz, *Presidency of Adams*, 399.
44 Ibid.
45 Ibid.
46 Ibid., 397.
47 Jefferson to Gideon Granger, August 13, 1800, Jefferson to Gerry, January 26, 1799, and Jefferson to Samuel Adams, February 26, 1800, in *The Works of Thomas Jefferson*, ed. Paul L. Ford (New York: G. P. Putnam's Sons), 7:138–141, 15–26, 450–453, 114–115.
48 McCullough, *John Adams*, 543–547.
49 Dumas Malone, *Jefferson and the Ordeal of Liberty* (Boston: Little, Brown, 1962), 481.
50 Ferling, *Adams vs. Jefferson*, 151.
51 Ibid.
52 As quoted in Larson, *Magnificent Catastrophe*, 180.

53   McCullough, *John Adams*, 543–547.

54   Ferling, *Adams vs. Jefferson*, 146.

55   Ibid., 147.

56   McCullough, *John Adams*, 536–537.

57   Jerry W. Knudson, *Jefferson and the Press: Crucible of Liberty* (Columbia: University of South Carolina Press, 2006), 42–43.

58   Jeffrey L. Pasley, *"The Tyranny of Printers": Newspaper Politics in the Early Republic* (Charlottesville: University of Virginia Press, 2001), 185–186.

59   Cunningham, *Jeffersonian Republicans*, 213–214.

60   Pasley, *Tyranny of Printers*, 188.

61   Ibid., 105–106, 126.

62   As quoted in Cunningham, *Jeffersonian Republicans*, 250.

63   The above discussion of Bishop relies on David Waldstreicher's book, *In the Midst of Perpetual Fetes: The Making of American Nationalism, 1776–1820* (Chapel Hill: University of North Carolina Press, 1997), 177–182.

64   For a discussion of this, see Sean Wilentz, *The Rise of American Democracy: Jefferson to Lincoln* (New York: W. W. Norton, 2005).

CHAPTER 8   TIE VOTE: THE ELECTORAL COLLEGE IN 1800

1   Douglas R. Egerton, *Gabriel's Rebellion: The Virginia Slave Conspiracies of 1800 and 1802* (Chapel Hill: University of North Carolina Press, 1993). Also, Callender to Jefferson, September 13, 1800, Jefferson Papers; John Randolph to Joseph H. Nicholson, September 26, 1800, Nicholson Papers, Library of Congress. Also, see Egerton's "Gabriel's Conspiracy and the Election of 1800," *Journal of Southern History* 56 (May 1990): 207; Herbert Aptheker, *American Negro Slave Revolts* (New York: International Publishers, 1963), 219–228; and Winthrop Jordan, *White over Black: American Attitudes toward the Negro, 1550–1812* (Chapel Hill: University of North Carolina Press, 1968), 393–396.

2   Jefferson to Monroe, July 14, 1793, as quoted in Aptheker, *Slave Revolts*, 42 and 41–42.

3   Jefferson to S. George Tucker, August 28, 1797, as quoted in Jordan, *White over Black*, 386.

4   *Gazette of the United States*, September 13, 1800, as quoted in Aptheker, *Slave Revolts*, 150.

5   *Virginia Herald*, September 23, 1800, as quoted in Jordan, *White over Black*, 396.

6   As quoted in Dumas Malone, *Jefferson and the Ordeal of Liberty* (Boston: Little, Brown, 1962), 480.

7   Murray to Adams, December 9, 1800, as quoted in Aptheker, *Slave Revolts*, 227.

8   See Egerton's "Gabriel's Conspiracy," and his *Gabriel's Rebellion*, especially 3–49; in the latter, see also 182–185.

9   Stanley Elkins and Eric McKitrick, *The Age of Federalism: The Early American Republic, 1788–1800* (New York: Oxford University Press, 1993), 737.

10   *Letter*, in *The Papers of Alexander Hamilton*, ed. Harold C. Syrett (New York: Columbia University Press, 1961–1987), 25:186–234; and Ron Chernow, *Alexander Hamilton* (New York: Penguin Books, 2004), 620–621.

11   As quoted in David McCullough, *John Adams* (New York: Simon & Schuster, 2001), 550.

12   As quoted in Elkins and McKitrick, *Federalist Era*, 739.

13   John Ferling, *Adams vs. Jefferson: The Tumultuous Election of 1800* (New York: Oxford University Press, 2004), 141–143.

14   As quoted in Darren Staloff, *Hamilton, Adams, Jefferson: The Politics of Enlightenment and the American Founding* (New York: Hill & Wang, 2005), 48–49.

15   As quoted in Malone, *Jefferson and the Ordeal*, 443.

16   William Little, H. W. Fowler, and J. Coulson, comps., *The Oxford Universal Dictionary on Historical Principles* (Oxford: Oxford University Press, 1955), 29.

17   Philip J. Lampi, "Election of 1800 Re-visited," unpublished paper presented at the American Historical Association Meeting, Chicago, January 9, 2000.

18   Congress in 1872 passed a law mandating that a single date be established for congressional elections. This was widely ignored; in 1876 ten of the thirty-eight states held elections on a date *other* than the Tuesday after the first Monday in November. It was not until "1960 . . . [that] all the states conform[ed] to the 1872 law." See Michael J. Dubin, *United States Congressional Elections, 1788–1997: The Official Results of the Elections of the 1st through 105th Congresses* (Jefferson, N.C.: McFarland, 1998), x.

19   U.S. Bureau of the Census, *Historical Statistics of the United States: Colonial Times to 1957* (Washington, D.C.: U.S. Government Printing Office, 1960), 681.

20   Ibid., and Lampi, "Election of 1800 Re-visited."

21   Ibid.; and electoral data from the American Antiquarian Society, First Democracy Project (http://www.americanantiquarian.org/fdp.htm). See also John H. Aldrich, "The Election in 1800: The Consequences of the First Change in Party Control," in *Establishing Congress: The Removal to Washington D.C. and the Election of 1800*, ed. Kenneth R. Bowling and Donald R. Kennon (Athens: Ohio University Press, 2005), 33.

22   *American Mercury*, September 4, 1800, as quoted in Noble E. Cunningham, Jr., *The Jeffersonian Republicans: The Formation of Party Organization, 1789–1801* (Chapel Hill: University of North Carolina Press, 1957), 219; see also 200–201, 204–210, and 217–218. For further discussion, see Ronald P. Formisano, *The Transformation of Political Culture: Massachusetts Parties, 1790s–1840s* (New York: Oxford University Press, 1983), 73; and Syrett, *Hamilton*, 24:444–453.

23   Stephen G. Kurtz, *The Presidency of John Adams: The Collapse of Federalism, 1795–1800* (New York: A. S. Barnes, 1961), 412–413.

24   Aldrich, "Election of 1800," 34; Lampi, "Election of 1800 Re-visited"; and John C. Miller, *The Federalist Era, 1789–1801* (New York: Harper & Row, 1960), 258.

25   Malone, *Jefferson and the Ordeal*, 462–463 and 492–493.

26   Election figures are from Lampi, "Election of 1800 Re-visited."

27   As quoted in Cunningham, *Jeffersonian Republicans*, 155.

28   *American Mercury*, September 4, 1800, as quoted in Cunningham, *Jeffersonian Republicans*, 219. See also 200–201, 204–210, and 217–218. Formisano, *Transformation of Culture*, 73; and Syrett, *Hamilton*, 24:444–453; Lampi, "Election of 1800 Re-visited."

29   First Democracy Project, American Antiquarian Society, Election of 1800.

30   Lampi, "Election of 1800 Re-visited." Rudolph M. Bell, in his *Party and Faction in American Politics: The House of Representatives, 1789–1801* (Westport, Conn.: Greenwood Press, 1973), 258–259, has a somewhat different total, twenty-one Republicans to twenty-five Federalists.

31 As quoted in Ferling, *Adams vs. Jefferson*, 156. See also Norman K. Risjord, *Chesapeake Politics, 1781–1800* (New York: Columbia University Press, 1978), 556; and Malone, *Jefferson and the Ordeal*, 460. The Federalists exaggerated their strength in the state. They polled 22.7 percent of the electorate in 1800. See the First Democracy Project, American Antiquarian Society, Election of 1800.

32 Editor's note in Syrett, *Hamilton*, 24:444–453; Dawson to Madison, December 12, 1799, and February 1, 1800, Madison Papers, Library of Congress; Jefferson to Monroe, January 12, 1800, in *The Works of Thomas Jefferson*, ed. Paul L. Ford (New York: G. P. Putnam's Sons, 1904), 7:401–403.

33 The figures are from Lampi, "Election of 1800 Re-visited."

34 As quoted in Cunningham, *Jeffersonian Republicans*, 189–190.

35 As quoted in ibid., 190–191.

36 First Democracy Project, American Antiquarian Society, Election of 1800.

37 McHenry to Wolcott, November 9, 1800, in *Memoirs of the Administrations of Washington and John Adams*, ed. George Gibbs (New York: W. Van Norton, 1846), 2:445.

38 U.S. Bureau of the Census, *Historical Statistics*, 681.

39 As quoted in Cunningham, *Jeffersonian Republicans*, 199.

40 Lampi, "Election of 1800 Re-visited."

41 As quoted in Lisle Rose, *Prologue to Democracy: The Federalists in the South, 1789–1800* (Lexington: University of Kentucky Press, 1968), 274. I have followed Rose's discussion of South Carolina politics in these several paragraphs.

42 Ibid., 274–276.

43 As quoted in ibid., 270 and 280–282.

44 Charles Pinckney to Jefferson, November 22, 1800, in *The Writings of James Monroe*, ed. Stanislaus M. Hamilton (New York: G. P. Putnam's Sons, 1900), 3:244–246. See letters of Peter Freneau from Columbia, South Carolina, in late November and early December 1800, in Miscellaneous Papers, Library of Congress. See also James H. Broussard, *The Southern Federalists, 1800–1816* (Baton Rouge: Louisiana State University Press, 1978), 30–31; Miller, *Federalist Era*, 267; Cunningham, *Jeffersonian Republicans*, 188–189, 231–236; and Syrett, *Hamilton*, 24:452.

45 As quoted in Cunningham, *Jeffersonian Republicans*, 236, 237, 238.

46 Ibid., 233. Cunningham claims that December 2, 1800, was the election day, while Ferling, *Adams vs. Jefferson*, 162–163, claims it was December 3, 1800.

47 Malone, *Jefferson and the Ordeal*, 491; and Nathan Schachner, *Thomas Jefferson: A Biography* (New York: Thomas Yoseloff, 1960), 646.

48 Malone, *Jefferson and the Ordeal*, 493; and as quoted in Ferling, *Adams vs. Jefferson*, 163–164.

49 Malone, *Jefferson and the Ordeal*, 495; and Ferling, *Adams vs. Jefferson*, 164.

50 See Kurtz, *Presidency of John Adams*, 412–414.

51 These are figures from the Office of the U.S. Clerk of the House at http://clerk .house.gov/art_history/house_history/index.html. This interactive site gives access to all historical election results of the House; each session is selected separately under the menu "Congress Overview." The figures differ in minor ways from those in other sources such as Manning Dauer, *The Adams Federalists* (Baltimore: Johns Hopkins University Press, 1968), 273–274. For the Sixth

Congress, see Bell, *Party and Faction*, 258–259; and for the Seventh, see Cunningham, *Jeffersonian Republicans*, 247. Cunningham warns that the figures are "only approximate," which underscores the notion that political affiliation was often worn very lightly in the early republic.

52 Lampi, "Election of 1800 Re-visited."

53 Cunningham, *Jeffersonian Republicans*, 246–248; and Lampi, "Election of 1800 Re-visited."

54 Lampi, "Election of 1800 Re-visited."

CHAPTER 9 THE CRISIS BUILDS

1 Dumas Malone, *Jefferson and the Ordeal of Liberty* (Boston: Little, Brown, 1962), 499.

2 Gallatin to his wife, January 15, 1801, in Henry Adams, *The Life of Albert Gallatin* (New York: Peter Smith, 1943), 252.

3 Gallatin to his wife, January 15 and 22, 1801, in Adams, *Life of Albert Gallatin*, 253, 255. Also see James Sterling Young, *The Washington Community, 1800–1828* (New York: Harcourt, Brace & World, 1966), 41.

4 See Henry Adams, *History of the United States of America: During the First Administration of Thomas Jefferson* (New York: Antiquarian Press, 1962), 1:11–14, for a description of the difficulties of travel.

5 *General Advertiser*, January 27, 1801.

6 M. Clay to Monroe, January 21, 1801, Monroe Papers, Library of Congress.

7 *General Advertiser*, January 26, 1801. That February, while balloting for the presidency was taking place, the House of Representatives appointed a committee to investigate the fires. After examining the testimony of a number of witnesses, the committee members found no evidence that the fire at the War Department was the result of "negligence or design," but they were unable to form any conclusions about the Treasury fire. See *Memoirs of the Administrations of Washington and John Adams*, ed. George Gibbs (New York: W. Van Norton, 1846), 2:478–481. Also, Elaine C. Everly and Howard H. Wehmann, "'Let Us to the Woods Repair': Moving the Federal Government and Its Records to Washington in 1800," in *Establishing Congress: The Removal to Washington, D.C. and the Election of 1800*, ed. Kenneth R. Bowling and Donald R. Kennon (Athens: Ohio University Press, 2005), 68–69.

8 See Jeffrey L. Pasley, *"The Tyranny of the Printers": Newspaper Politics in the Early American Republic* (Charlottesville: University of Virginia Press, 2001), chapter 8 and 185–186.

9 *General Advertiser*, December 17, 1800, and January 3, 1801.

10 Granger to Jefferson, October 18, 1800, Jefferson Papers, Library of Congress.

11 *General Advertiser*, December 11, 1800.

12 Ibid., January 7, January 10, and February 3, 1801.

13 *Salem Federalist*, January 29, 1801, as quoted in ibid..

14 It has only happened twice in American history that presidential elections had to be decided by the House of Representatives: once in 1801 and again in 1825.

15 Jefferson to Madison, December 19, 1800, in *The Works of Thomas Jefferson*, ed. Paul L. Ford (New York: G. P. Putnam's Sons, 1904), 7:470–472; Noble E.

Cunningham, Jr., *The Jeffersonian Republicans: The Formation of Party Organization, 1789–1801* (Chapel Hill: University of North Carolina Press, 1957), 240–241; John C. Miller, *The Federalist Era, 1789–1801* (New York: Harper & Row, 1960), 269.

16 William Smith to Ralph Izard, May 18 and November 8, 1796, in U. B. Phillips, ed., "South Carolina Federalist Correspondence, 1789–1797," *American Historical Review* 14 (July 1909): 784–785.

17 Theodore Sedgwick to Hamilton, November 19, 1796, with enclosures (Jonathan Dayton to Sedgwick, November 12 and 13, 1796; Sedgwick to Dayton, November 19, 1796), *The Papers of Alexander Hamilton*, ed. Harold C. Syrett (New York: Columbia University Press, 1961–1987), 20:402–407.

18 Hugh Williamson to Monroe, November 6, 1800, and Madison to Monroe, November 10, 1800, Monroe Papers, Library of Congress. See Madison to Jefferson, October 21, 1800, wherein Madison reported that Burr supporters were concerned that Southern states would fail to support the New Yorker.

19 John Ferling, *Adams vs. Jefferson: The Tumultuous Election of 1800* (New York: Oxford University Press, 2004), 177.

20 Jefferson to Burr, December 15, 1800, in *Political Correspondence and Public Papers of Aaron Burr*, ed. Mary Jo Kline (Princeton, N.J.: Princeton University Press, 1983), 1:469–470. Milton Lomask, in his *Aaron Burr* (New York: Farrar, Straus & Giroux, 1979), 1:273, argues that Jefferson "was not interested in giving Burr an 'active station' in the government, only in wringing from him an avowal of disinterest in the Presidency." Nancy Isenberg speculates on Jefferson's motives in *Fallen Founder: The Life of Aaron Burr* (New York: Viking Press, 2007), 206.

21 Burr to Jefferson, December 23, 1800, Jefferson Papers, Library of Congress.

22 Burr to Smith, December 16, 1800, in Kline, *Papers of Burr*, 1:474–475.

23 As quoted in Malone, *Jefferson and the Ordeal*, 494. Malone, quite rightly, wonders why it took Madison so long to reveal this.

24 Harper to Burr, December 24, 1800, in Kline, *Papers of Burr*, 1:474–475.

25 George W. Erving to Monroe, January 25, 1801, Monroe Papers, Library of Congress; and Diary of Gouverneur Morris, December 27, 1800, ibid., 475n.

26 As quoted in Isenberg, *Fallen Founder*, 210–211.

27 As quoted in ibid., 211.

28 Burr to Smith, December 29, 1800, in Kline, *Papers of Burr*, 1:478–479.

29 Smith to Burr, January 11, 1800 (misdated 1801) in ibid., 487–489.

30 Burr to Smith, January 16, 1801, and Burr to Jefferson, February 12, 1801, in ibid., 493 and 501.

31 Ferling, *Adams vs. Jefferson*, 183.

32 Editor's notes, Kline, *Papers of Burr*, 1:490, 492–493; Jefferson's note, February 12, 1801, in Franklin Sawvel, ed., *The Anas of Thomas Jefferson* (New York: Da Capo Press, 1903), 209–210; Hamilton to Gouverneur Morris, January 9, 1801, in Syrett, *Hamilton*, 25:304–305.

33 Morris to Hamilton, December 1, 1800, in Syrett, *Hamilton*, 25:266–268.

34 As quoted in ibid., 268–269n. See also Jefferson to Burr, December 15, 1800, in Kline, *Papers of Burr*, 1:469–470.

35 See Bruce Ackerman, *The Failure of the Founding Fathers: Jefferson, Marshall and the Rise of Presidential Democracy* (Cambridge, Mass.: Harvard University Press,

2005), for a discussion of the awkwardness of the timing of congressional sessions and the problems with "lame duck" sessions, 117–122.

36 Jefferson to Madison, December 19, 1800, *Works of Jefferson*, ed. Paul L. Ford (New York: G. P. Putnam's Sons, 1904–1905), accessed from the Online Library of Liberty, http://oll.libertyfund.org/title/757/87247.

37 *General Advertiser*, January 16, 1801, as quoted in Kline, *Papers of Burr*, 1:302–303n.

38 Hamilton to Gouverneur Morris, January 9, 1801, in Syrett, *Hamilton*, 25:304.

39 Adams to Elbridge Gerry, February 7, 1801, in *The Works of John Adams, 2nd President of the United States*, ed. Charles Francis Adams (Boston: Little, Brown, 1854), 9:97–98. Adams went on to say that if this occurred, it should "be followed by another election, and Mr. Jefferson would be chosen; I should, in that case, decline the election." John Ferling, in *John Adams: A Life* (Newtown, Conn.: American Political Biography Press, 2004), 407, claims that Adams during the vote of the House of Representatives "hoped the Virginian would win," while Abigail thought Jefferson "purer" than Burr but worried that he was a "visionary" and had "anti-Christian biases."

40 Jefferson's diary entry of April 15, 1806, in Sawvel, *Anas of Jefferson*, 237–241; Jefferson to John Breckenridge, December 18, 1800, to Madison, December 19 and December 26, 1800, and to Tench Coxe, December 31, 1800, in Ford, *Works of Jefferson*, 7: 468–469, 474–475, 157–163; Caesar Rodney to Jefferson, December 28, 1800, Jefferson Papers, Library of Congress.

41 *General Advertiser*, January 7, 10, and February 3, 1801.

42 Brackenridge to Jefferson, January 19, 1801, Jefferson Papers, Library of Congress.

43 Sedgwick to Hamilton, January 10, 1801, in Syrett, *Hamilton*, 25:310–313.

44 Harrison Gray Otis to Hamilton, December 17, 1800, and Sedgwick to Hamilton, January 10, 1801, in ibid., 25:259 and 310–313.

45 Virginia in 1800 had a population of well over 800,000, making it the most populous state in the nation. Pennsylvania was second and New York third, with each having at least 200,000 fewer inhabitants than Virginia. See U.S. Department of Commerce, *Historical Statistics of the United States: Colonial Times to 1957* (Washington, D.C.: Bureau of the Census, 1961), 13.

46 Bayard to Hamilton, January 7, 1801, in Syrett, *Hamilton*, 25:299–303. See also Gouverneur Morris to Hamilton, January 26, 1801, and John Rutledge, Jr., to Hamilton, January 10, 1801, in ibid., 25:329–330, 308–310.

47 As quoted in Miller, *Federalist Era*, 107.

48 Hamilton to Bayard, December 27, 1800, in Syrett, *Hamilton*, 25:275–277.

49 As quoted in Isenberg, *Fallen Founder*, 211.

50 Hamilton to Wolcott, December 16, 1800, Syrett, *Hamilton*, 25:257.

51 Hamilton to John Rutledge, Jr., January 4, 1801, in ibid., 25:293–298.

52 As quoted in Isenberg, *Fallen Founder*, 212–213.

53 Hamilton to Bayard, January 16, 1801, in Syrett, *Hamilton*, 25:319–324.

54 Hamilton to Wolcott, December 17, 1800, in Gibbs, *Memoirs of Administrations*, 2:458–460.

55 R. Troup to King, December 31, 1800, and February 12, 1801, in *The Life and Correspondence of Rufus King*, ed. Charles R. King (New York: G. P. Putnam's Sons, 1895), 3:358 and 390–391.

56 *The Federalist Papers*, ed. Clinton Rossiter (New York: New American Library, 1961), 414.

57 Ralph Ketcham, *Presidents above Party: The First American Presidency, 1789–1829* (Chapel Hill: University of North Carolina Press, 1984), 228.

58 Isenberg in *Fallen Founder*, 213, argues that Hamilton was motivated by his fear of losing control of his leadership in New York as well as in the Federalist party to Burr. However, while Hamilton had lost credibility with a number of Federalists, it is highly unlikely that Burr, after double-crossing the Republicans, would be able to assume a leadership role among the Federalists, most of whom, if they voted for him, were highly suspicious and antagonistic.

59 Gallatin discussed the various rumors and possible Republican strategies in letters to his wife, Hannah, in January and February 1801, in the Gallatin Papers, New-York Historical Society Collection. See also editor's note in Kline, *Papers of Burr*, 1:481–487.

60 Gallatin to his wife, January 15, 1801, in Henry Adams, *The Life of Albert Gallatin* (New York: Peter Smith, 1943), 254–255.

61 Gallatin to his wife, January 22, 1801, in ibid., 255.

62 James Bayard indicates this in his legal deposition in *Memoirs of Burr*, ed. Matthew L. Davis (New York: Harper & Bros., 1837), 2:122–137. See also Dawson to Madison, February 12, 1801, Madison Papers, Library of Congress.

63 "Plan" in *The Writings of Albert Gallatin*, ed. Henry Adams (Philadelphia: J. B. Lipincott, 1879), 1:18–23. Gallatin miscalculated. Virginia, North Carolina, Georgia, Kentucky, and Tennessee combined for only forty votes for the Jefferson-Burr ticket in 1800. See Manning J. Dauer, *The Adams Federalists* (Baltimore: Johns Hopkins University Press, 1968), 257.

64 Gallatin to his wife, January 22, 1801, Gallatin Papers, New-York Historical Society Collection.

65 Gallatin to his wife, January 15, 1801, in Adams, *Life of Gallatin*, 252–255, and John Dawson to Madison, February 12, 1801, Madison Papers, Library of Congress.

CHAPTER 10 THE CRISIS RESOLVED

1 Bruce Ackerman, *The Failure of the Founding Fathers: Jefferson, Marshall, and the Rise of Presidential Democracy* (Cambridge, Mass.: Belknap Press of Harvard University, 2005), 73.

2 See ibid., 55–76, for an interesting discussion of this possibility.

3 Maryland had a five-to-three Federalist majority in its delegation in House of Representatives until one Federalist, George Dent, decided to vote for Jefferson, resulting in a tie in the delegation. See Edward J. Larson, *A Magnificent Catastrophe: The Tumultuous Election of 1800, America's First Presidential Campaign* (New York: Free Press, 2007), 244.

4 As quoted in Nathan Schachner, *Thomas Jefferson: A Biography* (New York: Thomas Yoseloff, 1960), 657; and Nancy Isenberg, *Fallen Founder: The Life of Aaron Burr* (New York: Viking Press, 2007), 210. Also, Gallatin to his wife, February 12, 1801, and to James Nicholson, February 14, 1801, in Henry Adams, *The Life of Gallatin* (New York: Peter Smith, 1943), 260–262; *Annals of Congress*, February

9, 10, 11, 12, 13, 14, 16, and 17, 1008–1032; and Jefferson to Monroe, February 12, 1801, Monroe Papers, Library of Congress; and Samuel W. Dana to Oliver Wolcott, February 11, 1801, in *Memoirs of the Administrations of Washington and John Adams*, ed. George Gibbs (New York: W. Van Norton, 1846), 2:489–490.

5 Gallatin to James Nicholson, February 14, 1801, Adams, *Life of Gallatin*, 262; and John Ferling, *Adams vs. Jefferson: The Tumultuous Election of 1800* (New York: Oxford University Press, 2004), 187.

6 Samuel W. Dana to Wolcott, February 11, 1801, in Gibbs, *Memoirs of Administrations*, 2:489–490. See Jefferson's note of February 12, 1801, in *The Anas of Thomas Jefferson*, ed. Franklin Sawvel (New York: Da Capo Press, 1903), 209–210.

7 Jefferson to Benjamin Rush, January 16, 1811, in Ford, *Works of Jefferson*, vol. 11, accessible through the Online Library of Liberty, http://oll.libertyfund.org/index.php?option=com_staticxt&staticfile=show.php&title=807&search=%22benjamin+rhsh%22&chapter=88070&layout=html#a_2004788.

8 Jefferson to Monroe, February 15, 1801, in *The Works of Thomas Jefferson*, ed. Paul L. Ford (New York: G. P. Putnam's Sons, 1905), 7:490–491.

9 Monroe to McKean, July 12, 1800, Thomas McKean Papers, Historical Society of Pennsylvania.

10 Monroe to John Hoomes, February 14, 1801, in *The Writings of James Monroe*, ed. Stanislaus M. Hamilton (New York: G. P. Putnam's Sons, 1900), 3:258–259; McKean to Jefferson, February 20, 1801, Jefferson Papers, Library of Congress; J. Tyler to Monroe, February, 11, 1801, Monroe Papers, Library of Congress.

11 McKean to Jefferson, February 20, 1801, Jefferson Papers, Library of Congress; Monroe to Jefferson, January 20, 1801, in Hamilton, *Monroe*, 3:257.

12 McKean to Jefferson, March 19, 1801, McKean Papers. This is a re-creation of an earlier letter that McKean had destroyed once hearing of Jefferson's election. Jefferson requested the re-created draft in his letter to McKean, March 9, 1801, ibid.

13 Major T. M. Randolph to Monroe, February 14, 1801, Monroe Papers, Library of Congress.

14 *General Advertiser*, February 19, 1801.

15 Isenberg, *Fallen Founder*, 214.

16 *Washington Federalist*, February 12, 1801, as quoted in the *General Advertiser*, February 17, 1801.

17 George M. Dallas, ed., *Life and Writings of Alexander James Dallas* (Philadelphia: J. B. Lippincott, 1871), 112–113. A writer in the *General Advertiser*, February 16, 1801, urged patience: "When constitutional means fail us, it will then be time enough to resort to extremities."

18 Beckley to Gallatin, February 15, 1801, Gallatin Papers, New York Historical Society Collection.

19 Susan G. Davis, *Parades and Power: Street Theatre in Nineteenth-Century Philadelphia* (Berkeley: University of California Press, 1988), 53–57.

20 Lisle Rose, *Prologue to Democracy: The Federalists in the South, 1789–1800* (Lexington: University of Kentucky Press, 1968), 220–221.

21 Davis, *Parades and Power*, 195n.

22 Jeffrey L. Pasley, *"The Tyranny of the Printers": Newspaper Politics in the Early American Republic* (Charlottesville: University of Virginia Press, 2001), 187–190.

23 Gallatin to his wife, February 12, 1801, and to James Nicholson, February 14, 1801, in Adams, *Life of Gallatin*, 260–262; *Annals of Congress*, 6th Cong., 2d sess., February 9, 10, 11, 12, 13, 14, 16, and 17, 1008–1032; Jefferson to Monroe, February 12, 1801, Monroe Papers, Library of Congress; Samuel W. Dana to Wolcott, February 11, 1801, in Gibbs, *Memoirs of Administrations*, 2:489–490.

24 Bayard to McLane, February 17, 1801, Jefferson Papers, Library of Congress; Bayard to Samuel Bayard, February 22, 1801, in *The Papers of James A. Bayard, 1796–1815*, ed. Elizabeth Donnan (Washington, D.C.: American Historical Association, 1915). For the best account of Bayard resolving the deadlock, see Morton Borden, *The Federalism of James Bayard* (New York: Columbia University Press, 1955), 86–95. Also, Milton Lomask, *Aaron Burr* (New York: Farrar, Straus & Giroux, 1979), 1:280, 289–294.

25 Bayard to McLane, February 17, 1801, Jefferson Papers, Library of Congress; Bayard to Samuel Bayard, February 22, 1801, in Donnan, *Papers of Bayard*; Borden, *Bayard*, 89–90; *Memoirs of Burr*, ed. Matthew Davis (New York: Harper & Bros., 1837), 2:127–128; and editor's note in *Political Correspondence and Public Papers of Aaron Burr*, ed. Mary Jo Kline (Princeton, N.J.: Princeton University Press, 1983), 1:486–487. Also, George W. Erving to Monroe, February 17, 1801, Monroe Papers, Library of Congress; Thomas Mason to John Breckinridge, February 19, 1801, Breckinridge Family Papers, Library of Congress; Gallatin to James Nicholson, February 16, 1801, and to his wife, February 17, 1801, Gallatin Papers, New-York Historical Society Collection.

26 Bayard to Hamilton, January 7, 1801, *The Papers of Alexander Hamilton*, ed. Harold C. Syrett (New York: Columbia University Press, 1977), 25:299–303. See also Gouverneur Morris to Hamilton, January 26, 1801, and John Rutledge, Jr., to Hamilton, January 10, 1801, in ibid., 25:329–330, 308–310.

27 Larson, *Magnificent Catastrophe*, 268; as quoted in Ferling, *Adams vs. Jefferson*, 193.

28 Bayard to McLane, February 17, 1801, Jefferson Papers, Library of Congress; Bayard to Samuel Bayard, February 22, 1801, in Donnan, *Papers of Bayard*; Borden, *Bayard*, 89–90; Davis, *Memoirs of Burr*, 127–128; and editor's note in Kline, *Papers of Burr*, 1:486–487. Also, George W. Erving to Monroe, February 17, 1801, Monroe Papers, Library of Congress; Thomas Mason to John Breckinridge, February 19, 1801, Breckinridge Family Papers, Library of Congress; Gallatin to James Nicholson, February 16, 1801, and to his wife, February 17, 1801, Gallatin Papers, New-York Historical Society Collection.

29 Ferling, *Adams vs. Jefferson*, 192.

30 Deposition of Bayard, April 3, 1806, in Davis, *Memoirs of Burr*, 2:129–133. Bayard, at the time, was convinced that he had firm assurances from Jefferson. Bayard's demands on Jefferson were the very same ones Hamilton had called for in December. See Hamilton to Wolcott, December 17, 1800, in Gibbs, *Memoirs of Administrations*, 2:458–460.

31 Bayard to Allan McLane, February 17, 1801, Jefferson Papers, Library of Congress.

32 Jefferson's diary account, April 15, 1806, in Sawvel, *Anas of Jefferson*, 237–241.

This controversy may best be followed in Davis, ed., *Memoirs of Burr*, 2:112–137; and Borden, *Bayard*, 89–95.

33 Gallatin to Henry Muhlenberg, May 8, 1848, in Adams, *Life of Gallatin*, 248–251. Borden follows this interpretation in his *Bayard*, 91–93.

34 As quoted in McCullough, *John Adams*, 561–562.

35 Jefferson to Monroe, February 15, 1801, in *The Works of Thomas Jefferson*, ed. Paul L. Ford (New York: G. P. Putnam's Sons, 1904), 7:490–491.

36 Merrill D. Peterson, *Thomas Jefferson and the New Nation: A Biography* (New York: Oxford University Press, 1970), 676–677.

37 Ferling, *Adams vs. Jefferson*, 194.

38 Nancy Isenberg, *Fallen Founder: The Life of Aaron Burr* (New York: Viking Press, 2005), 217–218.

39 See James Roger Sharp, *American Politics in the Early Republic* (New Haven, Conn.: Yale University Press, 1995), 147, for speculation about Burr and the election of 1796.

40 William Cooper to Thomas Morris, February 13, 1801, in Davis, *Memoirs of Burr*, 2:113; Bayard to Hamilton, January 7, 1801, and Bayard to Hamilton, March 8, 1801, in Syrett, *Hamilton*, 25:299–303, 344–346; and Bayard to Richard Bassett, February 16, 1801, in Donnan, *Papers of Bayard*, 126–127.

41 Jefferson, "The Anas," January 24, 1804, in Ford, *Works of Jefferson*, vol. 1, accessible through the Online Library of Liberty, http://oll.libertyfund .org/?option=com_staticxt&staticfile=show.php%3Ftitle=800&chapter=85778& layout=html&Itemid=27.

42 Isenberg, *Fallen Founder*, 251.

43 Adams to Gerry , December 30, 1800, Gerry Papers, Library of Congress.

44 Isenberg, *Fallen Founder*, 224; Ferling, *Adams vs. Jefferson*, 201–202.

45 As quoted in Sharp, *American Politics*, 226.

46 Larson, *Magnificent Catastrophe*, 274.

47 The above quotations are from McCullough, *John Adams*, 564–565. McCullough opines that there was no "evidence" to indicate that Adams was "downcast" or "bitter." See 565–566.

48 As quoted in Larson, *Magnificent Catastrophe*, 269.

49 McCullough, *John Adams*, 565–567.

50 *The Life and Selected Writings of Thomas Jefferson*, ed. Adrienne Koch and William Peden (New York: Modern Library, 1944), 322–324.

51 As quoted in Ferling, *Adams vs. Jefferson*, 189.

CHAPTER 11 THE REVOLUTION OF 1800

1 Jefferson to Spencer Roane, September 6, 1819, in *The Portable Thomas Jefferson*, ed. Merrill D. Peterson (New York: Viking Press, 1975), 561–564. See Ellen Lewis and Peter Onuf, eds., *The Revolution of 1800: Democracy, Race, and the New Republic* (Charlottesville: University of Virginia Press, 2002) for a discussion by a number of historians who examine the "wide range of possible outcomes" of that election (xiii).

2 As quoted in Carl Jillson, "Fighting for Control of the American Dream: Alexander Hamilton, Thomas Jefferson, and the Election of 1800," in *Establishing*

Congress: The Removal to Washington, D.C., and the Election of 1800, ed. Kenneth R. Bowling and Donald R. Kennon (Athens: Ohio University Press, 2005), 17.

3   Jefferson to Benjamin Smith Barton, February 14, 1801, in *The Works of Thomas Jefferson*, ed. Paul L. Ford (New York: G. P. Putnam's Sons, 1904), 7:489–490.

4   Jefferson to Elbridge Gerry, March 29, 1801, in ibid., 9:240, accessible online at http://oll.libertyfund.org/?option=com_staticxt&staticfile=show.php%3Ftitle=757&chapter=87297&layout=html&Itemid=27.

5   Jefferson to Maria Eppes, February 15, 1801, Jefferson Papers, University of Virginia.

6   As quoted in Merrill D. Peterson, *Thomas Jefferson and the New Nation: A Biography* (New York: Oxford University Press, 1970), 931.

7   Nancy Isenberg, in her *Fallen Founder: The Life of Aaron Burr* (New York: Viking Press, 2007), writes, "First and foremost, despite what all of our standard history texts assume, there was no national Republican Party in 1800 or 1804; there was a Virginia Republican Party and a New York Republican Party, each of which sought, with jealous determination, to broaden its power" (255).

8   William W. Freehling, *The Road to Disunion: Secessionists at Bay, 1776–1854* (New York: Oxford University Press, 1990), 147.

9   As quoted in Jerry Knudson, *Jefferson and the Press: Crucible of Liberty* (Columbia: University of South Carolina Press, 2006), 53.

10 As quoted in John Ferling, *John Adams: A Life* (Newtown, Conn.: American Political Biography Press, 2009), 404.

11 Office of the Clerk, House of Representatives, http://clerk.house.gov/art_history/house_history/index.html. See also Lampi, "Election of 1800 Re-visited," paper presented at the American Historical Association Annual Meeting, Chicago, January 9, 2000, 8.

12 Lampi, "Election of 1800 Re-visited," 8.

13 Jeffrey L. Pasley, "'A Journeyman, Either in Law or Politics': John Beckley and the Social Origins of Political Campaigning," *Journal of the Early Republic* 16 (Winter 1996): 531–569; Noble E. Cunningham, Jr., "John Beckley: An Early American Party Manager," *William and Mary Quarterly*, 3rd ser., 13 (January 1956): 40–52; Edmund Berkeley and Dorothy Smith Berkeley, *John Beckley: Zealous Partisan in a Nation Divided* (Philadelphia: American Philosophical Society, 1973).

14 Noble E. Cunningham, Jr., *The Jeffersonian Republicans: The Formation of Party Organization, 1789–1801* (Chapel Hill: University of North Carolina Press, 1957), 190, 194.

15 As quoted in Jeffrey L. Pasley, *"The Tyranny of the Printers": Newspaper Politics in the Early American Republic* (Charlottesville: University of Virginia Press, 2001), 121.

16 Ibid., 111, 121, and 123.

17 Richard P. McCormick, "New Perspectives on Jacksonian Politics," *American Historical Review* 65 (January 1960): 294–295.

18 Ibid.

19 Richard P. McCormick, *The Second American Party System: Party Formation in the Jacksonian Era* (Chapel Hill: University of North Carolina Press, 1966), 29 and 343.

20 Bruce Ackerman, *The Failure of the Founding Fathers: Jefferson, Marshall, and*

the Rise of Presidential Democracy (Cambridge, Mass.: Belknap Press of Harvard University, 2005), 5; Cunningham, *Jeffersonian Republicans*, 260.

21 Jackson to Joseph Conn Guild, April 24, 1835, as quoted in Richard Latner, *The Presidency of Andrew Jackson: White House Politics, 1829–1837* (Athens: University of Georgia Press, 1979), 127. The emphasis is mine.

EPILOGUE

1 See Bruce Ackerman, *The Failure of the Founding Fathers: Jefferson, Marshall, and the Rise of Presidential Democracy* (Cambridge, Mass.: Belknap Press of Harvard University, 2005), 116–162, for a discussion of the Federalist Judiciary Act of 1801 and the Republicans' repeal of the act.

2 See Ron Chernow's *Alexander Hamilton* (New York: Penguin Books, 2004), 647–722, for an account of Hamilton's life after the election of Jefferson. See also Forrest McDonald's *Alexander Hamilton: A Biography* (New York: W. W. Norton, 1982); and John Chester Miller, *Alexander Hamilton: A Portrait in Paradox* (New York: Harper & Bros., 1959).

3 As quoted in McDonald, *Hamilton*, 356.

4 Chernow, *Alexander Hamilton*, 671.

5 Ibid. Between 1803 and 1845, all of the states created from the Louisiana Territory came in as slave states.

6 Ibid., 674–678.

7 Nancy Isenberg, *Fallen Founder: The Life of Aaron Burr* (New York: Viking Press, 2007), 164.

8 Chernow, *Alexander Hamilton*, 657–713; and McDonald, *Hamilton*, 356–361. Joanne B. Freeman, in *Affairs of Honor: National Politics in the New Republic* (New Haven, Conn.: Yale University Press, 2001), 163, quotes a friend of Hamilton's on the night before the duel that he had declared that he had resolved "not to fire at Col. Burr the first time, but to receive his fire, and fire in the air."

9 As quoted in Chernow, *Alexander Hamilton*, 718.

10 As quoted in ibid., 719.

11 As quoted in ibid., 718.

12 The above paragraphs on Burr's life have been drawn from ibid., 672–722; Stanley Elkins and Eric McKitrick, *The Age of Federalism: The Early American Republic, 1788–1800* (New York: Oxford University Press, 1993), 744–746; Isenberg, *Fallen Founder*, 223–414; and Milton Lomask, *Aaron Burr: The Years from Princeton to Vice President, 1756–1805* (New York: Farrar, Straus & Giroux, 1979), 296–369.

13 The above discussion of Adams is drawn from John Ferling, *John Adams: A Life* (Newtown, Conn.: American Political Biography Press, 2009), 417–437; David McCullough, *John Adams* (New York: Simon & Schuster, 2001), 568–576; and Joseph Ellis, *Founding Brothers: The Revolutionary Generation* (New York: Vintage Books, 2000), 206.

14 As quoted in McCullough, *John Adams*, 613; Ferling, *Adams*, 430.

15 McCullough, *John Adams*, 615; Ferling, *Adams*, 436–437.

16 Ferling, *Adams*, 428–429; McCullough, *John Adams*, 595.

17 McCullough, *John Adams*, 572.

18 Ellis, *Founding Brothers*, 212.
19 McCullough, *John Adams*, 537.
20 Ellis, *Founding Brothers*, 212.
21 As quoted in Merrill D. Peterson, *Thomas Jefferson and the New Nation: A Biography* (New York: Oxford University Press, 1970), 920. Peterson writes that Jefferson's "popularity, though shaken, remained high during his last months in office," 918.
22 Ibid., 927–928.
23 Ibid., 926, 923–924.
24 McCullough, *John Adams*, 587.
25 Peterson, *Thomas Jefferson and the New Nation*, 990.
26 Ibid., 988.
27 As quoted in Ellis, *Founding Brothers*, 223.
28 Ibid.
29 As quoted in McCullough, *John Adams*, 622.
30 Ibid., 581–585.
31 The above material on the correspondence between Jefferson and Adams draws from Ellis, *Founding Brothers*, 233–242.
32 Jefferson to John Adams, January 11, 1816, in *The Portable Thomas Jefferson*, ed. Merrill D. Peterson (New York: Viking Press, 1975), 550–552; and Ellis, *Founding Brothers*, 237–239.
33 Ellis, *Founding Brothers*, 237–239.
34 As quoted by Peterson, *Thomas Jefferson and the New Nation*, 1009.

BIBLIOGRAPHIC ESSAY

Scholars working in the early republic period of American history are blessed with a wealth of primary and secondary sources. This essay is selective in that it will focus primarily on those sources that formed the nucleus of research materials that informed the writing of this book.

The Library of Congress is the starting point: a treasure trove of archival material, it includes the Breckinridge Family Papers, the Campbell-Preston Family Papers, the Elbridge Gerry Papers, the Harry Innes Papers, the Thomas Jefferson Papers, the James Madison Papers, the James Monroe Papers, and the J. H. Nicholson Papers.

Other collections consulted were the Adams Family Papers (on microfilm) and the Albert Gallatin Papers, at the New-York Historical Society; and the Thomas McKean Papers at the Historical Society of Pennsylvania.

The *Annals of the Congress of the United States* (Washington, D.C.: Government Printing Office, 1847–1851) is valuable for the speeches and votes in the House of Representatives during the Adams administration and especially for the balloting in February 1801. Other beneficial document sets are: Philip S. Foner, ed., *The Democratic Republican Societies, 1790–1800: A Documentary Sourcebook of Constitutions, Declarations, Addresses, Resolutions, and Toasts* (Westport, Conn.: Greenwood Press, 1976); James D. Richardson, ed., *A Compilation of the Messages and Papers of the Presidents* (Washington, D.C.: Bureau of National Literature and Art, 1911); and U.S. Department of Commerce, Bureau of the Census, *A Statistical Abstract Supplement: Historical Statistics of the United States, Colonial Times to 1957* (Washington, D.C.: U.S. Government Printing Office, 1961).

Newspapers contain vital public information about opinion and mood in the country. The Philadelphia *General Advertiser* and the Philadelphia *Aurora*, edited by Benjamin Franklin Bache and, after his death, by William Duane, were the most outspoken of the Republican papers. Duane of the *Aurora* was one of the Adams administration's most virulent critics. The chief newspaper for the Federalists was the Philadelphia *Gazette of the United States*.

Philip J. Lampi and the First Democracy Project at the American Antiquarian Society in Worcester, Massachusetts (http://www.americanantiquarian.org/), have compiled a marvelous and unsurpassed data set on state-by-state voting in the early republic that is essential for helping to understand the politics of the period. Supplementing this is Michael J. Dubin's indispensable *United States Congressional Elections, 1788–1997: The Official Results of the Elections of the 1st through 105th Congresses* (Jefferson, N.C.: McFarland, 1998).

In addition, there are numerous important published collections. For Thomas Jefferson, the ongoing *Papers of Thomas Jefferson* (Princeton, N.J.: Princeton University Press, 1950–), begun by Julian P. Boyd and now edited by Barbara B. Oberg, is a superb and exhaustive collection that will replace the older collections of Jefferson's writings. Of the older published collections, Paul L. Ford, ed., *The Works of Thomas Jefferson* (New York: G. P. Putnam's Sons, 1904), is the best. Lester J. Cappon, ed.,

The *Adams–Jefferson Letters: The Complete Correspondence between Thomas Jefferson and Abigail and John Adams* (Chapel Hill, N.C.: University of North Carolina Press, 1959), 2 vols., is an excellent collection of an extraordinary correspondence between two old colleagues. Jefferson's diary may be found in the Ford collection as well as in Franklin Sawvel, ed., *The Anas of Thomas Jefferson* (New York: Da Capo Press, 1903).

Two one-volume collections of Jefferson's correspondence and other papers are Merrill D. Peterson, ed., *The Portable Thomas Jefferson* (New York: Viking Press, 1975) and Adrienne Koch and William Peden, eds., *The Life and Selected Writings of Thomas Jefferson* (New York: Modern Library, 1944).

A modern edition of James Madison's papers, William T. Hutchinson et al., eds., *Papers of James Madison*, vols. 1– (Chicago: University of Chicago Press; Charlottesville: University of Virginia Press, 1956–) is the definitive source here. An earlier collection, Gaillard Hunt, ed., *The Writings of James Madison: Comprising His Public Papers and His Private Correspondence*, 7 vols. (New York: G. P. Putnam's Sons, 1900–1910), is still quite useful.

I have found the anthology of Stanislaus M. Hamilton, ed., *The Writings of James Monroe* (New York: G. P. Putnam's Sons, 1898–1903) to contain some helpful letters. A major player in Virginia Republican politics was John C. Taylor of Caroline, although his papers are scattered. Some important letters may be found in William E. Dodd, ed., "John Taylor Correspondence," *John P. Branch Historical Papers of Randolph Macon College* 2, nos. 3–4 (June 1908): 214–252, as well as in the Jefferson, Madison, and Monroe collections at the Library of Congress.

William Branch Giles, a Virginian who served in the U.S. House of Representatives during crucial times in the 1790s, was also a member of the Virginia legislature. His memoir, *Political Miscellanies* (Richmond, Va.: n.p., 1829) contains important information about the Virginians' strategy after 1798.

A Pennsylvania Republican's views and activities may be found in George M. Dallas, ed., *Life and Writings of Alexander James Dallas* (Philadelphia: J. B. Lippincott, 1871). Also, Henry Adams, ed., *The Writings of Albert Gallatin* (Philadelphia: J. B. Lippincott, 1879), contains some important letters detailing Republican strategy during the crucial period of January–February 1801.

Aaron Burr's career may be followed in Matthew Davis, ed., *Memoirs of Burr* (New York: Harper & Bros., 1836–1837) and in a modern edition of his works, Mary Jo Kline, ed., *Political Correspondence and Public Papers of Aaron Burr*, 2 vols. (Princeton, N.J.: Princeton University Press, 1983).

For the Federalists, an essential source is Charles Francis Adams, ed., *The Works of John Adams, 2nd President of the United States*, 10 vols. (Boston: Little, Brown, 1854), as is John Fitzpatrick, ed., *The Writings of George Washington* (Washington, D.C.: U.S. Government Printing Office, 1931–1944). A modern and indispensable edition of Hamilton's papers is Harold C. Syrett, ed., *The Papers of Alexander Hamilton*, 27 vols. (New York: Columbia University Press, 1961–1987), although Henry Cabot Lodge, ed., *The Works of Alexander Hamilton* (New York: G. P. Putnam's Sons, 1904) remains helpful.

Some older editions of prominent Federalists are often quite informative: Elizabeth Donnan, ed., *The Papers of James A. Bayard, 1796–1815* (Washington, D.C.: American Historical Association, 1915); George Gibbs, ed., *Memoirs of the Administrations of Washington and John Adams*, 2 vols. (New York: W. Van Norton, 1846);

Charles R. King, ed., *The Life and Correspondence of Rufus King*, 6 vols. (New York: G. P. Putnam's Sons, 1894–1900); and Ulrich B. Phillips, ed., "South Carolina Federalist Correspondence, 1789–1797," *American Historical Review* 14 (July 1909).

A number of books have looked at the origins of national politics in the 1790s, including: Stanley Elkins and Eric McKitrick, *The Age of Federalism: The Early American Republic, 1788–1800* (New York: Oxford University Press, 1993); James Roger Sharp, *American Politics in the Early Republic* (New Haven, Conn.: Yale University Press, 1995); and John F. Hoadley, *Origins of American Political Parties, 1789–1803* (Lexington: University of Kentucky Press, 1986). Joanne B. Freeman's book, *Affairs of Honor: National Politics in the New Republic* (New Haven, Conn.: Yale University Press, 2001), presents a provocative and insightful portrayal of the politics of the early republic as viewed through the lens of a code of honor. Noble Cunningham, Jr., *The Jeffersonian Republicans: The Formation of Party Organization, 1789–1801* (Chapel Hill: University of North Carolina Press, 1957), and John Chester Miller, *Federalist Era: 1789–1801* (New York: Harper & Bros., 1960) were two of the first books to offer a political synthesis of the 1790s. Ralph Ketcham, *Presidents above Party: The First American Presidency, 1789–1829* (Chapel Hill: University of North Carolina Press, 1984), examines the conception of the presidency as it developed from George Washington down to Andrew Jackson; and Rudolph M. Bell, *Party and Faction in American Politics: The House of Representatives, 1789–1801* (Westport, Conn.: Greenwood Press, 1973), provides an interesting quantitative analysis of voting in the House of Representatives in an effort to discover when political parties actually developed.

Focusing more on political ideology as it informed politics are Lance Banning, *The Jeffersonian Persuasion: Evolution of a Party Ideology* (Ithaca, N.Y.: Cornell University Press, 1978) and Richard Hofstadter, *The Idea of a Party System: The Rise of Legitimate Opposition in the United States, 1780–1840* (Berkeley: University of California Press, 1969). Gordon S. Wood's two books, *The Creation of the American Republic, 1776–1787* (Chapel Hill: University of North Carolina Press, 1969) and *The Radicalism of the American Revolution* (New York: Alfred Knopf, 1992) have played a major role in refocusing scholarly attention on republicanism as a defining touchstone of American politics. See also Edmund Morgan's *Inventing the People* (New York: Norton, 1988), which raises some fascinating questions about the meaning of the "sovereignty of the people."

A number of first-rate books dealing with the election of 1800 have recently been published. I have, however, in this book offered a somewhat different explanation of the meaning of those significant events in 1800–1801. The books are: Bruce Ackerman, *The Failure of the Founding Fathers: Jefferson, Marshall, and the Rise of Presidential Democracy* (Cambridge, Mass.: Belknap Press of Harvard University, 2005); John Ferling, *Adams vs. Jefferson: The Tumultuous Election of 1800* (New York: Oxford University Press, 2004); Edward J. Larson, *Magnificent Catastrophe: The Tumultuous Election of 1800, America's First Presidential Campaign* (New York: Free Press, 2007); and Susan Dunn, *Jefferson's Second Revolution: The Election Crisis of 1800 and the Triumph of Republicanism* (Boston: Houghton Mifflin, 2004). Ellen Lewis and Peter Onuf have edited an excellent anthology on the election, *The Revolution of 1800: Democracy, Race, and the New Republic* (Charlottesville: University of Virginia Press, 2002); while another helpful collection is Kenneth R. Bowling and Donald R. Kennon, eds., *Establishing Congress: The Removal to Washington D.C., and the Election of 1800* (Athens: Ohio

University Press, 2005). See also James Sterling Young, *The Washington Community, 1800–1828* (New York: Columbia University Press, 1966), which presents a fascinating description of the political culture in Washington in 1800. An invaluable unpublished essay on the election, generously made available to me, is Philip J. Lampi's "Election of 1800 Re-visited," paper presented at the American Historical Association Annual Meeting, Chicago, January 9, 2000.

Biographies are a critical source for understanding the election of 1800. Dumas Malone's sympathetic work on Jefferson is a monumental achievement, and his *Jefferson and the Ordeal of Liberty* (Boston: Little, Brown, 1962) is indispensable for understanding not only Jefferson's role but also the larger political scene that was unfolding. One-volume biographies by Merrill D. Peterson, *Thomas Jefferson and the New Nation: A Biography* (New York: Oxford University Press, 1970) and Nathan Schachner, *Thomas Jefferson: A Biography* (New York: Thomas Yoseloff, 1960) reveal important aspects of Jefferson's career and political motives.

Joseph J. Ellis, *American Sphinx: The Character of Thomas Jefferson* (New York: Alfred A. Knopf, 1997) and *Founding Brothers: The Revolutionary Generation* (New York: Alfred A. Knopf, 2000) offer insightful and thoughtful analyses of Jefferson's personality and character.

Darren Staloff's *Hamilton, Adams, Jefferson: The Politics of Enlightenment and the American Founding* (New York: Hill & Wang, 2005), while not a biography, analyzes features of Jefferson's personality and ideology, as well as that of Hamilton and Adams.

John Adams has been served well by recent biographers. David McCullough's *John Adams* (New York: Simon & Schuster, 2001) is an elegantly written and sympathetic work that humanizes Adams. John E. Ferling's *John Adams: A Life* (Newtown, Conn.: American Political Biography Press, 2009) is another recent and admirable biography. Peter Shaw's *The Character of John Adams* (Chapel Hill: University of North Carolina Press, 1976) is an insightful look into the subject. Two very informative books dealing with the Adams administration are: Manning J. Dauer, *The Adams Federalists* (Baltimore: Johns Hopkins University Press, 1968) and Stephen G. Kurtz, *The Presidency of John Adams: The Collapse of Federalism, 1795–1800* (New York: A. S. Barnes, 1961).

Like Adams, Hamilton has benefited from an outstanding recent biography in Ron Chernow's *Alexander Hamilton* (New York: Penguin Books, 2004). Two older biographies are also very valuable for helping understand an often vilified figure in the early republic: Forrest McDonald, *Alexander Hamilton: A Biography* (New York: W. W. Norton, 1979) and John Chester Miller, *Alexander Hamilton: A Portrait in Paradox* (New York: Harper & Bros., 1959).

A powerful argument for a more positive view of another popular villain of the period is Nancy Isenberg's *Fallen Founder: The Life of Aaron Burr* (New York: Viking Press, 2007). Milton Lomask's *Aaron Burr: The Years from Princeton to Vice President, 1756–1805* (New York: Farrar, Straus & Giroux, 1979–1982) remains very useful for understanding the New Yorker.

There are dozens of biographies of George Washington. Among those most helpful in this project were Joseph J. Ellis, *His Excellency: George Washington* (New York: Vintage Press, 2005); Richard Norton Smith, *Patriarch: George Washington and the New American Nation* (Boston: Houghton Mifflin, 1993); James T. Flexner, *George*

Washington, 4 vols. (Boston: Little, Brown, 1965–1972); and John Ferling, *The Ascent of George Washington: The Hidden Political Genius of an American Icon* (New York: Bloomsbury Press, 2009). And while not a biography, Marcus Cunliffe, *George Washington: Man and Monument* (New York: New American Library, 1960) offers some valuable insights into what Washington meant to the new republic.

Two recent books have examined Washington's views on slavery: Francois Fursterberg, *In the Name of the Father: Washington's Legacy, Slavery and the Making of a Nation* (New York: Penguin Press, 2006) and Henry Wiencek, *An Imperfect God: George Washington, His Slaves, and the Creation of America* (New York: Farrar, Straus & Giroux, 2003).

A recent biography, Walter Isaacson, *Benjamin Franklin: An American Life* (New York: Simon & Schuster, 2004), was useful in looking at Franklin's view of Adams.

Many biographies of lesser-known figures that played important roles in the run-up to the election of 1800 have been published. Among these are Edmund Berkeley and Dorothy Smith Berkeley, *John Beckley: Zealous Partisan in a Nation Divided* (Philadelphia: American Philosophical Society, 1973); Robert Ernst, *Rufus King: American Federalist* (Chapel Hill: University of North Carolina Press, 1968); Lowell H. Harrison, *John Breckinridge: Jeffersonian Republican* (Louisville, Ky.: Filson Club, 1969); James Tagg, *Benjamin Franklin Bache and the Philadelphia Aurora* (Philadelphia: University of Pennsylvania Press, 1991); Robins Dice Anderson, *William Branch Giles: A Study in the Politics of Virginia and the Nation from 1790 to 1830* (Gloucester, Mass.: Peter Smith, 1965); Henry Adams, *The Life of Albert Gallatin* (New York: Peter Smith, 1943) and Morton Borden, *The Federalism of James A. Bayard* (New York: Columbia University Press, 1955). The Adams biography also includes a number of letters from Albert Gallatin, while Borden's book is essential for helping to understand the motives of Bayard in those last critical days before the final vote in the House of Representatives.

In addition to the biographies, a number of state or regional studies are exceptionally beneficial. For the Southern states, they include: Richard Beeman, *The Old Dominion and the New Nation* (Lexington: University of Kentucky Press, 1972); James H. Broussard, *Southern Federalists: 1800–1816* (Baton Rouge: Louisiana State University Press, 1978); Rhys Isaac, *Transformation of Virginia, 1740–1790* (Chapel Hill: University of North Carolina Press, 1982); Norman Risjord, *Chesapeake Politics, 1781–1800* (New York: Columbia University Press, 1978); and Lisle Rose, *Prologue to Democracy: The Federalists in the South, 1789–1800* (Lexington: University of Kentucky Press, 1968). Joan Wells Coward's *Kentucky in the New Republic: The Process of Constitution Making* (Lexington: University of Kentucky Press, 1979) is helpful for that state.

Richard R. Beeman's book, *The Varieties of Political Experience in Eighteenth Century America* (Philadelphia: University of Pennsylvania Press, 2004), is an indispensable work that analyzes the political cultures of the various colonies and states that shaped the experiences and history of the public men of the 1790s.

All dealing with the question of the politics of slavery are William W. Freehling, *The Road to Disunion: Secessionists at Bay, 1776–1854* (New York: Oxford University Press, 1990); Herbert Aptheker, *American Negro Slave Revolts* (New York: International Publishers, 1963); Winthrop Jordan, *White over Black: American Attitudes toward the Negro, 1550–1812* (Chapel Hill: University of North Carolina Press, 1968); and Garry Wills, *"Negro President": Jefferson and the Slave Power* (Boston: Houghton

Mifflin, 2003). Douglas R. Egerton's *Gabriel's Rebellion: The Virginia Slave Conspiracies of 1800 and 1802* (Chapel Hill: University of North Carolina Press, 1993) is an excellent discussion of the impact of Gabriel's Revolt on Virginia in the summer of 1800. See also Paul Finkelman's excellent *Slavery and the Founders: Race and Liberty in the Age of Jefferson*, 2nd ed. (Armonk, NY: ME Sharpe, 2001).

In the Middle and New England states, the studies that have been helpful are: Ronald P. Formisano, *The Transformation of Political Culture: Massachusetts Parties, 1790s–1840s* (New York: Oxford University Press, 1983); Paul Goodman, *The Democratic-Republicans of Massachusetts: Politics in a Young Republic* (Cambridge, Mass.: Harvard University Press, 1964); John A. Munroe, *Federalist Delaware, 1775–1815* (New Brunswick, N.J.: Rutgers University Press, 1954); Carl E. Prince, *New Jersey's Jeffersonian Republicans: The Genesis of an Early Party Machine, 1789–1817* (Chapel Hill: University of North Carolina Press, 1967); Harry M. Tinkcom, *The Republicans and Federalists in Pennsylvania, 1790–1801* (Philadelphia: University of Pennsylvania Press, 1950); and Alfred F. Young, *The Democratic Republicans of New York: The Origins, 1763–1797* (Chapel Hill: University of North Carolina Press, 1967).

Recently there has been a growing interest among historians in going beyond the traditional focus on elites for a more inclusive approach and investigating other aspects of the political culture of the early republic. One collection worth examining is Jeffrey L. Pasley, Andrew W. Robertson, and David Waldstreicher, eds., *Beyond the Founders: New Approaches to the Political History of the Early American Republic* (Chapel Hill: University of North Carolina Press, 2004); it has a number of exceptional essays asking new questions and looking at a wider evidence base than the more traditional historical treatments. Among the outstanding books that use new approaches and ask new questions are: Christopher Grasso, *A Speaking Aristocracy: Transforming Public Discourse in Eighteenth Century Connecticut* (Chapel Hill: University of North Carolina Press, 1999); Albrecht Koschnik, *"Let a Common Interest Bind Us Together": Associations, Partisanship, and Culture in Philadelphia, 1775–1840* (Charlottesville: University of Virginia Press, 2007); Simon P. Newman, *Parades and the Politics of the Street: Festive Culture in the Early American Republic* (Philadelphia: University of Philadelphia Press, 1997); David Waldstreicher, *In the Midst of Perpetual Fetes: The Making of American Nationalism, 1776–1820* (Chapel Hill: University of North Carolina Press, 1997); Susan Branson, *These Fiery Frenchified Dames: Women and Political Culture in Early National Philadelphia* (Philadelphia: University of Pennsylvania Press, 2001); Susan G. Davis, *Parades and Power: Street Theatre in Nineteenth-Century Philadelphia* (Berkeley: University of California Press, 1988); Woody Holton, *Unruly Americans and the Origins of the Constitution* (New York: Hill & Wang, 2007); and Douglas Bradburn, *The Citizenship Revolution: Politics and the Creation of the American Union, 1774–1804* (Charlottesville: University of Virginia Press, 2009).

Thomas R. Slaughter's *The Whiskey Rebellion: Frontier Epilogue to the American Revolution* (New York: Oxford University Press, 1986) is the standard and outstanding account of an important event defining politics in the 1790s. And Paul Douglas Newman, *Fries Rebellion: The Enduring Struggle for the American Revolution* (Philadelphia: University of Pennsylvania Press, 2004) offers a first-rate study of the later Pennsylvania rebellion. Another older but reliable work is W. W. H. Davis, *The Fries Rebellion 1798–1799* (1899; repr. New York: Arno Press, 1969). Eugene Perry Link,

Democratic Republican Societies, 1790–1800 (New York: Octagon Books, 1942) is still the standard treatment of the Democratic Republican Societies.

A very impressive study of newspapers in the early republic is Jeffrey L. Pasley's *"The Tyranny of the Printers": Newspaper Politics in the Early American Republic* (Charlottesville: University of Virginia Press, 2001). Jerry W. Knudson, *Jefferson and the Press: Crucible of Liberty* (Columbia: University of South Carolina Press, 2006) focuses on the press during Jefferson's two terms in office.

American politics during this period was highly influenced by world events; for understanding the international aspect, two books by Alexander DeConde are invaluable. See *Entangling Alliance: Politics and Diplomacy under George Washington* (Durham, N.C.: Duke University Press, 1958) and *The Quasi-War: The Politics of The Undeclared War with France 1797–1801* (New York: Scribner & Sons, 1966). R. R. Palmer's *Age of the Democratic Revolution: A Political History of Europe and America, 1776–1800* (Princeton, N.J.: Princeton University Press, 1964) gives a valuable international perspective. Howard Mumford Jones, *American and French Culture: 1750–1848* (Chapel Hill: University of North Carolina Press, 1965); Lawrence S. Kaplan, *Jefferson and France: An Essay on Politics and Political Ideas* (New Haven, Conn: Yale University Press, 1967); Joseph Klaits and Michael H. Haltzel, eds., *The Global Ramifications of the French Revolution* (Cambridge: Cambridge University Press, 2002); Albert Hall Bowman, *The Struggle for Neutrality: Franco-American Diplomacy during the Federalist Era* (Knoxville: University of Tennessee Press, 1974); and William Stinchcombe, *The XYZ Affair* (Westport, Conn.: Greenwood Press, 1980) all examine the relationship between the United States and France.

Richard H. Kohn, *Eagle and Sword: The Federalists and the Creation of the Military Establishment in America, 1789–1802* (New York: Free Press, 1975) is the standard treatment of the development of the military during the decade of the 1790s.

The passage of and reaction to the Alien and Sedition Acts are the subject of James M. Smith's excellent and essential *Freedom's Fetters: The Alien and Sedition Laws and American Civil Liberties* (Ithaca, N.Y.: Cornell University Press, 1956).

INDEX